D0849599

Chewing THE
WAFER

LIVING A CHRISTIAN WORLD VIEW

WILLIAM C JEFFRIES

authorHOUSE®

AuthorHouse™
1663 Liberty Drive
Bloomington, IN 47403
www.authorhouse.com
Phone: 1 (800) 839-8640

Published by AuthorHouse 03/23/2020

ISBN: 978-1-7283-5693-8 (sc)
ISBN: 978-1-7283-5691-4 (hc)
ISBN: 978-1-7283-5692-1 (e)

Library of Congress Control Number: 2020905425

Print information available on the last page.

CONTENTS

OTHER BOOKS BY WILLIAM C JEFFRIES

Taming the Scorpion: Preparing American Business for the Third Millennium, Professional Press, Chapel Hill, NC,1996.

Hannibal, Hummers, and Hot Air Balloons: High Performance Strategies for Tough Times, ESI, Inc., Zionsville, IN, 2001.

Still True to Type, Buttermilk Ridge Publishing, Noblesville, IN, 2002, 2011.

Profiles of the 16 Personality Types, Buttermilk Ridge Publishing, Noblesville, IN, 2002, 2005, rev. 2009, 2010, 2011, 2018.

Trap Door to the Dark Side, AuthorHouse, Bloomington, IN, 2006. An admittedly dark, Jungian–based personal memoir of a Special Forces soldier, Captain Christian Madison, living and fighting side by side with a tribe of primitive Montagnards in South Vietnam and Laos during the Vietnam War.

Spirit of the Oryx, AuthorHouse, Bloomington, IN 2009. A sequel to *Trap Door to the Dark Side*, the Muslim, Christian, and Jewish eschatological views of the end times collide in this high-tech novel that follows the exploits of retired army ranger, Colonel Christian Madison, as he and his team of special operatives from the past struggle to restore the reputation of Madison's recently murdered former partner in Vietnam. In the process they are caught up in an international terrorist plot directed at the port of Ras Laffan, Qatar, in a sinister effort to plunge the entire Persian Gulf area into World War III.

Concord, AuthorHouse, Bloomington, IN, 2009. The third novel in the "Christian Madison series." This one is a murder mystery and political novel set during the Obama administration, involving the efforts of a secret band of American patriots known only as Concord, to stop a lawless federal government running amok.

Culture and High Performance: Creating a World Class Business and Organizational Culture, Buttermilk Ridge Publishing, Noblesville, IN, 2011. It is the leader's responsibility to create the kind of organizational culture necessary to achieve the desired strategy and vision of success. This is a handbook every leader needs to coach them through the process of culture development.

Psychological Type and Sales Mastery, ESI, Inc., Zionsville, IN, 2013. A step by step method for knowing your customers, meeting their needs through Psychological Type and Emotional Intelligence, and closing the deal.

Framing the Sacred: The Shadow of Death. AuthorHouse, Bloomington, IN, 2017. Iranian mullahs create a high-tech methodology for turning anyone, regardless of political affiliation or world view, into a potential terrorist. In this, the third of the "Christian Madison Series," retired Colonel Madison and his team of former Green Berets are tasked with stopping an attack on the US power grid and nuclear facilities. Published one week before the Las Vegas massacre, the technology discussed may help to explain why this massacre remains unsolved.

Inliers: The Curse of Polarity Thinking. Buttermilk Ridge Publishing, Noblesville, IN, 2017. A leader's handbook for removing the organizational impediments to exceptional performance. If you have read Malcolm Gladwell's influential *Outliers: The Story of Success*, this book is the natural sequel that ideally should serve as the prequel.

All books are available from the respective publishers, at many of your favorite book sources, and always at the "Bookstore" section on www.execustrat.com. Should you desire signed copies of any of the above books, please make that request at this website.

Sanctify Christ as Lord in your hearts, always being ready to make a defense to everyone who asks you to give an account for the hope that is in you, yet with gentleness and reverence.

(1 Peter 3:15 NKJV)

PROLOGUE

Whatever our profession or calling in life, our Christian faith should be evident in what we say and what we do; our world view should be crystal clear. Those who know me, expect my books to be about leadership, organizational performance, mental fitness, psychological type, and building high performance teams. This is a different kind of book for me to write; it is about taking our faith to work. There is certainly nothing special about me or what I do; that is the point. Even those of us living and working off the radar screen as cooks at Chick-fil-A, cashiers at Walmart, college professors, business leaders, union mechanics at Caterpillar, translators at the United Nations, engineers developing new products, safety inspectors at NASA, or for some of us, even serving as consultants and advisors to senior business leaders, heads of state, and foreign royalty, have an opportunity to have our lives speak for the Christ who redeemed us. After all, our Lord came to redeem all of life, not just the time we spend in church.

The question I continuously have to reflect upon is, am I an international consultant who happens to be a Christian, or a Christian who chooses to be an international consultant. Which option I choose has very specific implications for how I should live and work. In one way or another, that is the choice afforded to each of us. Which value system or set of underlying considerations drives you? From a more academic perspective, what world view underscores our lives? Even before we can identify our individual roles in life, we have to determine who we are as individual believers. What is our essential ontology, and why have we been created? Each of us should examine those things we do and the lives we live to be sure they have a firm biblical foundation and can be clearly reflective of a Christian world view. If they cannot, it is time for a career change. To that point, how does such a world view develop? Where does it come from?

Thus far, my public life has encompassed overlapping careers as a professional soldier, a college professor, a business leader, an organizational consultant, an editor, an executive coach, a public speaker, a political advisor, and a writer. In the past I have written eight books on organizational high performance, diversity, organizational culture, leading exceptional teams, psychological type, political policy, mental fitness in athletics, and emotional intelligence, basing these books on the work my company routinely does in over a hundred Fortune 500 Companies, seventeen US Federal Government agencies, numerous college and professional sports teams, all five US military services, and businesses and non-profit organizations (NPO's) in, so far, 36 countries. Many of the methods we use and the language we have developed to describe such processes have become the standards in the consulting and coaching professions. That is why ensuring that each of them is based on a biblical precedent is critical to living a practical apologetic. Along the way, I have also written four adventure novels, based very roughly on my experiences working alongside and consulting with Special Operations teams, three-letter federal agencies, and other elite organizations around the world from Switzerland to France to Qatar to Laos to Vietnam to even the USA. What has gone mostly unspoken in these various books, is the world view lying beneath them. Oh, it was always there and peeks out from time to time—**once you have a world view and really trust it, it should be hard for others to ignore**—but its influence was always subtle at best. Here I will be clear as to why we do the work we do, the tools we use, and the approaches we take.

What our world view is and how it was formed differs for each of us. God writes the overall story, but our individual scripts vary depending on the roles God has prepared us to act out in this world. That is why telling our personal stories and understanding the many inputs along the way are critical to understanding how our world view developed. In this book, I will be very clear about what that world view is, how with God's help it has formed the unspoken foundation for every aspect of my life and business, and why, such clarity is critical for each one of us who intends to be an honest heir of the Christ who redeemed us. Sometimes a Christian world view takes time to become ingrained and develops only after years of contact with diverse influences, both good and bad. Hundreds of scholars and theologians have written about world views, but very few have tried to explain how one's world view is formed and how it should underlie our "secular" work on a daily basis. That is the main contribution this book offers. **Without speaking a word, our lives, occupations, and the ways we choose to perform our roles at work and at home should articulate our Christian world view.** Sadly, the public and private arenas are too often posed as discrete, unrelated, entities. Let's change that misconception.

As one writer has expressed it, anyone's world view needs to answer the following questions:

> Is there a source of ultimate good—a God?
> If so, what is God like and how do I relate to God?
> If there isn't a God, does it really matter? Life still goes on.
> What is truth and can anyone really know the truth anyway?
> Where did the universe come from and where is it going?
> What is the meaning of life?
> Does my life have a purpose; if so, what is it?
> What does it mean to live a good life?
> Does it really matter in the end whether or not I live a moral life?
> Is there life after death?
> Are humans basically "just smart apes with superior hygiene and a
>   fashion sense"—or is there more to us than that? (Crossway, "The
>   Importance of World Views")

James Anderson is on the right track. These are certainly some of the elements encapsulated in a biblical frame of reference. Our lives should provide cogent answers to these questions and others before we ever open our mouths. When you go to a sporting event, many of you proudly wear your favorite team's jersey to show your support. Day by day, do those around you know what team you are on or which one you support? I'll get more specific as my argument unfolds, but you get the idea. Your world view directly influences how you answer those kinds of big questions, both in structured arguments and with choices you make in your life and business. Even more importantly, how you answer these kinds of questions can determine the level of your success when discussing your story with others. **That is what a practical apologist for the faith does in a systematic way every day, seeking to influence non-believers' minds as well as hearts.**

Along the way, I will suggest what it means to be such an apologist. No, not a formal philosopher or minister of the Word working with apologetics ministries, although that approach has also been part of the prologue to my personal story, but just average believers who understand the need to be crystal clear about our beliefs and be able to give clear rational responses to honest difficult questions when we are confronted. More to the point, I will argue that it is our Christian obligation day-by-day to ensure our work and the approaches we use to accomplish it, reflect our world view so that **others, just by watching us, will have a reason to ask about the faith that is within us** and demand a reason for why they should believe as well—that is what I call **living a practical apologetic.**

Let's get personal. If you were asked to reflect back over your life, which events would you find most poignant? The experiences we remember with the greatest clarity are usually those with the strongest emotions attached to them: the overcoming of great obstacles, the losses that left us bereft or heartbroken, and the moments we felt most alive or at peace (births, religious experiences, marriages, bankruptcies, infelicities, divorces, getting fired, nasty breakups, the death of a child, and for too many in the last hundred years, time spent serving their countries in combat). As you relate such events in your life to others, you have all used a phrase like, "As luck would have it," or as an excuse, "Look, it just happened." Even most young children's fairy tales begin with that innocent phrase, "Once upon a time." Often when reminiscing with friends, you started the conversation with "Remember when…?" When you start the conversation this way, you are in the process of beginning to tell a story. Even the writers of the *Old* and *New Testaments* get caught up in the cant of the day with their, "and it came to pass…."

And Cain talked with Abel his brother: *and it came to pass,* when they were in the field, that Cain rose up against Abel his brother and slew him (KJV, Genesis 4:8).

And it came to pass on a certain day, as He was teaching, that there were Pharisees and doctors of the law sitting by, which were come out of every town of Galilee, and Judaea, and Jerusalem: and the power of the Lord was present to heal them (KJV, Luke 5:17).

Indeed, the phrase translated as, "and it came to pass," is used 1,265 times by writers in the *Bible.* The secular world casually dismisses these times as mere happenstances. The Christian, however, has special insights on such occasions and understands that nothing simply haphazardly "comes to pass." While God's sovereignty impacts every event in life, the most poignant of these events occur when divine interventions, what the ancient Greeks would have called *kairos* (divine) time, intersect with the more mundane chronological order of events (*chronos*) time. Christians understand those intersections to be miracles, such as when Jesus' body on the cross was stretched out spanning both the vertical and the horizontal at the very intersection of *kairos* and *chronos*, and became the embodiment of the miracle that would change the world. Often these moments are times when God wants to make a point in our lives or allow us to make a statement in his name. Although the choices we make in these interstices are often unconscious and seem without specific causation or intent, all of them erupt from our basis world view. Sometimes, it is the least significant of events that can provide the greatest witness to God's sovereignty and make the most profound contribution to forming our more mature world view. Regardless of their apparent insignificance at the time, God has inked in each one on our day planner for a specific reason (KJV, 1 Thessalonians 5:13). It is our job to use each one effectively and to learn from them.

I have done my best here to capture just some of those personally poignant events in my life as a son, father, and husband—three labels I proudly claim—and in my professional roles as a soldier, coach, entrepreneur, international consultant, researcher, author, political advisor, and builder of exceptionally high-performing teams to demonstrate how one's world view develops over time. Those arenas often overlap as they should for any of us who claim the name, Christian. While some of the following stories may seem more personal and autobiographical than you might desire, that is not the point. I have taken this approach, not to talk about me or merely to relate personal events in my life—difficult for an Introvert to do, by the way—but to use the various anecdotes, often what seemed at the time insignificant occurrences in my story, as examples of ways in which our world views take shape and then announce themselves as we engage the world with the claims of Christ. These personal events form the spiritual DNA of our eventual world view. If we do it right, God will use such everyday mundane events in each of our lives for his purpose. Sometimes I have succeeded and sometimes I have failed. I am equally certain that too many times I have missed the opportunities that God provided. Often, it has little to do with what we say but how we live. Some of these examples just demand more personal backgrounding than others. Please forgive me in advance. Every story is another vector into my ultimate world view.

So, to reiterate, what I hope this book does is to provide a few examples of **practical apologetics**, the definition of which I believe will unfold as I relate experiences and tell a few stories. While my personal experiences are necessarily different from yours—in that regard you are probably very fortunate—I hope you will see how ostensibly unimportant "secular" experiences can provide the springboards for engendering and trumpeting a practical apologetic. Every "it came to pass" in our lives is an occasion to state our case for humbly claiming the name Christian. That is essentially the thesis of this book.

If we are committed Christians, every event in our lives and professions should be an occasion to reflect the Christ who redeemed us. We should <u>be</u> the Gospel.

For reasons that will become clear as you read, I'll call these occasions opportunities to **chew the wafer.**

DEDICATION

If I were to dedicate this book to anyone, it would be to all those who have asked me the tough questions over the years and forced me to put up or shut up.

ACKNOWLEDGMENTS

I appreciate greatly the conversations I have had with several people in the process of reviewing my thoughts. Cal Ray and Paul Jeffries provided wise commentary, biblical insights, and support for my ideas and several other individuals raised occasional reinterpretations of some scriptural passages I may have overlooked. I am also thankful to be a member of a sound *Bible* teaching church led by a senior pastor and elders who preach the gospel unapologetically week in and week out.

Most of all I am thankful for Cheryl, a loving wife who gives me the encouragement and freedom to try to be the man God wants me to become.

An excellent wife who can find?
She is far more precious than jewels.
The heart of her husband trusts in her,
and he will have no lack of gain.
She does him good, and not harm,
all the days of her life.
She seeks wool and flax,
and works with willing hands.
She rises while it is yet night
and provides food for her household.

She a opens her hand to the poor
and reaches out her hands to the needy.
(NASB, Proverbs 31)

CHAPTER I

"O Sing the Song of Odysseus"

In "Book Eight" of the epic poem, *The Odyssey*, the blind bard, Demodocus, is found in the process of singing (what today we would call narrating a story) the exploits of that war hero, Odysseus, the legendary King of Ithaca and hero of the Trojan Wars, during a grand feast in celebration of one more of his numerous victories. Everyone present seems to be enjoying the "singing" except for Odysseus, himself, who occasionally bursts into tears because of the pain and suffering of which the story reminds him. At every break in the singing, through a torrent of tears, Odysseus would raise his cup and pour libations to the gods, thanking them for their interventions in his life, but as soon as Demodocus begins again Odysseus pulls his cloak over his head to hide his tears. Odysseus—the hero of this tale—doesn't say a word, but his very actions betray his pantheistic pagan world view and the role his "many gods" seem to play in giving it meaning. As with Odysseus, all of these "and it came to pass" moments in our lives are meant for celebration of the one true God's deliverance, but some can easily devolve into sadness and regret when we recall their memory.

From the beginning of time, human beings have been story telling creatures. Animistic Aboriginal peoples in northern Australia drew some of the earliest pictures on cave walls to document their existence. Polytheistic Egyptians unknowingly followed their example by sketching

1

creative hieroglyphics on all their earliest structures to tell of floods, droughts, crop failures, unexplained phenomena in the skies, and the birth and burial of kings. It seems that telling the story of who we are and why we are here is part of human history. Horses do not sketch diagrams on stable walls, koalas do not carve their initials in the trunks of eucalyptus trees, and bears certainly do not keep diaries while they hibernate. Humans are the only creatures capable of creating and seemingly compelled to tell stories. The statements such living histories make often form the clearest expressions of one's world view.

What began as an oral tradition, simply telling stories to others or reciting the exploits of heroes to crowds in mead halls, eventually found its way into writings. Creating documents to capture such stories, however, is a relatively modern invention. The oldest surviving great work of literature is the epic of *Gilgamesh*, the ancient poem heralding the exploits of the semi-mythical King Uruk of Mesopotamia, written in Akkadian in the late second millennium BC. Two thousand years later in the epic poem *Beowulf* and in the Greek and Latin epics like *The Odyssey* and *The Iliad*, the bard, or storyteller, becomes the *de facto* creator of culture as he recounts the exploits of great warriors, their values, and why they act as they do. Each is an expression of the prevailing world view of their time.

Far more important in many ways to our culture than mere historians, when the bard or storyteller weaves his narratives, he captures the emotions of the moment as well as the deeds of the heroes involved. When an historian dies, it can be a sad event and his or her family no doubt mourn, and maybe someone authors an obituary. So important, however, is the role of the storyteller in these epic sagas, that when he dies, as one who is known as the "Shaper" does in *Grendel*, the 1971 story of *Beowulf* written by John Gardner from the monster's point of view, the culture dies with him, demonstrating even from ancient times the power of stories to transform individual lives and whole cultures and the devastating loss that occurs when no one is present who is capable of telling our stories. These are some of the reasons we should study literature from the past. Not just to learn how to chant rhymes in Middle or Old English, or recite Shakespearean sonnets to our lovers, but to introduce us to mankind's plight through history and see how we have chosen to relate to the universe around us, either by ourselves, alone, or in reliance upon something or someone far greater than ourselves. These works of literature are early repositories of their cultures' respective world views.

Over a thousand years later, when Chaucer penned *The Canterbury Tales*, he opens with:

> *When that Averylle with his shoures soote*
> *The droughte of March / hath perced to the roote*
> *And bathed every veyne in swich lycour*
> *Of which vertu engendred is the flour*
> *What zephirus eek with his sweete breeth*
> *Inspired hath in euery hold and heeth*
> *The tendre croppes / and the yonge sonne*
> *Hath in the Ram / his half cour yronne*
> ....
> *Thanne longen folk to goon on pilrymagges.*
> (The *Hengwrt Manuscript*)

Once we struggle through the Middle English, we find in just these few eight lines that the very seasons make one think of death (the coldness, sterility, and drought of March), and the subsequent rebirth, and resurrection (April). God's story is even rooted in nature itself. The rain prompts images of growth and regeneration—a gift from heaven. Even nature in this created universe echoes Christ's sacrifice on the cross (the greatest intersection of *kairos* and *chronos* of all time). The upshot is that during the springtime (a time symbolic of new life and resurrection) in each of our lives, when we are suddenly awakened to the created world around us, **every one of us is urged to make such a pilgrimage—a personal journey to understand our faith—to show the world the sacrifice of Christ for all mankind.** The rest of this fragmentary epic poem is geared to getting to know the lives and world views of numerous pilgrims making the pilgrimage to the shrine of St. Thomas Becket at the Cathedral of Canterbury—a cross section of society that includes a priest, a cook, a pardoner, a soldier, a miller, a squire, a scandalous divorcee, and

23 other occupations, at least one tale for each day of the month in the author's original plan. **The stories range the gamut from the humorous to the bawdy to the contemplative to the religious emphasizing that the Christian world view must be capable of embracing all of life's experiences**. Indeed, Chaucer includes himself in this spiritual journey, as his original plan called for telling two of the tales as himself—a poet and the storyteller—who is also a committed pilgrim. A reminder that we are all in this together.

Everything we do and every story we tell should speak of our kinship with Christ and reflect our world view. To help us understand that we are all on a journey in life, the poet introduces us to each one of the pilgrims as she or he tells their tales. We get to hear their personal stories. Taken as a body these tales reflect the various Christian, pagan, and naturalistic world views of their day. In the process of telling their stories, each pilgrim reveals her or his individual relationship with Christ and the organized church of Chaucer's day. The very fact that the poem remains just a literary fragment of Chaucer's original intent (he seemed at first to plan for every pilgrim to tell four stories), makes the point that **there are many more stories to be told, especially ours.** How we tell those stories at work and at home will reflect our world view and the narratives that contributed to its formation.

This is rarely the approach taken by professors of literature as they explicate the Chaucerian text from the perspectives of their own routinely Humanistic world views and revel in simply studying the vernacular of the day, but it goes to the heart of the poet's intent. The poem is an early study of mankind and our relationship to God. To prevent boredom during the long trip and make their time together more poignant, at the suggestion of the narrator, **the pilgrims agree that along their pilgrimage they will take turns telling stories, and that whoever tells the best tale wins a free meal at the Tabard Inn**, upon their return. Stories are critical to our culture and individual lives. **Be thinking about what your story might be. In the end times, when Christ returns, you will be asked.**

More to our purpose, just think of all the stories (parables) Jesus told to me his point. These forty-six ostensibly mundane stories in the *New Testament*, range from the simplicity of a poor widow's baking bread in her humble dwelling to the richness of the prodigal son's being welcomed home by his father. Jesus didn't flaunt theology in his audiences' faces but instead rooted the values he stood for and the God with whom he shared divinity in a series of homely stories that common people in his age as well as ours could understand. Yet, as simple as these stories are, in sum they embody almost all of Jesus' fundamental teachings. The casual reader can naively see these stories just as examples of various things that Jesus observed or did—miracles that he performed—and equate his coming to earth as merely a reflection of what he did; after all, he did die on the cross and rise again. To be sure, no one else has ever done that. But before that seminal event, think of all the times people flocked to Jesus to ask him to DO something for them: make them see, cast out a demon, make them walk, bring their child or brother back to life, save their boat, cure their leprosy, keep them from sinking, or feed over 5,000 followers. They constantly expected him to do something or to show them a sign. From time to time Jesus, Himself, has to remind them that,

> An evil and adulterous generation seeks for a sign, but no
> sign will be given to it except the sign of Jonah. So he left
> them and departed (ESV, Matthew 16:4).

Even his mother initially fails to grasp the divine nature of Jesus' existence. Recall her request during the marriage feast of Cana: "And when they wanted wine, the mother of Jesus saith unto him, they have no wine." (KJV, John 2: 3). The person who knows him most intimately treats him like a supernatural butler, a kind of 1st century Grub Hub. "Go get wine, son." Jesus can just shake his head and reply, "Woman, what have I to do with thee?" (KJV, John 2: 4). It is not until the 6th chapter of the Book of John, when Jesus is confronting potential followers and church leaders that he begins to articulate his ontological case for existence. **This is the beginning of his practical apologetic.** When the pharisees ask him for more supernatural bread, Jesus replies with the first of seven (a number in scripture that is always intended to make us sit up and pay attention), "I am" statements in the Gospel of John: "I am the bread of life: he that cometh to me shall never hunger, and he that believeth on me shall never thirst" (KJV, John 6:35). Later in that Gospel, he affirms that he is:

The Light of the World, John 8:12,
The Gate, John, 10:9,
The Good Shepherd, John 10:11,
The way the truth and the life, John 14: 6,
The vine, John 15:5, and
The resurrection and the life, 11:25-26.

He did not just arise from the dead and walk out of his tomb. Oh, that event was foundational proof of who Jesus claimed to be as the long awaited Messiah and what he told his followers he would do, "Destroy this temple, and in three days I will raise it up" (ESV, John 2:19), but **it is not what he did but who he is that changed the world**; he IS the resurrection and the life. **What Jesus affirms again and again, is that we should be far less concerned with what he did than who he was; and because of who he was, what we can become. Jesus lived his world view.** From a practical apologist's point of view, Jesus was much more concerned with ontology—the nature of being—than he was with what we want him to do for us. Indeed, almost with an eye to affirming this ontological approach to his being, each book of the *Old* and *New Testaments* affirms a different identity or aspect of ontology for Jesus:

Genesis: He is the Creator,
Exodus: He is the Passover Lamb,
Leviticus: He is the Atoning Sacrifice, The High Priest,
Numbers: He is the Smitten Rock, and the One Lifted Up in the Wilderness,
Deuteronomy: He is the True Prophet,
Joshua: He is The Captain of The Lord of Hosts, hence, the Captain of our Salvation,
Ruth: He is the Kinsman Redeemer,
1 & 2 Samuel: He is the Prophet of the Lord,
1 & 2 Kings: He is the Reigning Lord,
1 & 2 Chronicles: He is the Glorious Temple,

Ezra: He is Ezra's Restorer,

Nehemiah: He is The Rebuilder of Walls,

Ester: He is the Advocate for His People

Job: He is the Dayspring from on High, The Everlasting Redeemer

Psalms: He is The Lord who is our Shepherd, the Only Begotten of the Father, the Chief Cornerstone, the Shepherd of our Souls

Proverbs: He is Our Pattern,

Ecclesiastes: He is the Wisdom of God, He is Life's Goal,

Song of Solomon: He is The Lover and Bridegroom,

Isaiah: He is The Suffering Servant, the Wonderful Counsellor, The Mighty God, The Prince of Peace,

Jeremiah: He is the Righteous Branch,

Lamentations: He is The Weeping Prophet,

Ezekiel: He is The Son of Man,

Daniel: He is The Son of Man Coming in the Clouds of Heaven, He is the Smiting Stone, He is the Ruling Prince,

Hosea: He is The Bridegroom, Redeeming Husband of the Fallen Wife,

Joel: He is The Restorer, He is the Baptizer with the Holy Spirit,

Amos: He is The Burden Bearer,

Obadiah: He is the Mighty Savior,

Jonah: He is The Forgiving God, He is the Resurrection,

Micah: He is The Messenger with Beautiful Feet,

Nahum: He is The Avenger of God's Elect,

Habakkuk: He is The God of our Salvation, He is the Great Evangelist,

Zephaniah: He is the Restorer of the Remnant; He is the Instrument of Judgment,

Haggai: He is the Desire of all Nations, He is The Cleansing Fountain,

Zechariah: He is Israel's King and Savior coming in Humility; He is The Pierced Son,

Malachi: He is The Son of Righteousness with Healing in His Wings,

Matthew: He is The Messiah,

Mark: He is The Miracle Worker,

Luke: He is The Son of Man,

John: He is The Son of God,

Acts: He is The Ascended Lord,

Romans: He is Our Righteousness, He is The Justifier,
1 & 2 Corinthians: He is The Justifier,
Galatians: He is The One Who Sets Us Free,
Ephesians: He is The Christ of Riches,
Philippians: He is The God who Meets Every Need,
Colossians: He is The Fullness of the Godhead,
1 & 2 Thessalonians: He is the Soon Coming King,
1 & 2 Timothy: He is The Mediator Between God and Man,
Philemon: He is the Friend, closer than a brother,
Hebrews: He is The Blood that washes Away My Sins,
James: He is The Great Physician,
1 & 2 Peter: He is The Chief Shepherd,
1, 2, & 3 John: He is Everlasting Love,
Jude: He is The God our Savior, and in
Revelation: He is The King of Kings and Lord of Lords.

Who is he? He is the Great "I am"—the *author and consummation of ontology.*

> "And God said to Moses, I AM THAT I AM: and he said,
> Thus, shall you say to the children of Israel, I AM has sent
> me to you." (ASV, Exodus 3:14)

If he is to be a model for us, and if we are to have "that mind in us which is also in Christ Jesus" (ESV, Philippians 5: 2-11), it follows that as we live our lives, we can only pray that our lives in some small way can also model our fundamental Christian beliefs about reality, knowledge, being, and values—our world view—so that others, just by watching us will be prompted to ask why we make the choices we make at work, at school, and at home, and why we have such a faith and confidence in a home schooled carpenter's son, a young Jewish rabbi from an obscure Galilean village, who lived and died so long ago. **Our very being—how we live our lives at work and in our homes**—can be far more important than anything we say or do. That **is the foundation for practical apologetics.**

Spring ahead a few centuries with me and change countries. In the early twentieth century, as part of the cosmic battle for C. S. Lewis' soul began to unfold while he was serving as a Don at Oxford's Magdalen College (one can almost see Archangel Michael contending with Satan for his soul during that period), he reminded us that stories have the power to present truths in a probative way; in short, that "reason is the natural organ of truth, but imagination is the organ of meaning." Even for that stodgy British professor, storyteller, and theologian, who is widely recognized as one of the most influential expositors on Christianity in the modern age, he found that when truths are put into imaginative form, they can be driven not only into the mind but also into the heart; his Narnia series is perhaps the finest memorial to that understanding. Just last summer, while reading *The Lion the Witch and the Wardrobe* (the 2nd book in that series) for the umpteenth time, I was struck by the profound theological insights that Lewis weaves into this simple "children's" story. Yes, Aslan is a fearsome lion, yet he is so much more. He is also the sacrifice, the lamb, slain for all in his kingdom. Children come to love him and weep as he lies dying, sacrificed on the Stone Table. Predictably, however, Lewis does not leave him helplessly stretched out there for the vultures to consume. Nor does scripture leave Jesus as just a metaphor for the lion of Judah. That was just the start of the story.

> In Revelation 5, Jesus is the long-awaited Lion of the tribe of Judah.

> John weeps because no one was found worthy to open the scroll of God's judgment or even to look inside it. Then one of the elders says to John, "Do not weep! See, the Lion of the tribe of Judah, the Root of David, has triumphed. He is able to open the scroll and its seven seals" (Revelation 5:4–5). Both genealogies in Matthew and Luke record that Jesus is a descendant of the tribe of Judah. When Jesus is revealed as the promised Lion of the tribe of Judah, it reveals His deity. He is the true king and the One to whom belongs the long-awaited obedience of nations. Yet it is not His fierceness or the

force of His power that makes Him worthy. **In that act of grand inversion, the Lion has triumphed because He became a Lamb** (Revelation 5:6–10; John 1:29). Jesus Christ is worthy because He lived a perfect, sinless life and in shedding His blood defeated sin and death. His death and resurrection have resulted in a protection for His people and an eternal kingdom that will honor and worship God. Ruling this kingdom will be Jesus, the Lion of the tribe of Judah. (Got answers.com).

"The Lion and the Lamb," the contemporary song by Bethel Music, captures this dichotomy in profound ways:

> Our God is a lion
> The Lion of Judah
> He's roaring with power
> And fighting our battles
> Every knee will bow before Him
> Our God is a lamb
> The lamb that was slain
> For the sins of the world
> His blood breaks the chains
> Every knee will bow before the lion and the lamb
> Every knee will bow before him.

In a remarkable inversion of potential, Jesus now relies on each of us to tell that story. We are the pilgrims on our journey and those around us are dying to hear our stories. And, yes, there will be prizes at the end of our journey. The Apostle John calls them crowns. Thus, I would argue, it behooves us to be effective storytellers as well, in order to pass on to subsequent generations the unlikely ways in which Christ has redeemed individual lives and built his culture—the local church.

That is why, in our coaching and training, helping organizational leaders become more powerful storytellers is foundational to our business. Following in that tradition, therefore, most of what I will do in the following pages is simply tell stories. Sometimes I'll interpolate and cull out what I believe are the appropriate scriptural implications; the other times it's on you. **Be constantly alert to look for the relationship between mundane personal events in your story and the ways in which you respond to them and the more profound world view implications they should herald.**

Believers corporately celebrate the Lord's supper or participate in the Eucharist, depending on your denomination's or sect's tradition, by eating a piece of bread or taking a simple wafer in remembrance of Jesus' body that was broken for us and by drinking wine or grape juice as a metaphor for the blood of Christ shed for us (KJV, Luke 22:19-20). But day by day, making the significance of this sacrament real in our lives for others to observe, what I will call, "*chewing the wafer,*" is an individual responsibility.

CHAPTER II

Story Telling and leadership

Let's jump right in. If we are faithful to our callings, whether that is as an athlete, cook, consultant, team lead in a Target Super Store, home schooling parent, soldier, plumber, chiropractor, practicing engineer, blogger, government bureaucrat, lawyer, teacher, financial analyst, student, bitcoin trader, senior business leader, or in my case a business consultant, coach, and writer—dare I even include in this number some believers actually serving as politicians?—every aspect of our lives and work should reflect our Christian world view. We do not have to be pastors, priests, missionaries, or elders to proclaim our faith in Christ. **Every occupation, profession, job, and calling, the tools we use, and the decisions we make in such positions, intentionally or unintentionally, will reflect our world view.** What does yours reflect?

Because so many sources rightfully highlight the power of stories to transform lives and cultures, we make it part of our business expertise at Executive Strategies International (ESI) to coach organizational leaders to become better storytellers. That such a starting point is central to our world views, but is usually unspoken, may not be readily apparent. **What may seem just a secular activity often has an underlying world view precedent.** It is part of our insinuating a practical apologetic in our consulting and training work. Our experience indicates that whether one is preaching a sermon, leading a team, trying to close a sale, hosting a podcast, supervising a shift, giving a Ted Talk, commanding a military unit, or exercising authority over an entire organization, much like Chaucer's pilgrims, "**whoever tells the best story wins**." Annette Simmons' book of the same name subtitled, "How to use your own stories to communicate with power and impact," makes a similar point.

I am sure that some of you have been asked, when seeking membership in a local church, to tell your story, in short how you came to your faith. Others of you when attending a social event and are introduced to others have been asked, "So…what do you do?" Just this month, while helping to facilitate an Ethics and Leadership Conference for high school juniors and teachers in Indiana, I was asked to begin by telling the assembled group who I was and what I did. On such occasions, you are being asked to tell part of your story, so others can get to know you on a deeper more personal level. On many occasions, you have begun with articulating your very being: I'm an engineer, I'm a landscaper, I'm a financial advisor with Capital One, I'm a homemaker, I'm a student, I'm an intelligence specialist, I'm an ICU nurse, I'm a dentist. You have just unwittingly become an amateur philosopher, identifying with your basic ontology. **With a little more basic knowledge and some good coaching you can become a practical apologist.** Proclaiming your Ontology (your essential being or identity) is just step one.

In a similar vein, being an effective leader requires us to be capable of telling our organization's story as well with power and sincerity, wrapping ourselves in our Vision and Core Values (our ethic), packaging our drive for innovation, demonstrating our desire to serve our customers and communities, and perhaps communicating our drive to generate new revenue streams with passion and conviction. The data demonstrates and our experience affirms **that the best storytellers are often the most successful organizational leaders**. Those who cannot craft a compelling story watch their market share dwindle, Wall Street analysts stifle yawns, their best employees leave, and their congregations nod off in the pews. Coaching others in how to tell effective stories, is just one of many ways I will discuss that our Christian world view should provide the philosophical underpinnings of the techniques we choose to use in our "secular" jobs. As the quotation marks suggest, I will also argue **that it makes very little sense to try to separate the "secular" from the sacred. For the Christian, the two should intertwine**. In that vein, our lives should tell our stories and be reflective of our Christian world view. The very ways in which we live, work, and demonstrate our expertise to the world should mark us for the Christ who redeemed us.

How can this happen practically? Let me start with a simple story. A few years ago, I was consulting for a large Arab-owned multi-national energy company in Doha, Qatar, as the organization was making its transition from serving multi-national corporations as a federal government agency under the direct control of Emir Hamad bin Khalifa Al Thani, to becoming a publicly held corporation with complex global ethical obligations. We had just spent the previous three days helping this company's very diverse leadership team develop a Business Strategy, create a compelling Vision of what success would look like five years out, agree upon a set of Core Values that a mostly Muslim leadership team from Qatar, Yemen, Saudi Arabia, India, Pakistan, and the UK could embrace, and establish a set of Operating Principles and Norms that would help them achieve the Metrics they had laid out for success. Collectively, these steps assist organizations in achieving what we call a culture of High Performance (See my book, *Culture and High Performance: Creating a World Class Business and Organizational Culture*). There was nothing ostensibly "Christian" about my approach; indeed—and with this assertion some of you may take umbrage—to do so in any business engagement but particularly in such a theologically, culturally, and politically charged environment would have been disingenuous, unprofessional, and unproductive, ensuring my failure to engage them and accomplish my assigned task. I am a business consultant, after all, not an ordained preacher, evangelist, or missionary. However each of these aspects of organizational performance has, as I will demonstrate as we proceed, a Christian foundation. That point aside, recall that **my premise is that our lives should reflect in all our work our basic Christian world view**.

Our training was being held at the Diplomatic Club in Doha, Qatar, a palatial structure reflecting beautiful Yemeni architecture overlooking the Persian Gulf. During our lunch break on the third day, a wealthy sheik, relative of the Emir, and senior business leader in the newly formed organization, approached me and asked me to step outside with him onto the veranda. He began by saying, "Dr. Jeffries," "Bill, please," I gently corrected him, touching my heart with my right hand as I spoke. Smiling, he continued, "Bill, thank-you, I do not mean to be rude or to pry but I perceive by your conversation and approach over the last few days that you are a Christian; am I correct?" Frankly a little surprised by his comment and not pressing him at the time as to why he believed that was the case, I assured him that he was correct. "Yes," I said, "what we would call an evangelical Christian." Continuing, he said, "I am a Muslim, a Sunni by tradition, and my wife is a Christian, a Baptist whom I met while attending Cambridge University and later the British School of Economics several years ago. We fell in love despite our theological differences and have been married now for eleven years and have two children, a boy and a girl. I want to be the best husband for her that I can be. Can you please offer me some suggestions as to how I can appreciate her Christian faith and become a better husband to her and father to our children?"

Wow, what an opportunity, unexpectedly dropped onto my plate over lunch! How would you begin? What would you say? These are the very moments for which scripture commands us to be prepared. By the way, let me be quick to add that the openness he expressed is not the norm for a Yemeni Arab Muslim, whether Sunni or Shia and certainly not from a Saudi Wahabist, but it is not that unusual for well-educated Muslim businessmen of any sect in Qatar, Ajman, Dubai, and the UAE, who have observed American business and financial success for years and wondered about the reasons for it, for them to be open to such polite conversation, always much more compelling when they institute it, not us. **Working with them, living an authentic value-centered Christian world view is far more impactful than preaching. It is up to us to live lives that make others ask the right questions.**

Over some freshly caught Arabian Gulf hamour (grouper), we spent the next hour discussing the similarities and differences between a Christian approach to values, marriage, and gender and a Muslim understanding of the same issues. Admittedly, our conversation initially dealt primarily with more philosophical and rational questions—a thoroughly apologetic approach—but with a little nudging began to turn toward biblical implications, such as the model for the covenantal nature of Christian marital unions. In the brief time we had together, we examined the Sunni view of Islamic eschatology and compared it to the unreformed evangelical Christian view of the same times in the future. Muslims are routinely interested in how future events will reveal the consequences of our particular faiths. In the process we explored how the covenantal Christian view of marriage is meant to reflect Christ's relationship to His followers (the Church) and how that relationship will be revealed in the end times—The Marriage Supper of the Lamb.

This is the kind of Vision—what succeeding looks like in the long term in our business jargon—that we teach as part of our "secular" formula for organizational success. So impactful was our brief conversation, apparently, that he invited me over to his home that evening for dinner. For those of you who have worked in that part of the world, you realize what a rare honor it is to be invited to an Arab's home, particularly spontaneously. It just does not happen. That night over more in-depth conversations regarding the story of my faith, the exclusivity of Jesus' claim (John 14:6), and some delicious Macbus, the national dish of Qatar, he asked me to go "dune bashing" in the Mesaied with him and his son the next time I returned to his country. **He was open and questioning of someone who understood his "story" and expressed an authentically lived one of his own**. That is the practical apologetic key that opens so many doors. Our stories count!

Should such a conversation seem daunting or even intimidating to you, let me admit that it does take some time to prepare. I suggest that Nabeel Qureshi's *Seeking Allah and Finding Jesus*, would be a great place for you to start to provide the necessary background for such a discussion. Even Professor Malcolm Clark's more secular *Islam for Dummies* can be a very basic source of information. The point is that we can't just wing it. **We must have done our homework.** Our conversation was an exercise in theological baby steps to be sure, but it laid the foundation for what I hoped will be a stronger marital relationship and family and perhaps chart the path for his own personal pilgrimage toward the Christian faith. Clearly his wife had opened the door with her story, because of what the sheik had seen in her life and unconditional love, and he sensed a resonance with my approach to Story Telling, Vision, Values, Norms, and Role definition. **It was not a time for preaching or simply presenting the Gospel in traditional terms**—as you may have learned in a "witnessing training class" held at your church. **This opportunity demanded a practical apologetic approach.** That is what we can always hope for when our work and lives properly reflect our Christian world view.

It goes without saying, I trust, that in order to have such a conversation, Christians need to be well-grounded in their own faiths, know their own scriptures, and be open to learning about others as well. **Adherents to other religions often put us to shame in their diligence to know and proclaim their faiths to the world.** Many Muslims have memorized large sections of their Holy Scriptures, and in some cases the entire *Qur'an,* as well as being conversant with the applicable Hadith. Other "People of the Book," Orthodox Jews, have traditionally memorized the entire *Torah,* and many Hassidics and other Orthodox Jewish men to this day wear their scriptures around their heads in Phylacteries during weekday prayers, showing that the teachings of their scriptures (particularly Deuteronomy 16: 13-21) symbolically protect their mind and reasoning capability and, most importantly, ought to be manifested publicly in their lives. Find me a Christian who has actually read the entire *Bible* cover to cover—yes even the seemingly boring books of Ruth and Ester and wading through all the begets and begots in Numbers and the many laws in Leviticus—let along read, studied, and practiced "rightly dividing" it (2 Timothy 2:15), and I will buy you a cup of Dunkin Donuts best cold brew.

Too many of us professing Christians are lazy and uninformed, waiting to be told on Sunday mornings what is important to know and which verses to memorize. It should come as no surprise then that becoming capable of presenting an apologetics approach to scriptural truths to others seems such a daunting task, not only to individual Christians but also for far too many leaders in the local church. We are afraid of what we will not know and are more than willing to pawn off the task to others or deem it to be an unimportant tangent to our faith. Get busy!

> **Study** to show thyself approved unto God, a workman that needeth not to be ashamed, rightly dividing the word of truth (KJV, 2 Timothy 2:25).

When we are clear about our own world view, it will naturally permeate everything we do, teach, and say, every tool we use, and business practice and teaching methodology that we employ. As Ravi Zacharias reminds us in some of his most profound podcasts and U-Tube presentations, whatever our world view, it must provide rational answers for at least four basic questions formed around "**origins, meaning, morality**, and **destiny.**" The point that Ravi makes most poignantly is that not only can each individual aspect of our existence be captured and explained in these four considerations, but there must be coherence among all four. When that coherence exists, others cannot help but see it, even in our "secular" work.

Depending on one's world view, a person may be able to form a reasonable answer to one or two of these considerations, but **only the Christian world view permits such coherence among all four.**

How would you answer an honest questioner regarding the Christian view of:

Where this world came from
Where life came from
What the purpose is of life
Why human life is valuable
How we determine right and wrong
Where we as a people are headed

Why the culture of the USA might be different from that of France, Saudi Arabia, India, Indonesia, Somalia, China, Mali, or Israel?

What is your story? By working with you or simply watching you day by day, would I be compelled to ask you?

CHAPTER III

Taking Your World View to Work

As I was mulling over the last chapter, I got a text from a friend who is an innovative and thoughtful entrepreneur and educator asking me if I could suggest a Christian World View based ethics curriculum that he could use to launch an ethics program in his newly established university. Great timing. The answer I sent him back was far more than he wanted to hear, I am sure, but is rooted in the following story.

Let me start with some fundamentals. Several years ago, while I was assigned as Director of Ethics at a branch of National Defense University in Norfolk, VA, I was invited as an adjunct professor to teach a course entitled Ethics and Law in Higher Education at Old Dominion University in Norfolk. It was intended to be a one semester capstone course required for all graduate students seeking their Ph.ds in Education from that university. I was asked to team-teach the course with an attorney, who was then the President of Virginia Commonwealth University. Together, over the semester, we crafted a number of difficult case studies that posed potential ethical and legal dilemmas that professors, administrators, and others involved with higher education might have to face because of their positions and then discuss them from two vantage points: the legal implications, on which my attorney colleague would take the lead, and the ethical implications which were primarily my purview. Ethics and law are often "two paths that diverge in a yellow wood" (See Robert Frost's "The Road Not Taken") and arrive at two very different locations. The seminar discussions, as you may have already surmised, were vigorous and at times contentious. I am a Christian; to the best of my knowledge, he was not.

Each of us had some time before we delved into the actual case studies to take a few periods during the semester to address our individual approaches to these dilemmas and provide the necessary academic background for our approaches. We didn't need a textbook; the daily news gave us far more examples than we needed. Part of my approach was to lecture on the rudiments of several world views—particularly Deism, Naturalism, Existentialism, Monotheism, Atheism, New Atheism, and Christianity—that underlie our ethical biases. One of my graduate students found this approach, in her words, "life altering" and, as it happened, had some close family ties with Rev. Pat Robertson, who had years earlier founded a private Christian University in Virginia Beach, VA, called CBN University—these days known as Regents University. She apparently had a conversation with him regarding our class, and he subsequently had one of his staff give me a call. During a brief telephone conversation with the meeting planners at CBN, I was invited to speak on ethics at an upcoming convocation being held at the university. When I arrived a few weeks later, I saw the large placard out in front of the auditorium announcing my talk as "A Defense of Christian Ethics." That title posed an ethical dilemma for me.

A year earlier, I had the pleasure of spending a couple hours in the office of Dr. John Silber, the brilliant and iconoclastic President of Boston University, who had purged the faculty of dozens of intellectual charlatans and resurrected a university atrophying from incompetence, immoral behavior, and academic lethargy and helped to transform it into the premier research university it is today, very similar to what President Mitch Daniels, former Indiana Governor, has accomplished at Purdue over the last several years. In our discussions, Silber expressed to me his belief that ethics should be thought of as a unitary field, much like physics. In brief, it makes very little sense to talk about the physics of flight, the physics of soccer, the physics of the MLB Home Run Derby, or the physics of driving a car at 85 mph as though they were based on different principles of logic. The same forces that impact my Dodge Charger as I evade the speed traps on I-65 while heading to a Yankees-White Sox game on the south side of Chicago, impact LeBron as he drives to the basket, our son Austin as he competes in shooting competitions in Kentucky, our son Paul as he skis a double black diamond down the French side of Chamonix, my chiropractor daughter Tiffany as she adjusts your neck, my daughter Ainsley as she zip lines over her Wild and Free retreat in Virginia, and also impacted the brave engineers and Thai SEALs who rescued twelve young soccer players and their coach from certain death in a flooded cave in Thailand in 2018. Physics is physics.

Silber's premise stayed with me as I delved more deeply into the subject matter, myself and began to see the folly of separating Professional Ethics into different disciplines. To be sure, you can find dozens of books on "Christian" Ethics authored by revered theologians and scholars on Amazon; that's their problem, not mine. **They all muddy the issue and create problems for a practical apologist.** Most people will readily assent to the proposition that there is just one physics with different specific applications. In a similar vein, ethics—that branch of philosophy devoted to the examination of universal principles of conduct—is a unitary field. As we will see, how we approach that relativity is dependent on our world views. Correctly understood, there is but one ethic, one set of principles that should guide human conduct. Consistent with that view, there are then a variety and relativity of applications of ethics to different fields of enquiry. This premise is fundamental to living a practical apologetic.

As I began speaking with my initially shocked audience of mostly divinity students and pre-law majors at CBN-Regents, I said, "Let me begin by stating for the record that the sign out front is incorrect. **There is no such thing as Christian Ethics.**" As students began to squirm and glanced uneasily around the room at one another and a few looked searchingly for Rev. Robertson, I continued by alleging that the same principles—I would argue ethical absolutes—that underscore political ethics, journalistic ethics, business ethics, medical ethics, military ethics, and scientific ethics, also underscore what we glibly refer to as Christian Ethics. When we fail to recognize that fundamental principle, **we relegate Christian Ethics**

to just a limited subset of ethical behaviors applicable to a limited arena of existence and therefore subject to Naturalistic considerations. It is akin to saying there are Ethics, and oh yeah, there are those other "Christian" ethics, a subset of the real deal. **As practical apologists for the faith, we dare not concede that point. Ethics is ethics.** Silber later was asked to speak at the U. S. Military Academy, and he captured many of these same observations in his speech on "professional" ethics in general, entitled "The Ethics of the Sword," in which he made a similar point regarding "military ethics."

That very understanding contributed to the ongoing development of my story. Years earlier, when I was on the faculty of the United States Military Academy at West Point directing the yearling (sophomore) courses in Comparative World Literature, I and several others from our department were summoned by the Head of my academic department and the Dean of the Academic Board to a meeting in the Dean's office. They explained to those of us present that the Secretary of the Army had just mandated the creation of an ethics curriculum at the Academy, and they informed us that I, and a few others on the English Department faculty, had been identified to help launch the initiative. I was honored to be asked, but also knew that such an undertaking was not just a matter of selecting textbooks and creating a basic syllabus. In my mind, selecting the course of study was secondary to other concerns. The quality of our preparation and pedagogical approach would determine our outcomes, and I was painfully aware that there were some very different world views represented in that conference room.

I told those present that while I believed that such a course of study was imperative for the proper development of future leaders of the army, and that I was excited to be considered among those to launch such an initiative, that before we could teach a course in ethics, because that discipline was a subset of a larger discipline, we should start at a more basic level and first teach an introductory course in philosophy. Such an academic foundation was necessary in order to ground students in the systematic approaches taken by the great thinkers of all ages who had wrestled with the questions of Metaphysics (what is real), Epistemology (the theory of knowledge),

Ontology (the nature of being), and Axiology (fundamentals of ethical reasoning). These are also the weight supporting pillars of every credible world view. In short, Ethics is just a subset of the academic discipline of Philosophy. They said, they understood the need to lay such a foundation and that we should go ahead and do that also.

As our conversation continued, I chimed in that before we could even immerse students in an Introduction to Philosophy, we needed to ground them in logic and critical thinking and ensure they understood the elements of Western syllogistic reasoning that had informed the arguments of all the great philosophers down through the ages who would routinely challenge one another for potential logical violations of coherence among their systems of thought. Again, affirming nods all around the conference table, but then the Dean dropped the bomb and said we needed to accomplish it all in one semester. So, the task became how to distill the essence of at least three semesters of difficult undergraduate academic work into one term. That was the challenge our department accepted.

First came the selection of the faculty. At the time, almost all West Point teaching faculty were active duty military officers, the majority of whom were themselves West Pointers. All had attended various prestigious graduate schools and had obtained at least a master's degree in their discipline and were subsequently assigned to teach in the Department of English at the Academy for three years. Before we could get military faculty with graduate degrees in philosophy or ethics through the graduate school academic pipeline, we would have to transition existing instructors of English already assigned to the department into that role. One does not just take history majors and ask them to teach a college-level course in advanced math or nuclear physics. In a similar vein, one does not take several mid-grade army officers with graduate degrees in Language, Literature, Literary Criticism, or Fine Arts and suddenly commission them to teach a credible college-level course in philosophy and ethics. We had to prepare them intellectually and pedagogically. We conveyed this concern to our Department Head who agreed completely with our observations. I said while I myself had always had a great interest in philosophy and had read widely in the discipline, that I had very little formal education in the subject. He said, "We'll take care of that"; sounds so simple—but that is the army way. Give us a mission, and we will find a way to accomplish it.

The Academy brought in three superb mentors to work with us: Professor Bob Gurland, who at the time was the multi-talented Chairman of the Philosophy Department of NYU (by theology, training, and upbringing a widely-read but admittedly a non-observant Jew and a world-renowned mathematician), the Deputy Chairman of the Philosophy Department at Princeton University (a self-described smorgasbord Roman Catholic), and William Barrett (the leading Existentialist philosopher of the time), the author of *Death of the Soul, Irrational Man,* and 17 other highly respected philosophical works. Their three world views could not have been more disparate. The three of them met with about ten of us off and on weekly for over a year, grounding us in the history and methodologies of philosophy and ethics. They essentially taught us the course we would be teaching our students the subsequent semester. It was a year-long tutorial from some of the brightest minds in the country—no doubt the finest non-degree-granting graduate education anyone could have ever received. What these three academic mentors forced us to do was not only to understand the various philosophical thought forms through the ages from the Pre-Socratics to more contemporary Post-Modernists but to be able to argue their respective merits and demerits as well as the ethical stances that just naturally arose from each of their philosophies and underlying world views.

Throughout history, each philosopher in his or her own way has grappled with the question of origins (where did mankind come from?), the meaning of existence (why are we here?), the nature of morality (where did such a concept arise and why is it important?), and what is the destiny of individual humankind and culture (what happens when a person dies?). In short, during this whole process, I had the opportunity to come to grips with my own world view and learn how to defend my Christian world view against all comers, regardless of their presuppositions. **Unbeknownst to the Academy, they were helping to prepare me to become a staunch practical Christian apologist.**

Our immediate goal in teaching philosophy and ethics at West Point was to prepare future army leaders to be thoughtful, responsible ethical decision makers. To be more specific, they had to be able to understand the ethics of *jus ad bellum* (Just War Theory) and the ethical obligations of an army officer to grapple intellectually with topics such as just war criteria, the appropriate or inappropriate uses of military interventions, the ethics of preemptive or anticipatory attacks, the policy of noncombatant immunity, the relative moral equality of competing combatants, and how to make life-changing ethical decisions on the battlefield. Such issues impact a host of other concerns such as the future impact of Just War theory on how this nation should deal with all the numerous forms of warfare in the future: asymmetric, guerilla, cyber, conventional, psychological, jungle, desert, and others. In brief, grounding our students in the philosophical foundation of the military ethic and the world view that undergirds it, was our major focus. These were the central issues with which such a course in ethics had to grapple. In recent conversations at military ethics conferences, with those currently teaching in that department, I have been pleased to learn that the same approach to the teaching of ethics that we launched in the 1980's is mostly still in place over thirty years later. Kudos to those who followed in our wake for their academic diligence. The one major difference is that currently several of the instructors at West Point, as well as even more at the other major service academies, are non-Academy graduates and several are civilian professors with no military credentials whatsoever. That difference can be problematical.

All this is but the back story for the answer I sent to my local entrepreneuring educator friend, that far more important than the curriculum was the individual or individuals whom he chose to teach such a course, because that individual must have a solid grasp of the history and development of philosophy through the ages, an understanding of the major schools of derivative ethics, and, since he wanted the program to be a Christian world view based ethics curriculum, the presenter must also have a firm grasp of all the competing world views and be capable of articulating the Christian position regarding each of them.

Should that same topic interest you, by the way, I suggest, as a starting point, reading Abdu Murray's *Grand Central Question*, in which Murray, a renowned Muslim lawyer who converted to Christianity, tackles each of the major world views from the stand point of the central question each tries to resolve and demonstrates why **the Christian world view is the only one that adequately answers every one of their major questions.**

CHAPTER IV

World Views Redux

Now that you have heard the term "world view" a few times, let me return to where I began to be sure we have the same understanding of terms. I want to be academically clear and scripturally accurate but also very practical. What is a world view and why is knowing what yours is so important? If you go to every high school freshman's (and apparently SIRI's and Alexa's) favorite research source, Wikipedia, to define the term, the overly stuffy perfunctory definition you will find there is that a world view is "a fundamental cognitive orientation of an individual or society encompassing the whole of an individual's or society's knowledge and point of view." Excited yet?

My definition will be less pedantic but more useful. **A world view is an overall philosophical and religious way of looking at the world and those around you. It must make sense of what you experience as reality and what you believe to be true.** Nowhere is such a consideration more important than in matters of faith. Think of it as a set of colored glasses you wear—your world view colors everything you see, think, and do, before the brain even begins to process the incoming data. The glasses that a Christian wears color reality in a very different way from those worn by atheists, agnostics, or adherents of other religions around the world, even other monotheistic ones such as Islam and Judaism. As such, this overall approach to life weaves together all the aspects of existence that provide an individual with a more-or-less coherent philosophical frame of reference underlying all thought and action.

Underscoring these aspects of reality are all the presuppositions (fundamental world view assumptions) which we hold (consciously or subconsciously) about the make-up of our world. Building on Zacharias's four pillars of a world view (origin, meaning, morality, and destiny), one must answer several more specific related questions:

1. What is the prime reality?
2. Who or what is man?
3. What is the purpose of life?
4. What happens to us at death?
5. What is the basis of morality?
6. Why should we care?
7. Is there such a thing as moral obligation?
8. What is the meaning of history?
9. Why are we here?
10. Why is human life to be respected or revered?

A typical academic approach to studying world views would identify them as: Positivism, Constructivism, Post-positivism, Participatory, and Pragmatism. Again, that is academically accurate but a bit too stuffy and not very practical. I'll leave them for you to research if you are so inclined. I instead prefer to discuss world views by exploring a series of other more easily defined and practical "isms" related to the nature of faith: Theism, Naturalism, Postmodernism, Atheism, Agnosticism, Pantheism, Existentialism, and a specific version of Theism—Christianity. That approach can be heavy enough lifting for most of us.

But we are getting ahead of ourselves—back to my colleague's query. The underlying question that must be considered in structuring the methodology and content of any course in ethics, is why are we offering it? That is the question I posed to the local college president. If he instituted such an academic course of study, what would be its Purpose? What would his Vision of success be? Once that Vision has been clarified, how would he know that the program of instruction had achieved it? The very Purpose of such a course of instruction and what a Vision of success would look like, if it were it done right, would then determine the methodology. Once we answered those questions, we could commence.

When we spoke with the Dean of Students at West Point, for example, regarding why we were being tasked to launch such an initiative in ethics, he explained that events as far removed from the 1980's as the March 16, 1968 massacre of over 300 unarmed Vietnamese villagers in the Son Tinh District village of My Lai, South Vietnam, the 1970 shooting of unarmed college students demonstrating against the War in Southeast Asia at Kent State by the Ohio National Guard, as well as other less well publicized demonstrations and administration building sit ins related to that unpopular war on campuses such as those staged at Berkley and Wisconsin-Madison indicated that the then contemporaneous training approaches to engraining the military ethic and associated values in draftees had apparently been inadequate. Even though Lieutenant William Calley, the American officer in charge of the American infantry unit that entered the village of My Lai and allowed the atrocity to take place, was an OCS (Officer Candidate School) commissioned officer—what the troops sarcastically called a 90-day wonder—not even an ROTC graduate—and most significantly not a West Pointer trained and educated for four years— and the troops at Kent State were in the National Guard (what the troops at the time sarcastically referred to as "weekend warriors")—not regular army soldiers, because West Pointers were meant to set the standard for the profession, the decision had been made at the Department of Defense level to start the ethics education with them. The metaphor the SECDEF used was that West Point graduates were meant to be the drop of dye dropped into a glass of water that would eventually color the entire glass. Our job was to disperse the dye.

Let's return to the present. When I queried the local college president regarding why he wanted to include a course in ethics based on a Christian world view, he said that his Purpose for launching such a program of study was to prepare his students to make better decisions when they graduated and entered the organizational world or went on to higher education. Great answer and one that, knowing him and his Christian world view, I expected him to offer up.

Trust in the Lord with all your heart,
and do not lean on your own understanding.

In all your ways acknowledge him,
and he will make straight your paths.
(NIV, Proverbs 3:5-6)

The law of the LORD is perfect,
reviving the soul;
the testimony of the LORD is sure,
making wise the simple;
the precepts of the LORD are right,
rejoicing the heart;
the commandment of the LORD is pure,
enlightening the eyes;
the fear of the LORD is clean,
enduring forever;
the rules of the LORD are true,
and righteous altogether.
(KJV, Psalm 119:105)

CHAPTER V

Ethical Decision Making

Let me expand on this particular case of living a practical apologetic in our professional lives. As an analogy to creating such a program of ethics based on the Christian world view, consider this story about another rather specialized example of planning. When one plans for an airborne combat operation—something, in the past, I had some expertise in doing—one does not plan for such an operation, as you might expect, step by step from beginning to end. You do not begin with where the troops are currently located, give them a mission, issue ammo and carefully packed chutes, load them down with the appropriate gear and ammo, transport them to the flight line, stage them for loading the aircraft, arrange them in "sticks" for the jump, fly to the tactical site, stand up, hook up, jump out of the planes, land, hide the chutes, assemble for the operation, and then engage the enemy tactically. You start, instead, at the end, planning for the tactical operation on the ground and the engagement with the enemy. Then you back plan every event required to get the appropriate troops with the appropriate weapons, equipment, and ammunition and the appropriate tactical plan at the appropriate place and time. You begin with a Vision of the end results and then plan back to the beginning. The end always determines the appropriate beginning and the required behaviors to get there. Almost sounds like a biblical model.

In a similar vein, when developing a strategic plan for a business, the savvy leader does not start with current results, and then plan year by year for five to ten years into the future. What happens with such a plodding beginning-to-end approach is that everything tends to change along the way; when you finally get to the fifth or tenth year out, the reality does not match your plan. Military planners know this as Helmuth von Moltke's (famous Prussian strategist before WWI) warning that "no plan ever survives contact with the enemy." The wise leader starts by "Futuring;" by that we mean, envisioning and analyzing a series of the most likely potential futures and then deciding which one best matches the anticipated political, economic, business, and sociological realities. Once we know the most probable end states, we can back plan to get there— similar to the Airborne example above. For the business world, that means finding a skilled futurist before the planning process commences. From the standpoint of theology, **that is why a special blessing is promised to the believer who will study the Book of Revelation** (KJV, Revelation 1:3)— **not just a potential future, but what God tells us <u>will</u> happen one day**. Thank-you John of Patmos. That is the believer's Vision of ultimate success: Satan defeated once and for all, Death destroyed, earth renewed, and believers in eternal communion with God. Genesis begins on a created earth and Revelation ends on a renewed (recreated) earth. Having such a clear understanding of end time events—what will happen in the future— helps to underscore how we should live our lives to get there. I'll come back to that biblical injunction in much more detail, because it directly impacts the development and practical consequences of our world view.

Let's apply that analogy to the teaching of ethics. The tactical plan on the ground (a Vision of what success would look like and an approach for achieving it) always precedes the operations, logistics, and delivery plans. **The same is true of preparing to engage others holding competing world views with your own. Yes, you must know yours inside and out, but you better understand theirs as well.**

Given my colleague's desire to enable students to make better, more ethical, decisions in the real world upon graduation—on their jobs—let's start there—on the ground in confrontation with their "enemy." As graduates they will be taking jobs in various businesses and careers, each with its unique specialized ethical challenges. For some that challenge may be trying to satisfy an irrational customer, helping innovation teams develop new products, putting up drywall for a construction project when they suspect the framing may be damaged, supervising several plumbers out on the job site, confronting a supervisor as to why she was cutting corners on a building project, running a used car business when they suspect that part of their inventory may have come from flood-ravaged areas of Houston, developing a website for clients with whom they may have fundamental moral differences, serving as a software designer for Facebook, or maybe even acting as a quant for Fanny Mae. Is it possible to describe a consistent decision-making methodology that one can use when faced with an ethical dilemma of any variety? I say yes, and again, it had a biblical premise when we designed it.

Let me begin generically by suggesting that regardless of one's world view, there are certain pertinent questions one should raise. As one answers these questions, the Christian must always be cognizant of how she or he is being perceived by others and how a follower of Lord Jesus should behave. If we are dedicated followers of Christ, our work, of course, should never be thought of as separate from our faith (see Sebastian Traeger's and Greg Gilbert's *The Gospel at Work: How the Gospel Gives New Purpose and Meaning to Our Jobs*). However, one does not merely have to preach to one's co-workers or customers, hang *Bible* verses on the office carrel wall, or pester them to join you in church or at your local *Bible* study to express one's Christian world view; although, there are times when those more direct witnessing approaches may also be quite appropriate. Rather, **we are all called to "be" the gospel.** It is an ontological approach I am suggesting, not an epistemological (theory of knowledge) one. **For many colleagues and customers with whom you associate on a daily basis, you may be the only gospel they ever hear or see in action**. My colleague who asked me the initial question is also the author of the book geared largely to young people entitled, *You're Always Being Interviewed*. For the Christian, the equivalent is "you are always being watched," and you should always be in the process of becoming more Christlike.

In the same way, let your light shine before others, so
that they may see your good works and give glory to your
Father who is heaven (ESV, Matthew 5:16).

From the *New Testament* perspective, this is fundamental to ongoing
sanctification, and imperative if we are going to be able to represent a
practical apologetic. As a starting point, let's take a topic as fundamental to
organizational life as effective problem solving. If our Christian world view
can be foundational here, it can be reflected in almost any other aspect of
our business life; so I will start very generally. Regardless of one's world
view, to be an effective decision maker, one should consider asking each
of the following questions:

1. <u>What does the data say</u>? What are the facts bearing on the problem?
   Try "five-sensing" the situation: what can you see, feel, taste, hear,
   or maybe even smell regarding the perceived situation? That is
   why Existentialist philosopher Jean Paul Sartre, in the early 20th
   century, suggested to us that the most perplexing epistemological
   issue in life is that "something is there." This remains the most
   perplexing question facing philosophers and evolutionists who
   concoct one debunked argument after the next to try to explain
   what they find. In short, mere existence (what is there) is the
   beginning of any reputable intellectual search, regardless of one's
   world view. We can see that "something," either specifically or
   more generally, but we must start with what is.

2. <u>What might the data mean, and what are some of the possibilities
   inherent in that data</u>? So, something exists, either specifically
   (data or facts) or more generally (ideas and theories), so what?
   What theories might be applicable? What theoretical models
   make sense? Are there certain best practices in your industry or
   business? How has a similar problem in your area of influence
   been handled before? What is the big picture, after all? Are there
   existing regulations or administrative procedures that dictate a
   particular approach? What is the purpose of your having to make
   this decision in the first place?

3. Given that existence is there (admittedly a weird tautology), that something IS, <u>how can we examine and evaluate it</u>? We can't do the "evaluation" until we have something to assess. How do you plan to analyze the quality of the data? How will you separate fact from speculation? Is it a fact or mere supposition? What analytical process such as, Force Field Analysis, FMEA (Failure Model and Effects Analysis), T-Model, Kepner Trego, Root Cause Analysis, Six Thinking Hats, etc. do you tend to use?

4. <u>What will the impact be on others</u> based on your decision? Are there lives at risk in this decision? Is safety a consideration? Is the environment at stake? How might this situation impact your employees, your customers, your competition, your family, your team, your community, or maybe even your nation? Are there uncontrolled viruses running rampant? Who is impacted?

This is a simple "secular" model based on psychological type (See my *Still True to Type* for an in depth discussion of this subject) that recognizes the need to involve all four dominant personality preferences when deciding: **S**ensing (data, facts, specifics), i**N**tuition (ideas, theories, concepts, possibilities), **T**hinking (using your favorite objective, impersonal B-School model, like Kepner Tregoe or a Force Field Analysis), and **F**eeling judgments (impact on others). We designed the following model over two decades ago and simply called it the **Z Model**:

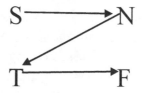

We encourage the discussion of these personality preferences always to be in just that order: **S** to **N** to **T** to **F**, for reasons discussed above, to ensure that all elements of decision making are involved. Nothing overtly theological here, just a reflection of existential reality as a starting point. As recent neurological research has begun to uncover, this is also the process that the brain, uses to understand existence and meaning and know what to do with it. If it is true, it must be of God.

What exists? **S**

What might that mean? **N**

How do we begin to analyze that existence and meaning? **T**

Are there interpersonal, moral or ethical implications of our analysis? **F**

These are also essentially the implications embedded in the four levels of the cerebral cortex, as it seems to rise in structural complexity from combinations of **SF** to **ST** to **NF** to **NT**. One step lays the foundation for the next. This approach simply follows the way in which the brain has been designed. If you want to flesh out this procedural approach check out Walter Lowen's *Dichotomies of the Mind* and much of the more recent practical research by Dario Nardi. These days this model is generally accepted in the organizational world and can be found in your favorite search engine as the **Zig-Zag** decision-making model. **We embrace it not just because it reflects reality but because it follows a biblical pattern**; more of that later when I discuss Emotional Intelligence (EI) and the biblical model behind it, as well. But this is just the starting point. As always, for us to use them, these ostensibly secular models must have biblical predicates.

All these epistemological considerations are critical to make any decision but take on special meaning when morality or ethical concerns are under the spotlight. Since consulting on ethical decision-making is part and parcel of our business, it is important that our approaches in this arena can be rooted in scripture. For that reason, we teach this model in our business consulting. Indeed, having just returned from working with an animal health business in Fort Worth, Texas, I had the leadership team use this **Z** model to inform the decisions being made regarding what new products to launch, how much to invest in new product development, how to distribute bonuses to deserving employees, and several other business issues. The previous month, we used the same decision-making model to help a defense contractor on the west coast analyze the approaches taken by its numerous innovation teams, and are currently working with a major engineering firm supporting NASA in Houston, Texas evaluate the safety concerns of the current Artemis Mission to return to the moon in 2022 and future manned Orion launches to Mars. The organization's specific technology is irrelevant; the model works because it reflects our basic created humanness—what it means to have been "fearfully and wonderfully made." This is just the purely secular starting point and is useful regardless of one's world view. As we move into the arena of ethics, the model necessarily gets more complex, particularly when one desires to be seen as living on the basis of a Christian world view.

Let's move beyond the routine. As described, the above model is a general decision-making model usable for any issue and <u>not tied to any specific world view</u>. Ethical decision-making is a special case of the above, and begins to be able to reflect, even more clearly, the essential elements of one's world view. Having an appropriate model for making ethical decisions is more complex and needs to include additional considerations besides what merely "works." In that regard, I will define *ethics as a rational reflection about what it would be right or wrong to do*. When moving into this arena of problem solving, we encourage all organizations, regardless of nationality, culture, or possible world view to ask the following additional questions:

1. How do you define the current dilemma?
2. Have you defined the problem accurately?
3. How would you define the problem if you stood on the other side of the fence?
4. How did the problem occur in the first place?
5. To whom and what do you give your loyalty as a person?
6. To whom do you owe your loyalty as a member of your profession?
7. What is your intention in making this decision?
8. How does your intention compare with the probable results?
9. Whom could your decision harm or help?
10. Would it be appropriate to discuss your decision with other parties?
11. Are you confident that your decision would be as valid long term as it seems now?
12. Could you disclose without qualms your decision or action to your boss, your commander, your family, your team lead, your human resources professional, your legal advisor, or even to a minister, priest, or other religious advisor? If not, are your reasons justifiable?

13. What is the symbolic potential of your decision if understood? What if it were misunderstood?
14. Under what circumstances would you allow exceptions to your decision?

To reiterate, these additional fourteen considerations are helpful regardless of one's world view. Using the Airborne Operation analogy described above, now it is time to "back plan" how you will do what you do. The ethical dilemma you may face is equivalent to the tactical situation on the ground. Once you know your world view, how would that particular world view and its implicit values color your response to each of the questions above?

As if such generic decision making were not already complicated enough, **the Christian world view demands a third set of considerations**. A Christian application of ethics is not just a rational reflection of what is right or wrong but is more "revelational" in quality (ie. God's disclosure of Himself and His will to His creation). Reason gathers the key information described above (facts, options, background); reason identifies the key epistemological issues; logic analyzes the individual elements (goals, biases, means, motives, and consequences); and reason formulates certain principles, rules, and practices. But, and this is a huge BUT, **reason is not the sole source of the principles by which the Christian makes moral or ethical decisions**. The Christian has Holy Scripture as a starting point as well, but therein lies the need for further extrapolation.

When it comes to Scripture, not all ethical "norms" discussed are equally authoritative. Hold your fire; let me explain. Hermeneutics plays a key role here. A lot depends on the substance, the person, the period, and the culture involved. One cannot simply close one's eyes, riffle through the *Bible,* and at let a finger land on a random verse and then act accordingly. This is not a magic act by Ben and Teller. There are certain exegetical and more generally hermeneutical considerations that apply when working out of a Christian world view. Some of the following considerations come into play.

1. Does the apparent principle appear in the *Old Testament* or the *New Testament*? Which *Old Testament* teachings are affirmed by Jesus in his ministry, and which have been fulfilled or superseded by Grace?

2. Which principles offer clear imperatives, and which are just examples? Scriptural imperatives always take precedence over examples, just as absolutes should always override particulars (see chapter XXXIII).

3. Direction vs. inference. What is the motive of the teaching? Is it didactic or explanatory?

4. Are the specific examples of behavior merely historical or cultural or do they stand for universally binding principles?

5. Does the supposed principle appear in a single passage or in multiple passages? Far too many *faux* theologies and alleged moral practices and ethical principles sprout from a single verse of misinterpreted scripture. Cultish thinking thrives on this approach. As a general rule of thumb, the *Bible* interprets itself.

6. Is there a scriptural mandate for or against your proposed decision?

7. Is the scripture silent on the issue? If so, you should probably do the same.

8. What is the type of biblical literature you are reading? Is it poetry, parable, wisdom, apocalyptic, history, gospel, epistle, etc.?

9. We must interpret scripture within the context of the passage. Is it meant to be taken literally or figuratively? Always start with the literal and then check to see the degree of figurative language used to gain additional insights.

10. Be sure to distinguish between promises made to Israel and those made to the Church. Here is where Reformed and un-Reformed theologians often come to fisticuffs. As I read and interpret scripture, not all the promises made to Israel automatically transfer to the Church.

11. After the Day of Christ (review Thessalonians and Revelations), when you have to tell your story—give an answer for why you acted as you did—what would you say? Be careful, crowns may be at stake here.

Only by careful study and attending to the leading of the Holy Spirit can we ascertain which take precedence over which. For the Christian, the involvement of the Holy Spirit is the other silent partner in our ethical decision making. We dare not leave him out.

What I trust is beginning to evolve is the awareness that to be a consistent ethical agent, the Christian does not have to have attended divinity school, handed out tracts in the mall, have an advanced degree, or been found shouting, "Repent for the end is near" while wearing a sandwich board on the corner of Wabash and 10th Avenue, but does have certain obligations. The task falls to each of us. Regardless of our jobs or professions, whether as a leader, a writer, professor, a consultant, a story teller, a furniture refinisher, a blogger, a soldier, Lyft driver, and many others to be sure, if we are to be consistent with our world view, there will be opportunities for our faith to be seen, without our sporting a cross on our lapels. **Ethical decision making is one of those specific cases where our Christian world view should always be readily apparent.**

Some few of us may have the opportunity to take a knee on the playing field and Tebow for the crowd, and others after a significant victory may be able to say during an ESPN interview or being inducted into the Baseball Hall of Fame, "First let me give thanks to my Lord and Savior Jesus Christ." God bless you Mariano! Still others may have just gone yard in Yankee Stadium and as they cross home plate point up to the sky with two index fingers to give thanks. Some may even be privileged to serve as Vice President of the United States and suggest to the President that every staff meeting begin with prayer; thank-you Mike Pence. Meanwhile, the rest of us will be working quietly behind the scenes and simply living our practical apologetic for others to observe. What others see should be what they get, in our personal associations and in our professional lives.

Let me offer a seemingly purely "secular" story of what I am claiming. While teaching philosophy and ethics at West Point, I had the opportunity to participate in the creation of the ten-part PBS television series called *Ethics in America*, an Annenberg Project directed by Fred Friendly, who was at the time the President of CBS News. This was a 10-hour TV and video series designed for the general public's viewing and, in particular, to be used by college and high school students to tackle the major ethical dilemmas of the day. The series, which is still available today on-line and in DVD's, includes the following programs and subject matter:

"Anatomy of a Hostile Takeover" (Ethics in Business)
"Do Unto Others" (Personal Ethics)
"Does Doctor Know Best?" (Ethics in Medicine)
"The Human Experiment" (Ethics in Scientific Research)
"The Politics of Privacy" (Ethics in Journalism)
"Public Trust, Private Interests" (Ethics in Government)
"To Defend a Killer" (Ethics in Criminal Law)
"Truth on Trial" (Ethics in Civil Law)
"Under Orders, Under Fire" (Ethics in the Military, Part I)
"Under Orders, Under Fire" (Ethics in the Military, Part II)

Each program had a prominent law school professor serve as a moderator and a panel of experts from various disciplines, all big name players at the time, such as news anchor Peter Jennings, *60 Minutes* lead investigator Mike Wallace, army Chaplain Timothy Tatum, Senator (Democrat VP Candidate) Geraldine Ferraro, Surgeon General Dr. C. Everett Koop, Supreme Court Justice Antony Scalia, army General William Westmoreland, oil magnate and entrepreneur T. Boone Pickens, Chairman of Berkshire Hathaway Warren Buffett, Planned Parenthood President Faye Wattleton, House Speaker Newt Gingrich, Dr. Lester Thorow, the Dean of MIT's Sloan Institute, Senator Barney Frank, Father J. Bryan Hehir from the Catholic Conference of Bishops, Attorney Rudy Giuliani, and many others.

My role was to act as one of several subject matter experts who helped script some of the hour-long television programs and during the actual televised segments to sit in the audience and quietly assist in signaling the moderator when to go to each participant to ensure the greatest diversity of thought and differences of opinion in order to flesh out the topics for the audiences. While preparing for this work, I was occasionally asked to speak on topics related to ethics in various locations anywhere from the

Hastings Institute on the Hudson to discuss legal and medical ethics, to Vassar to lecture on ethics in the humanities, to several Modern Language Association conferences in New York City, Chicago, and Los Angeles to discuss the ethics of literary criticism, and even to one debate on the campus of Harvard University to discuss the role of the military in combat.

Most of the time, because I was not on official government orders or representing the Academy or the army, *per se,* I left my military uniform in my closet and wore a modest suit and tie to fit in with the academic crowd. On one occasion, at Harvard University, I took a different tact. I had been asked to participate in a discussion with several prominent ethicists on a topic of which I had some professional experience—the ethics of unconventional warfare. Because of the subject matter of this debate, I chose to wear what were called my Class A's—my dress green military uniform—with several rows of US combat ribbons on the left breast and several Distinguished Unit, Presidential, and Foreign Awards for valor on the right breast pocket. It was just my normal every day "work" uniform that I would wear while teaching classes of cadets at West Point. When he saw me walk into the meeting, one of the distinguished panel members refused to participate in the debate because, as he phrased it, it wouldn't be fair to him and the others, because I was wearing my ethic. Let me say that again: "**I was wearing my ethic.**" The other speakers were not, and if they chose to reveal their individual belief systems or personal world views during the debate, would have to argue persuasively for their points of view. In his opinion, I would have a head start on each of them before I opened my mouth. In many ways he was right. My uniform shouted Duty, Honor, and Country before I said a word.

What did he mean, and why was he concerned about my uniform's announcing my ethic? Think of the four fundamental issues underlying every world view that Zacharias proposes. Recall also the fifteen questions I suggested earlier that need to be raised in any ethical decision. As you do your job, lead your families, or attend classes what core values do you stand for on a daily basis? How would those with whom you work or associate know it? To what do you owe allegiance? To whom do you owe loyalty as a human being and as a profession? Before whom do you bow? **Day by day,**

do you wear your ethic? More prosaically, are you wearing your team's jersey? If I were working with you, would I recognize your world view through your actions and know which side you are on?

For those who wear the army uniform, as I did for twenty-four years, there is an Oath of Office we each swore to or affirm at our initial commissioning and with each subsequent promotion. The statements are simple, yet fundamental to the military ethic:

> I ___, do solemnly swear (or affirm) that I will support and defend the *Constitution* of the United States against all enemies, foreign and domestic; that I will bear true faith and allegiance to the same; that I take this obligation freely, without any mental reservation or purpose of evasion; and that I will well and faithfully discharge the duties of the office on which I am about to enter.

> So help me God.

Adherence to this oath undergirds one's service to the country and is represented symbolically by the uniforms he or she wears. Furthermore, once in the military, every soldier swears to uphold what is known as the "Code of Conduct." By implication then, by wearing the uniform, I declare that...

I am an American fighting in the forces that guard my country and our way of life,
I am prepared to give my life in their defense.

I will never surrender of my own free will. If in command, I will never surrender the members of my command while they still have the means to resist.

If I am captured, I will continue to resist by all means available. I will make every effort to escape and aid others to escape. I will accept neither parole nor special favors from the enemy.

If I become a prisoner of war, I will keep faith with my fellow prisoners. I will give no information nor take part in any action which might be harmful to my comrades.

If I am senior, I will take command. If not, I will obey the lawful orders of those appointed over me and will back them up in every way.

Should I become a prisoner of war, I am required to give name, rank, service number, and date of birth. I will evade answering further questions to the utmost of my ability. I will make no oral or written statements disloyal to my country and its allies.

I will never forget that I am an American, fighting for freedom, responsible for my actions, and dedicated to the principles which made my country free.

I will trust in my God and in the United States of America.

When I wore the uniform, those values and their implicit underlying world view and ethic were unmistakable. When I walked into a room, before I ever said a word to anyone, my world view was symbolically announced and should have been crystal clear. What my fellow panelist objected to was that, if he chose to declare his values or declare his personal world view as part of our debate, it might take him substantial time to articulate it with clarity. What I stood for was clear, just by wearing the uniform—my appearance. And he was right. I and three others debated for the audience and **his chair stayed empty. That is also a statement of the ultimate credibility of one's world view. When your chair stays empty, you forfeit the right to validate your point of view, and everyone knows it.**

I remember well during one challenging temporary duty assignment I had touring selected nuclear missile silos in the Dakotas, hearing my teammate, Cardinal John O'Connor, ask a young air force major if it was difficult for him to be a Catholic Christian in the military. The officer smiled and with naïve honesty simply said, "No, your Eminence. Not at all. No one ever knew it." If one is a Christian, that's a problem.

How about you? On a daily basis, just living your life, and doing your job, if you are a believer, does anyone know it? Does your appearance and behavior—just being there—announce your ethic, or is your chair empty? As I saw one church marquis in Rockhill, South Carolina put it several years ago, **"If you were hauled into court and accused of being a Christian, would there be enough evidence to convict you?"**

> Whoever says he abides in Him ought to walk in the same
> way in which He walked (NKJV, 1 John 2:6).

CHAPTER VI

The Theory of Knowledge

I am not going to wax too theoretical on you, but in order to lay the foundation for living a practical apologetic, some theory might be helpful. We help the organizations that hire us establish a set of Core Values and to be able to articulate a Vision of ultimate success. We believe ardently that truly exceptional leaders in any organization lead on the basis of such imperatives. Our experience with dozens of Fortune 500 Companies, all five military services, and with countless senior executives whom we coach bear out this bias. Most importantly we take this approach because, as with all of our methodologies, we believe it is biblically based. Since the *Bible* begins this way, we probably should as well. To highlight that rationale, let me relate another brief story.

When our youngest son attended the International School of Indiana, a superb IB (International Baccalaureate) educational program, one of the required courses in high school was Theory of Knowledge (TOK). It is a course that many of the students from more than fourteen different countries in his class were not particularly excited about taking, because it seemed far less "practical" than advanced algebra, spherical trig, world history, calculus, French II, or Mandarin Chinese. For many students as well as some parents, many of whom were expats working for Dow or E. I. Lilly, the program seemed to be too theoretical. Indeed, initially we were not too excited by the requirement ourselves, but the course is required for an IB diploma. We are thoroughly aware of how easily those who teach such courses, as the resident content authority figures, can insinuate their personal world views into class conversations but at the same time recognized that the ability to understand the concepts discussed, particularly those with which we might personally disagree, is critical to the formation of one's personal world view. This understanding is particularly critical for those students who do not have such routine discussions at home. Furthermore, we were confident that our teachings at home and the practical apologetic by which we tried to live would be an adequate counterweight to several possibly antagonistic views.

In retrospect, I would argue it is one of the most practical courses any high school student can take, because it required students to come to grips with what they actually believe about the nature of reality, the fundamentals of knowledge and thought forms, the origins of being, the world in general, and their place in it. My wish is that such a course would be required of all high school students in this country, but alas, such was not the goal of John Dewey at the turn of last century; we will get to him. As a mini version of an introductory college philosophy course, TOK forced students to confront the principles of ethics and philosophy in ways that most secondary schools never do, which is why our young women and men graduating from even the very best high schools in the USA—particularly church sponsored ones—and matriculating at universities are woefully unprepared for the systematic onslaught against their values by Naturalistic and Humanistic professors and other authority figures on campus, not to mention their peers. One of the graduate schools where I spent six years, Duke University—a Methodist founded university—is just the latest to ban Young Life, a Christian association, from meeting on campus because they dared to affirm the biblical principle that marriage is between one man and one woman. Duke should probably turn their beautiful campus cathedral into a museum, as most thoroughly secularized European countries have already done, Poland being the one contemporary exciting public Christian exception.

As with all such programs, however, the impact of the Theory of Knowledge depended on the person teaching it. Our son's teacher was a very bright, dedicated teacher, the assistant Head of School as I recall, but one with whom I personally would have had some fundamental philosophical as well as theological differences, but he was a skilled educator and taught the program in a very professional and usually even-handed way. The course often provided material for rich conversations at home in the evenings. I remember several occasions as our son would pour over the readings and write essays, our having discussions about the origins of morality, the fundamentals of ethics, and our need, as Christians, to be able to offer sound biblically founded answers to the questions posed by skeptics.

I would often tell our kids—a few actually listened—that **I am a non-Naturalistic deontological absolutist.** More specifically, that label, which I proudly wear, implies that I am a rules-deontologist with a contextualist leaning (ie, the context of any specific circumstance determines which rules are applicable). Initially their eyes tended to cloud over like yours just did, but eventually most came to understand why such a description is critical to embracing and expressing our Christian world view and why understanding such terms is critical to your story as well, particularly if you want to be able to engage others with different world views.

Yes, exploring some of the underlying philosophical concepts regarding world views is very important. Distinguishing between terms such as jural and telic, Teleological and Deontological, Cognitive and non-Cognitive, Naturalistic and non-Naturalistic and several other pairings in the discipline is not just grist for a *Jeopardy* word game or an exercise in leafing through an on-line dictionary, but a fundamental basic vocabulary for Christians to understand so we can present our arguments with greater clarity. When one is more concerned with the telic aspects of a stance than the jural, for example, one looks at outcomes rather than the obedience to a code or set of rules—so much for the Code of Hammurabi, the Ten Commandments, or the U. S. *Constitution.* Know any of them? When one is a Teleologist, one is ends oriented with right and wrong primarily dictated by anticipated results, what some philosophers commonly describe as the greatest good for the greatest number (a view which, for example, could justify taking all the organs from one healthy person and parsing them out to fifteen persons experiencing organ failure to save them), while if one is a Deontologist, one recognizes that the rightness or wrongness of an act imbues within the act itself and the context in which it occurs, not just potential results.

When one claims to take a Cognitivist approach, one holds the view that morals and ethical dialogue state something verifiable or falsifiable; whereas, if one is a non-Cognitivist, one believes that **there is an unbridgeable gap between fact and value, science and supernatural belief.** I trust you are beginning to appreciate the significance of understanding on which team you play and its implicit game plan. If you are interested in learning more about such philosophical distinctions, which I would argue is much more than mere esoterica but an apologetic requirement, start at Appendix I and then read diligently. While there are many good introductions to the subject matter, a good starting point is Robert Solomon's *Introducing Philosophy* (purely secular and scholarly) and podcasts by theologian R. C. Sproul, particularly the one entitled "Christian Ethics." Even though I'll ding him for his title, his content is excellent. Yes, even Tom Morris's *Philosophy for Dummies* can get you started and perhaps whet your appetite to read further.

In being clear to express a Christian world view, **perhaps most important of the philosophical contraries is the distinction between Naturalism and Non-Naturalism**; I'll return to this distinction several times in the following chapters. Anyone desiring to become a practical apologist needs to be thoroughly grounded in this distinction, as it underscores many of the arguments against your beliefs that you will receive. An ethical Naturalist believes that all ethics or values can be reduced to the level of empiricism. Such a belief denies the *prima facie* distinction between establishing a fact about the world and making a value judgment about that fact. For the Naturalist, then, it follows that the supernatural (our Christian faith, to be specific) is an illusion and the concept of a holy and righteous God is pure folly. As the late Naturalist, theoretical physicist, and atheist Stephen Hawking (If you are not familiar with Hawking, think about the TV series, *Big Bang Theory*) would phrase it when discussing his own upcoming death in an interview with the editor of *The Guardian*, "I regard the brain as a computer which will stop working when its components fail. There is no heaven or afterlife for broken down computers; that is a fairy story for people afraid of the dark." Despite his demise, Naturalistic scientists continue to genuflect in front of him and bow before his vaunted intellect. For the philosophical Naturalist, moral judgments are nothing special but just a subclass of facts about the natural world; whereas, for the Non-Naturalist (yes, that's me and I would argue should be for all those desiring to live a Christian world view), values are distinct from factual considerations—they have a different genesis. Thought forms have life and death consequences.

Some of the brief stories that follow will untangle many of the implications of such distinctions. Knowing that the founder of our education system in the USA was John Dewey, one of the most famous of philosophical Naturalists at the turn of the century, it should come as no surprise that **God has been permanently expelled from our public schools. That was Dewey's long-range Pragmatist goal**. Public education in the USA is based on his Naturalistic philosophy with the end of using public education to impose every variety of atheistic social engineering on the youth of America. The disaffected high school students of one era, banned from participation in religious practices in school—even ridiculed if not proscribed from mouthing the word God in the Pledge of Allegiance— become the Naturalistic teachers, university professors, business leaders, judges, and politicians passing laws impugning the Christian world view of the next. That the Christian world view is under direct assault by the media, the courts, the entertainment industry, university professors, and far too many politicians these days, should be no surprise. **Our tax money has been used to train them to marginalize us.**

Before proceeding, it is also necessary to distinguish between two other terms: morality and ethics. The two are often confused and routinely misused by leaders in the business world, the public square, and theologians as well as far too many professors of philosophy, who should know better. Too often, when they are not just simply equated and glibly used interchangeably, the two are superficially reduced in common parlance to ethics' being the theory and morals' being the application of a theory. That distinction is too sophomoric and misleading. The two words have different origins, even in language and the cultures spawning them. This distinction is critical for the Christian to understand when debating with those holding different world views. The word "morals" is derived from the Latin word *mores*; whereas, the word "ethics" comes from the Greek word *ethos*. Not only were the two cultures vastly different but so were the historic predicates behind the language. Understanding the distinction is critical for being able to live one's Christian world view with clarity and consistency.

Let's start there. The Latinate word *mores,* alludes to a set of behaviors, accepted standards of behavior, and ways in which people act which are often dependent on their location, their culture, their education, their religious training, their tribal concerns, their traditions, and how they are otherwise raised. The *mores* (hence moral standards and practices) of New Englanders, therefore, may be different from the *mores* of North Carolinians, Texans, Brazilians, Koreans, Singaporeans, Watutsis, or Yemenis. No surprise there. In the USA, for example, various geographical locations and states even have different legal standards for moral issues as fundamental as when death occurs: "heart stoppage," "brain death," or my favorite, "when the vital spirits flee the body" (of course that is Texas). Those still considered to be alive in one state can be declared legally dead in another. Similarly the mores of Midwesterners (flyover country—hence we can be ignored) are very different from those of Californians, the Pennsylvanian Amish, New Englanders, or Hollywood A-Listers. Often those whom we elect to represent us from these different areas reflect the dominant morality of the voting populace in those areas. Certain political parties count on that distinction to win votes. Some habits get ingrained over time and become the accepted moral standards of a group and, consequently, are hard to argue against.

The United States' Founding Fathers recognized the potential impact of these prevalent moral distinctions early on and instituted the Electoral College in Article II, Section 1 of the US *Constitution* to prevent the tyranny of democracy—the state of affairs where the values (morals) of 51%

of the population could easily take away the rights of the other 49%. Their fear of majoritarianism or the *mobile vulgus* (the fickle crowd) was why they joined Plato in rejecting democracy in lieu of a republic. Plato (whom you will meet again in Chapter XXXIII) made the powerful and coherent argument that democracies are susceptible to "tyranny of the majority" and rule by demagoguery. These days, for example, the routine voting population of just five states is larger than the other 45 states combined and could drive the outcome of a national election based solely on popular votes. To ensure that the moral compulsions of just a few large populated states with clear moral biases could not run roughshod over other more sparsely populated states with vastly different moral consensuses, the US Founding Fathers argued against such a pure democracy in favor of the republic they instituted. Hence this clear distinction between morals and ethics was present at the founding of the USA as well as embedded in the ancient Greek and Latin civilizations.

Mores, ergo the derived morals of a specific group, are by their very nature "relative" in that they depend on many aspects leading up to their codification. I expect morals to differ depending on where I am and the prevailing culture in which I am immersed. Some US states, for example, ban abortion after a child has had a specific time in the womb to develop, and others have elected leadership—New York, New Jersey, and California leap to mind—who argue to allow for infanticide even after a live birth. Let's take this moral difference to work. When meeting a businesswoman in NYC, Zurich, Seattle, London, Frankfurt, or Paris for the first time, I would courteously, without thinking, extend my hand in greeting. If I should be introduced to an Arab businesswoman in Qatar, Ajman, Saudi Arabia, or another surrounding Arab country, I will perhaps nod my head in her direction but always wait for her to extend her hand first (if, at all), letting me know it would not be immoral for her to do so with a man, and that I could shake her hand. On the other hand, when meeting a businesswoman in Brazil for the first time, I would not think twice about her giving me a warm embrace. The Founding Fathers in the USA further recognized these relativistic moral differences by retaining certain rights for the states (which may vary greatly depending on the values of their residents) while only assigning a limited number of specific moral considerations to the federal government. The 10ᵗʰ Amendment to the *Constitution* codifies that fundamental distribution of moral powers.

Ethics, on the other hand, are not relative. Ethics, in the original Greek, are a system of clearly articulated absolutes underlying superficial moral distinctions. The origin of the word *ethos* goes as far back as the early Greek writings of the *Odyssey* and other great epic poems. The *ethos* (more properly, *ethikos*) of a Greek household—where Odysseus lived for example—was located at the very center of the house, the *oikos*, closest to where the family lived, inside the safety of the walls. It was literally the "horse stall," the place where the horse was safely kept. The horse was housed at the very center of the *oikos* for protection because of its value to one's very existence. That was important for safety because the horse was the source of so much of life's bounty, transportation, agricultural, war fighting capability, and many other areas of life. We often joke these days about a dog or cat being a "member of the family." To the early Greeks, that critical member of the clan was the horse. Their very existence depended on protecting it. By extrapolation then, your *ethos,* or in translation your ethic, should be the center of where you live—what is most important to you. It is critical to your existence and your very ontology (existence). Everything else should be built around it.

Regardless of one's upbringing, culture, nationality, theology, or education, certain "horse stalls"—centers of existence—exist. They are the absolutes embedded in the very DNA of the Christian world view. That human life is to be cherished is an absolute ethic shared by almost every culture (eg. John 15:13). Protection of the innocent is a generally universal ethic. Respect for the elderly is an absolute ethic. Providing for the disabled and the unfortunate is in most cultures an absolute, and these absolutes—the universal ethics—exist across religions and nationalities. What makes the difference is how those ethics are imposed—the relative individual moral understandings involved. The question is where do you live? What is the center of your being? That center—those absolutes—must form the heart of your world view and should be demonstrated by your life: **"And he is before all things, and in him all things hold together"** (KJV, Colossians 1:17).

Let's take a specific example of the above, respect for the elderly, and see how those distinctives are expressed cross-culturally. One might think that such an ethical absolute would be a no-brainer in most cultures, but it is an ethic that has different moral implications and associated behaviors swirling around it, depending on the culture. In the USA, for example, and much of western Europe, we claim to honor the elderly and demonstrate that ethic by providing basic medical, financial, and personal care for them as they grow older. When they are too infirm to take care of themselves, families often "stash" them, I'm sorry, arrange for them to be housed and cared for by others, in an elder care facility or nursing home, and the family visits them on holidays—if they are lucky. In much of Asia, the elderly are truly esteemed and their opinions sought out and honored. They are always the patriarchs or matriarchs of a family and live with them to help to provide moral stability in the home. A practical consequence of such a distinction is that in North America, when a worker reaches 60 or 65 they are often offered a package or a chance retire with a pension or go on social security—something they, themselves, have paid for over the years. In Japan, when they reach that age, these same seniors are routinely sought out and hired and promoted, because with age should come respect and veneration for their wisdom and experience.

In parts of northern Alaska, on the other hand, when an aged male Aleut becomes too infirm to care for himself, out of respect for his age and personal dignity, he traditionally was placed on an ice floe and sent out to die with dignity by himself, without having to be observed or gawked at sorrowfully by others in his tribe during his terminal suffering. He can remain independent and not be ashamed of his inability to care for himself until he dies. The ethic in each case may be the same, respect for the elderly; the associated morals, however, are very different. Which is correct? Which is right? Which honors more the ethic that says that the elderly and infirm should be cared for and respected? Is the rectitude inherent in the act itself (Deontology), or is right or wrong determined by the ends (Teleology) and the outcomes? How we address those fundamental issues depends on one's world view underlying the practices. How you decide and live out such issues screams your world view to others.

Let me return to why I include this story. All this is prelude—the back story to use a contemporary term—to why we teach organizations that to be responsible corporate citizens, caring not only for their employees and the communities and business it serves, but how they should be known by those outside their organization. Leaders should be careful to establish a set of Core Values that inform their organization's corporate ethic. Our approach is distinctly secular but, as always, has a Christian world view, a biblical, precedent. It is just one more way we seek to live out a practical apologetic through our work. How do you accomplish that goal in your personal and public lives?

The individual morals of employees and leaders in most organizations and businesses are naturally very different depending on their religion or lack thereof, upbringing, ethnicity, cultural heritage, and other considerations, but can ultimately be irrelevant to the organization's Core Values. We explore those individual values and then assist the organization in determining which are most important to the organization's Purpose and public stance the organization wants to take and which Core Values the entire team can agree to honor, despite their individual moral differences. We help organizations, particularly their senior leadership, have the kind of honest conversations that define their ethic by unearthing those underlying values by which they wish to be known and within which they can act consistently with integrity with both their employees and stakeholders.

During such discussions, if organizational leaders do not themselves as a team raise them as part of the analysis, we can always raise the values implicit in a Christian world view as alternatives to consider—because they are central to western culture—and if applicable, encourage them to argue for or against including such values in their business model. Even if that opportunity does not present itself, the very fact that our methodology begins with Vision and Values is rooted in the Christian world view. That our approach will be based on a Non-Naturalistic Deontological one is implicit to our business model and the soul of our practical apologetic. During the discussions, I can present it—with much less jargon—as the reason why it is foundational to our being known as so successful in the professional community and encourage organizations to adopt similarly consistent values when working with employees and customers. That is living a practical apologetic through our business. You can do the same in yours.

Whether we are believers or not, can we sometimes doubt that we are right and vacillate as leaders when making decisions? Certainly, but that is why having a publicly stated ethic—a set of agreed upon Values—is crucial to an organization's success and a leader's personal integrity. A stated public model encourages personal compliance. Much as the Christian should be known for her or his values, a responsible organization should announce its Values and ask to be held accountable to them. What a great approach for the Christian to model. The organizational world knows that should they choose to work with us at ESI, that we believe that exceptional performance begins with their leaders' having established a clear Vision of what success looks like (an organizational eschatological approach, if you will), a set of clear Core Values (its axiological stance) that establishes an organization's Ethic, and a set of Operating Principles or Norms (think of these as the behavioral moral implications) by which employees will treat each other day by day. Great leaders lead on the foundation of Vision and Values. That is also the philosophical main frame of a Christian world view.

Our own company's Core Values are stated as Passion, Vision, Integrity, Innovation, Teamwork, and Joy. Each is foundational to the kind of work we do and how we want to be known to our clients. The last one usually gets an organization's attention, and they are often curious to know why Joy is so important to our work. I'll let you gnaw on that one and come up with your own rationale. The reason is based on far more than simply loving to do the kind of work that we do and exuding enthusiasm and excitement as we help to change lives and organizations for the better. In case you are curious, give a read to C. S. Lewis's work, *Surprised by Joy* in the process. With all the Lord has done for us, how could a Christian not be joyful? That same "Joy" entered our family's personal story in a very practical way many years ago. That a non-existent nurse named Joy just happened to appear on the scene and gave just the right instructions to the attending nurses when one of our sons was in a life-threatening position when very young, and then disappear, never to be seen again, and not have her name appear on any hospital registry of employees, also has some pertinence here. **Moments of *kairos* intervention are all around us, if we will just pay attention.** But that is a different story. Do our work and principles of organizational existence properly reflect our world view? Our clients sit as our judge every day. Do yours?

When William Shatner presented us with the "Heartbeat of America Award" on his TV special some years ago, for being the company that has done the most to restore American business since the terrorist attacks of September 11, 2001, he cited our Core Values as what enabled us to be so successful.

> So, whether you eat or drink, or whatever you do, do all
> to the glory of God (KJV, 1 Corinthians 10:31).

CHAPTER VII

Spanky's Men's Room

It is ironic how it is often the smaller things, which at the time may have seemed insignificant, that stay with one and become the most poignant events in our developing stories. I remember well my time in graduate school at Duke University, while studying for my doctoral prelims in English, being drawn to the American novelist John Updike's works because of his ability to weave stories of the conflicts arising between faith and unbelief. Some of us who had been in Professor Duffy's classes on literary critical theory or Professor Strandberg's courses in Modern American Fiction would gather on our own time for hours in remote student lounges or carrels in the library, sprawled out on blankets in Duke Gardens, and occasionally meeting in various off campus graduate student haunts like Shooters or Francesca's in Durham or Chapel Hill to argue the merits of his writing or critique his fictional expressions of faith. Unlike many of the sciences and courses in the STEM disciplines where facts are generally indisputable and correct answers can be known with little doubt, the humanities require discussion, analysis, challenge, interpolation, and thoughtful examination and exegesis.

Some of our most profound learnings in grad school occurred outside the classrooms of the ivy-covered Allen Building on Duke's west campus. Since I have a passion for understanding both faith and fiction, I may have been the instigator for these informal gatherings, and it was probably no surprise to any of my fellow doctoral candidates and anyone who knows me today that Updike became one of my favorite modern authors. At one time, I even considered writing my doctoral dissertation on Updike's canon. Had I not stumbled across Thomas Pynchon, who manages to intertwine the Second Law of Thermodynamics (entropy)—my first undergraduate degree was, after all, in engineering—faith, history, theology, physics, and philosophy in *The Crying of Lot 49*, *Gravity's Rainbow*, and *V.*, I am sure I would have done so.

Appreciating and deciphering Pynchon's canon, however, proved to be quite the challenge, as one must continuously pirouette on the precipice of numerous disciplines to understand him. As an author who always was and from time to time still remains more of a recluse than even the late J. D. Salinger, Pynchon could never be pinned down for an interview. Since tracking down others with more ominous intent who never wanted to be found was my specialty in Vietnam, Laos, and other unfriendly countries during part of my career in the army, I thought I would stage an academic coup and be the first researcher to find and corner him in order to pummel him with numerous questions I had about his world view, his understanding of contemporary Christianity, his fictional use of the second law of thermodynamics, his historical understanding of the development of V2 rockets in *Gravity's Rainbow,* and the novel's literary kinship with James Joyce's *Ulysses.* What a great introduction to a doctoral dissertation and future book that coup would have been!

One summer, while in graduate school preparing for my subsequent teaching assignment on the faculty of West Point, I managed to track Pynchon as far as Juarez, Mexico, where persistent rumors had it that he hung out in August. The novelist William Styron, the author of *Sophie's Choice, The Confessions of Nat Turner, Darkness Visible,* and a dozen other great novels, all of which in various ways demanded that readers consider the persistent interplay between history, philosophy, personal faith, conflicting world views, and life's diverse challenges, was the writer in residence at Duke University for a couple years while I was there in grad school and a frequent guest in my home on weekends. He had become a good friend telling me at one time during a barbecue at my house in Durham that I was one of the few graduate students he had ever met who truly appreciated his mastery of language and the subtleties of his metaphysics as we would haggle over our competing world views.

Over coffee one afternoon at Francesca's Dessert Shop in Durham, he suggested to me that I might be able to corner the elusive Thomas Pynchon if I was willing to make the trip to Juarez. Styron claimed to know of one or two of Pynchon's favorite obscure back street bars where he could chill without being recognized. That was all the challenge I needed, so I hopped a military flight from Pope AFB in North Carolina to El Paso, Texas for a few days to stay with a friend at Fort Bliss, situated just across the border from Juarez, Mexico.

One evening, after walking over the Paso Del Norte Bridge to Juarez from neighboring El Paso, I wandered in and out of a few seedy bars along "The Strip" looking for someone who matched the sketchy description I had of him. Spotting a solitary American with a New York Yankees ball cap pulled down low over his eyes while nursing a Dos Equis and pretending to be playing solitaire at a wooden table in the rear of the bar, I sauntered over and, although uninvited, plunked myself down in a chair across the table from him politely saying, "Mr. Pynchon, what a pleasure to bump into you like this." Culling out a reference from his novel, *V.* I continued, "Just like old times in Malta with the Whole Sick Crew, huh?" He was notably surprised but remained composed and pleasant enough for a couple minutes before politely excusing himself to go to the "head." That word sealed his identity for me, knowing, as I did, that Pynchon had spent two years in the navy. Since he did not return for several minutes, I followed him in to the grubby *bano,* only to find that he had escaped through the men's room window. When I followed him out, I found myself in one of the very dark and unfriendly alleys of Juarez—not a very hospitable place to be found alone even thirty years ago before Juarez had become a totally crime ridden, cartel dominated city. I beat feet back across the Rio Grande and returned to the friendlier environs of El Paso and took a cab to my friend's government housing quarters at Fort Bliss.

My fascination with Pynchon and the theological implications of his complex world view remained, but my personal searches for this recluse ended with an empty stall in Spanky's men's room. Pynchon remained the consummate recluse for many years but since the publication of *Mason Dixon*, his most significant work of fiction after *Gravity's Rainbow*, he has become grudgingly more or less accepting of his public role while living in New York City. When he finally agreed to a brief interview with the media after the publication of his detective story, *Bleeding Edge*, in late 2013, he joked that some folks had gone to great lengths in the past to interview him, even to following him out a window of a Mexican bar. Guilty as charged. But I digress; faith sometimes leads us down dark and potentially dangerous alleys, not too far removed from John of the Cross's (Juan de la Cruz) *Noche Oscura* ("Dark Night of the Soul"). One of those alleys led me back to John Updike and his passion for combining faith, life, and fiction, in his Christian world view, an approach that would help define my role as English professor for the next several years, until God's plans for my plot changed.

Three years later, while a tenured English professor serving as the course director for Comparative World Literature at the United States Military Academy at West Point, I invited John Updike to the Academy to speak on the character of modern fiction for two advanced English electives I was then teaching entitled, "Faith and Modern American Fiction" and "Narrative Style and Religious Meaning." In the question and answer session following Updike's presentation, a cadet asked him how he could write such quasi pornographic novels, as *A Month of Sundays*, and still claim to be a Christian. Updike did not try to defend the book as anything but what the cadet claimed it was but merely replied, "Young man, I assure you, on Sunday mornings, I can with a clear conscience, recite the Creed at the top of my voice." This may not be a satisfactory biblical definition of Christianity for many of you, but if one *truly affirms* what the Creed (Apostles, Nicene, or Athanasian depending on one's denomination or ecclesiastical leanings) affirms—the word *Credo* in Latin, after all means, "I believe"—it comes pretty close: **If you declare with your mouth, 'Jesus is LORD,' and believe in your heart that God raised him from the dead, you will be saved**" (ESV, Romans 10:9). Updike's works—almost all of which are Pulitzer or Nobel quality fictional stories—probe the heart and soul in ways that demand a theological as well as a literary response from the reader. Welcome to the community of faith, John. The question we are probing here, however, is how do we take that Sunday morning statement of belief to the rest of our life Monday through Saturday?

While no John Updike, I faced a similar dilemma when writing my first novel in what has become known among my fans as the "Christian Madison Series," *A Trap Door to the Dark Side*. Admittedly having written it during a particularly dark period of my own life, it is a personal memoir of a Special Forces soldier immersed in the little heralded and very dark and often obscene war in Laos, Cambodia, and Vietnam in the late 1960's—a war that I had some very personal knowledge of and one that this country has tried very hard to ignore and forget. Recently, on National POW Remembrance Day in the USA, the 3rd Friday in September (has any Millennial or Gen-next even heard of that day, let alone cared about it?), I walked into a Zionsville, Indiana Starbucks wearing a black T-shirt with a large POW-MIA picture on it with the words, "All Gave Some; Some Gave All," and the young heavily tatted and variously pierced barista smugly asked, "Wasn't that war a long time ago, buddy?" At least he could read. I find that is a plus for many in his generation; fortunately it wasn't in cursive. I tried hard to remember the "with gentleness and reverence" clause in 1 Peter 3:15 and simply said, "It was for some of us, my young friend. Be glad you were not alive back then or you might never have come home and had the chance to pour me an iced Grande Komodo Dragon." I'm sure he didn't have a clue as to what I was talking about and just calmly returned to mixing someone's caramel Frappuccino. So much for a tip. War itself, regardless of the motivations of the parties involved, is always a quasi-pornographic experience for those involved and for a nation's collective conscience; hence, individuals' reactions to those events—the stories they tell—the shadow they cast, must reflect that darkness in order authentically to do justice to the reality of what is too frequently soul numbing violence. Nowhere is the desire to live a clearly expressed Christian world view more important.

War, particularly unconventional asymmetric warfare, for those who are caught up in it, is often a personal journey into a dark, dangerous, and formidable alley and always a plunge into that dark side that the good Doctor Carl Jung discussed; one that demands that we partner with such darkness temporarily in order to survive and with God's help emerge whole into the light. We are not destined to dwell permanently in that *Noche Oscura*. Those who cannot do so suffer from a lifetime of PTSD and other debilitating afflictions. *Trap Door to the Dark Side* is not a book I would want friends or loved ones to think truly represents me or just the sum of my personal experiences and values, or even to read, for that matter, but it is a story that certainly gathered a large cult of followers when it first appeared and continues to attract the attention of Jungian scholars who want to understand the power of the Shadow archetype to foster personal growth and transform behavior. For the less literate, the *Star Wars* movie series delves into that same dark archetype—"Luke, I am your father"—and those who survive must learn how and when to go into temporary partnership with the dark side in order to surface the more positive "Force." The Christian realizes that the mythical Jedi's "May the Force be with you," in a different world view is affirmed as, "If the Lord wills," or my dad's favorite, "If the good Lord's willing and the creek don't rise." Even what may seem at the time as a throw away comment can reflect our world view.

It is, however, a story that pounded on my door and demanded to be written to honor the dark reality experienced by too many of my warrior brothers with very different world views—a reality that pursued many of them back to "civilization," destroyed marriages, and impacted their lives. To be faithful to the experience of war, a work of fiction or even a personal memoir must reflect such darkness honestly. *Trap Door* is a plunge into the depths of one's personal Shadow. It is one that needed to be written to purge the demons from many friends' souls, many of whom make appearances in different guises. Such honesty sometimes unearths the obscene that makes one cling to the fragile borders of morality. The only thing that allows us to emerge into the light is God's graciousness and the power of a Christian world view to reground us. As Bev Shea used to sing so gloriously, "His eye is on the sparrow and I know…he watches… me" (Matthew 6:25-26).

Depending on our faith backgrounds and cultural leanings we tend to assume automatically that certain subjects ought naturally to be off limits for those claiming membership in the Christian community of faith. That is a sad misunderstanding and one that those from non-Christian world views love to try to exploit. Updike, from his perspective, wanted to reclaim the entire gamut of life and art for his faith by articulating life's struggles from a Christian world view. While clearly a writer of fiction—just a professional storyteller—and not a Christian apologist, Updike would be pleased to be included in the number of those who want to reclaim the entire culture for Christ. My early spiritual mentor, Fran Schaeffer, dedicated his entire life to do just that. In our sessions working with skeptics and questioning youth as well as older intellectuals at L'Abri in Huemoz, Switzerland and elsewhere—providing honest answers to honest difficult questions—our persistent efforts were dedicated to helping university students and questioning intellectuals from numerous countries and academic institutions understand the power of the Gospel to embrace all of life's experiences: emotionally, psychologically, intellectually, philosophically, ethically, artistically, musically, and rationally.

Many individual stories were sketched during those times in the magnificent Swiss Alps. One day, while on one of our many hikes in the region of Huemoz-sur-Ollon, home of the Swiss L'Abri, which was at first based out of the Chalet les Melezes, a questioning student, a young German graduate student studying religion at the university of Heidelberg, as I recall, raised Karl Barth's Neo-Orthodox claim to Dr. Schaeffer, that faith should be separated from reason. As Barth stated it, faith was just an "irrational leap of faith," and the subsequent Naturalistic Existential belief that Christianity demanded from believers a "Leap of Faith" was born. Many Christians to this day throw that phrase around as though it were actually sound theology. Fran called us over to the edge of one of the nearby cliffs and had us look down over the precipice. He responded to the German student in the following story that is captured in the "Afterword" to his *He is there and He is not silent.*

Suppose [Fran began] we are climbing in the Alps and are very high on the bare rock, and suddenly the fog rolls in. The guide turns to us and says that the ice is forming and that there is no hope; before morning we will all freeze to death here on the shoulder of the mountain. Simply to keep warm the guide keeps us moving in the dense fog further out on the shoulder until none of us have any idea where we are. After an hour or so, someone says to the guide, "Suppose I dropped and hit a ledge ten feet down in the fog. What would happen then?" The guide would say that you might make it until the morning and thus live. So, with absolutely no knowledge or any reason to support his action, one of the group hangs and drops into the fog. This would be one kind of faith, a reckless [irrational] leap of faith.

Suppose, however, after we have worked out on the shoulder in the midst of the fog and the growing ice on the rock, we had stopped, and we heard a voice which said, "You cannot see me, but I know exactly where you are from your voices. I am on another ridge. I have lived in these mountains, man and boy, for over sixty years and I know every foot of them. I assure you that ten feet below you there is a ledge. If you hang and drop, you can make it through the night, and I will get you in the morning.

I would not hang and drop at once but would ask questions to try to ascertain if the man knew what he was talking about and if he was not my enemy. [**This is exactly what the practical apologist wants to happen after all— question us!**]. In the Alps, for example, I would ask him his name. If the name he gave me was the name of a family from that part of the mountains, it would count a great deal to me. In the Swiss Alps there are certain family names that indicate mountain families of that area. In my desperate situation, even though time would be running out, I would ask him what to me would be the adequate and sufficient questions, and when I became convinced by his answers, then I would hang and drop (pp. 99-100).

This is the God whom the Christian world view honors when our lives answer others' "adequate and sufficient" questions—what I call living a practical apologetic. Even a cursory understanding of world events suggests that we are also in danger and our time may be running out. He is not only THERE (that is the metaphysical reality), but He has been far from silent over the ages (Romans 1:20). In the person of his son Jesus, he has been where we are and can say, trust me. I know exactly where you are because I have been there one time myself. **At his first advent, Jesus demolished the need for a leap of faith and created a step of certainty.**

If Christianity is not capable of honestly engaging and providing answers to every aspect of our human existence, it is not a credible world view. Too often we try to separate the heart and the head when dealing with our faith. Scripture does not allow for such bifurcation. Schaeffer would also claim to be able to shout the Creed at the top of his voice. Most importantly, as Dr. Schaeffer would go on to ask later in his life, if those traditional creedal assertions are true, each of us must pose the question, *How Should We Then Live?* **How does faith consort with daily, often obscene reality? How do we live a practical apologetic?** While the language and examples Fran used in his many books are largely dated these days, the truths he expounded are not and are simply reworked into contemporary thought forms and references by writers such as Os Guinness in his social commentaries, Abdu Murray in *Saving Truth: Finding Meaning and Clarity in a Post-Truth World*, and a few others.

> But sanctify the Lord God in your hearts: and be ready always to give an answer to every man that asketh you a reason of the hope that is in you <u>with meekness and fear</u> (KJV, 1 Peter 3:15).

It's remembering those last four words that gives me the greatest trouble.

CHAPTER VIII

"I Show You Doubt to Prove That Faith Exists"

Not too long ago, we celebrated the death—yes, Christians often do that—of a young man named Tyler Trent at our church in Carmel, Indiana. If his name is somewhat familiar to you, it is because Tyler became known statewide in Indiana and later throughout much of the country when he was named from his wheelchair as the Captain of the unranked Purdue Boilermakers football team before their huge upset of number 2 ranked Ohio State in October of 2018 (see his book, *The Upset*). After being diagnosed not once, not just twice, but yet a third time with terminal bone cancer, Tyler celebrated his trust in Christ and his enduring faith in God's perfect will for his life in ways that the college and professional sports world, indeed, much of the entire nation, came to admire. In fact, the Forward to *The Upset* was written by Scott Van Pelt, the well-known anchor for ESPN (not an organization particularly renowned for its Christian world view).

Unable even to speak in the later stages of the rare bone cancer, osteosarcoma, that had ravaged his young body, and usually in excruciating pain, Tyler would mount his famous smile and hold up one, four, and then three fingers signaling, "I...love... you." Many in the media never really caught on and questioned his persistently positive demeanor, and predictably all those traditional questions of why a good and gracious

God allows such suffering surfaced in the media and in some of your homes. Even those most positive about their faiths can occasionally find themselves questioning the goodness of God and his personal involvement in our lives. Until God one day destroys cancer forever, indeed in the end times destroys death itself, the question for all of us must be, "how should we then live?" during times of uncertainty, suffering, and apparent abandonment, even in the midst of the agony of disease or injury? *How can we "chew a wafer" with thanksgiving when we are drowning in pain?* A recent book by Mark Vroegop, senior pastor of College Park Church in Carmel, Indiana addresses this very subject in his *Dark Clouds, Deep Mercy.* Tyler Trent reaffirmed the pattern in ways that make those of us who are blessed with better health shamefaced for our apathy. Sometimes one's practical apologetic is lived most clearly when suffering is at its peak. Yes, we celebrated Tyler's death because, as he often phrased it, *"Whether alive or dead, I win. I am either here on earth with those whom I love or in Heaven with my Lord and Savior, Jesus Christ."* "Tyler Strong—Boiler up!"

These days, Ravi Zacharias, Lee Strobel, Nabeel Qureshi, John Lennox, Norman Geisler, John Ankerberg, Tanya Walker, Wayne Grudem, Ken Ham, Michael Ramsden, and several other contemporary Christian apologists probe these questions of faith in various aspects of our human existence. What we practical apologists for the faith suggest and, yes, I humbly include myself in that number, is that **we should not simply melt into the culture and refuse to be known for our beliefs.** There is nothing insipid about "belief" as described in the *New Testament.* The word for "believe" in Greek, *Pisteuo (pistevo),* is an active verb implying that such should be a Christian's attitude as well—active not passive. Just one of many examples of this active faith is Jesus' healing of the Centurion's boy, recorded in the Gospel of Matthew (8: 5-13). The centurion showed that he trusted Jesus' ability to heal when he dared to ask Him to heal his son. And when Jesus said, "I will come and heal him," the Centurion further showed his trust by saying, "I am not worthy that you should come under my roof; only speak a word and my boy will be healed." This is a soldier I can relate to. Jesus confirmed his active trust in verse 13 when he said, "'as you have trusted, let be it done unto you.' And his boy was healed in that hour." This is active (*pisteuo*) belief, not just a passive understanding.

Indeed, that sense of the verb is echoed throughout the entire Gospel of John.

It always struck me as very worshipful yet rather paradoxical that sincere Roman Catholics would historically approach the Eucharist with mouths open and have the priest place the communion wafer on their tongues, unwilling even to touch something so holy. In one regard, putting what I believe is the unbiblical doctrine of transubstantiation aside, their reverence for the Body of Christ—the Host—was always impressive to me and seemed to serve as witness to the world of their reverence for all that the Lord had done for us, despite who we are and what we have become through disobedience. Christ is infinite and holy, and we mortals are not. On the other hand, though, such an act of separation between Creator and creature, God and penitent, is a misreading of scripture and a grievous reflection of centuries of our culture's separation from all that is holy—a belief as anachronistic as the old rusting rood screens separating the laity from the clergy and the penitent from the altar—man from God—the remnants of which are still found in isolated European Roman Catholic and Church of England sanctuaries—and our unwillingness as believers to engage the world. It denies what our role should be as lights shining in a very dark world, a world where **Christ has torn down that wall of separation**, just as the Temple veil was rent in twain at the time of the crucifixion.

> And behold, the curtain of the temple was torn in two, from top to bottom. And the earth shook, and the rocks were split. The tombs also were opened. And many bodies of the saints who had fallen asleep were raised, and coming out of the tombs after his resurrection they went into the holy city and appeared to many.
>
> When the centurion and those who were with him, keeping watch over Jesus, saw the earthquake and what took place, they were filled with awe and said, "Truly this was the Son of God!"
> (ESV, Matthew 27: 51-54)

In one of John Updike's short stories, "The Music School," a writer named Alfred Schweigen tells about hearing a priest describe the post Vatican II (1959) change in his church's attitude toward the Eucharist. With just one Vatican decree, the worshipper was suddenly allowed to touch the Host. As Updike phrases it, **the wafer was not meant to melt in some insipid way in the believer's mouth but was instead meant to be taken in our hands, placed in our mouths, and chewed and swallowed like the bread of life for which it stands. That is active kinetic belief.** In that regard, believers are all Alfred Schweigen, called to be crucified with Christ. We are not meant to be passive observers in God's kingdom, but actively engaged to redeem it. **Chewing the wafer means to "redeem the time"** (Ephesians 5:16), **to "occupy until He comes"** (Luke 19:13), **to help reclaim the entire culture for Christ—defending Christianity against all objections, intellectual ones included.** This is why, as I have insinuated, there is no such thing as "secular" work. To redeem the time, to be ready at all times to give a reason for the faith that is within us, means that **Christ expects every aspect of our daily lives to reflect our world view** and ongoing cruciform sanctification (KJV, Galatians 2:20).

As an introvert, I have always tended to keep most things from my past to myself, but from time to time in our family conversations I would let a story or two that no one had been aware of slip out, particularly events from my youth and during my time in the US army. My kids from time to time would encourage me to jot down some of the more memorable ones so they will not be lost once I am no longer around to relate them. To some extent my four adventure novels serve that purpose, and some of the events and plots, the often treacherous dark alleys that Colonel Christian Madison and his team have to weave their way through in *Trap Door to the Dark Side, Spirit of the Oryx, Concord*, and *Framing the Sacred* accomplish that purpose anonymously, as C. S. Lewis would approve. Taken as a developing unfinished opus they form the outline of a somewhat fictional autobiography. Some of those stories may actually be true, or at least may weave partially fictitious activities and plots around authentic characters and settings that were all too true in the past—all of which contributed in some small way to crafting my Christian world view. It is just that the names have been changed to protect those involved—both the guilty and the innocent. Until someone straps me up to a polygraph, I guess readers will have to be the judge as to which are and which are not true.

Some stories, however, need to be told in context as they actually occurred and ought not to be embellished or fictionalized, despite Lewis' praise for such fictional art, in order to express the world view that they rest upon. They are the stories I try to relate here to demonstrate the correspondence between mundane life events and the formation of a Christian world view. Each, at least in my mind, reflects the need we have to **chew the wafer—to engage the world with our faith**. Nowhere is that approach more important than in our professional lives.

An acquaintance of mine, a member of the Cherokee Nation, relates the story of a Native American elder who told his grandson about two wolves who struggle continuously in every human heart. "One wolf is named Evil," he began, "personifying anger, jealousy, envy, and pride, and the other is named Good, personifying joy, love, peace, faith, and humility." The grandson innocently asks his grandfather, "If they are constantly struggling, which wolf eventually wins?" The elder replies, "The one you feed." The Biblical equivalent is Galatians 5:17. **"For the flesh lusts against the Spirit, and the Spirit against the flesh; and these are contrary to one another, so that you do not do the things that you wish."** How true that is for all of us. Such a verse brings to mind all those medieval paintings showing a person with a good angel perched on one shoulder and an evil one on the opposite shoulder, each whispering partisan advice to the unwary mortal—each more than capable of seducing the mind and the heart. Which one we listen to depends on us and will necessarily reflect our world view for others to observe.

In one of Robert Browning's marvelous nineteenth century monologues, a skeptical reporter named Gigadibs—a "literary man," as the poet describes him—comes to visit Bishop Blougram, having heard that the well-known bishop may not have always lived a carefully observed "Christian" life style and may have dared to express doubts from time to time about his personal faith and the inerrancy of scripture. The whole monologue is well worth reading, but the gist is that the Bishop admits to the reporter that he does indeed have questions from time to time, but that very questioning nature is expected of thoughtful Christians who must rely on *sole fide* to justify their salvation. *Sola fide* or faith alone is a key point of difference not only between Protestants and Roman Catholics but also between biblical Christianity and almost all other religions and teachings. As the Bishop himself wisely confesses,

> You call for faith: **I show you doubt, to prove that faith exists.**
> **The more of doubt, the stronger faith**, I say, if faith o'ercomes doubt.
> "Bishop Blougram's Apology," in *Men and Women*

We need to be careful not to impugn those with whom we interact when Christian brothers and sisters seem to stumble in their individual walk or when those outside the faith express doubts about the authenticity of scripture, miraculous occurrences, and the historical accuracy of scripture or pose other difficult questions that seem to be attacks on our faith. Rather we should see those occasions as opportunities to engage them with the truth. They are only asking such questions or attacking us for something they have seen in our lives—our outworking of a practical apologetic. That's what we want. **You are the bait.** The more our lives reflect the Christian world view the more we will be questioned and frequently vilified. If unbelievers did not see something different in us, they would attack someone else. If you are going to soar like an eagle, expect hunters to gather. When we Christians get skeptical questions from those who observe our lives, those occasions are a reason to celebrate and engage them with the reasons we have for the faith that is within us. **Reel 'em in**. The Christian's clarion call is always *Sola fide*.

> For by grace are ye saved through faith; and that not of yourselves: it is the gift of God: Not of works, lest any man should boast.
> (ESV, Ephesians 2: 8-9)

CHAPTER IX

Abnormal Christianity

I'll leave the discussion of what "normal" Christianity is to those with degrees in theology, a DD after their names, a Rev in front, or a backwards collar encircling their necks, as well as some of the great authors from the past such as Augustine, G. K. Chesterton, Aquinas, Luther, and other brilliant Christian authors who have invested their lives in an understanding of our faith. Their works are there for those of us interested in their foundational insights. Most of them form the grist of the better schools of theology. This past summer, just to refresh my understanding of the basics of our Christian world view, I spent three months pouring over a few of them—the 992 pages of Daniel Akin's *A Theology for the Church*, the 1,299 pages of Wayne Gruden's *An Introduction to Biblical Doctrine*, and the much shorter *Catechism of the Catholic Church* (a mere 825 pages). Taken as an unofficial theological trilogy these works can form a solid inter-denominational foundation for a systematic cross-doctrinal understanding of the application of God's Word to our theologies. These are some of the better sources you can consult to help you understand why various denominations and sects emphasize some beliefs and traditions over others.

"Normal" Christianity must first interpret scripture accurately, and then systematic theology involves "an orderly, rational, and coherent account of the justification for the various doctrines of the Christian faith. It addresses issues such as what the *Bible* teaches about certain topics or what is true about God and his universe, its interaction with all areas of life—science, worship, philosophy, history, ethics, psychology, and so on," how the local church should understand, teach, and apply various scriptural principles, and why Roman Catholics and Protestants as well as individual denominations can differ so fundamentally in their practices and observations. When it is done right, systematic theology can then also lead to an authentic biblical understanding of the rudiments of a world view formation as we seek to set the biblical-theological framework of scripture over against all other world views and learn scripture's application to areas of faith that the *Bible* may not seem to address. Systematic theology is intended to present a well-thought-out biblical frame of reference for the practices and rites of Christianity, over and against all of its competitors, as it seeks to weave biblical truth into every domain of life. Sadly that does not always happen.

Would that I were qualified to write about such linkages, but that is not my expertise. All that is quite normal and essential to grounding one's personal faith in Christ, but also mostly tangential to understanding our Christian world view. This is the arena in which most *Bible*-believing churches rightly spend their time. As you expand your understanding of normal Christianity, I encourage you to spend a few days with the above texts, or some tertiary source as basic as C. S Lewis' *Mere Christianity*, or a few months reading over the many works of contemporary expositors of scripture found in your church's "bookstore." We all have our favorites and trusted experts, but I recommend checking out several podcasts by Ravi Zacharias and other giants of contemporary faith and then delve into one of the texts on systematic theology, to understand how scripture interacts with every aspect of the Christian's life. Then for a practical application of these principles in several aspects of life, sign up for some of the free on-line courses offered by Dallas Theological Seminary or some daily devotional such as David Jeremiah's or anything from Moody. One of the very best is David Platt's daily podcasts. David, the lead Bible teacher at McClean Bible Church in Vienna Virginia, is a perceptive and trustworthy expositor of scripture, with a strong following among urban professionals.

All of those learnings are critical to sound belief, but that's not what this brief chapter is about.

The more I think about the fundamentals of our faith and our current dispensational (that word alone probably helps you to color my theology) requirement to believe on the basis of faith alone the more I realize how extraordinarily abnormal that is and why it is so difficult for non-believers to understand. **From the first century, Christ has built his church using abnormal human beings**. He didn't choose the ecclesiastical elite, the scholarly, the esteemed intellectual, or the politically connected. They largely rejected Him, as many from the same groups do today. He came to a Roman Centurion—what today would be an army company commander (I like to think he was similar to a contemporary army Ranger; Hooah!)—a handful of fishermen, a tax collector, a despised and rejected Samaritan woman (most likely the village tramp), a sweaty vile-mouthed shepherd or two, a tent maker, the blind, the infirm, and the crippled. Most extraordinarily, he came to a young recently betrothed Jewish female virgin. He didn't come just to the ones you might expect to form the foundation of his church; no DD's after any of their names. He certainly didn't come to the extant Jewish church hierarchy. They sought to undermine his ministry and eventually put him to death. His whole methodology was inverted.

One of my professors of modern American fiction while I was studying for my doctorate at Duke University was Dr. Victor Strandberg. While a renowned literary scholar, humanist, and a caring and urbane gentleman, Vic would probably be quite surprised to learn that he has been cited in a book about practical Christian apologetics (I'll be sure to send him a copy), but one of his insights in class is pertinent to our discussion. In our multi-year deep dive into modern American fiction, Professor Strandberg often led us to examine several fictional examples of what he called the "Inverted hero," the one you would least expect to be the hero in works of fiction but who was, in works ranging from T. S. Eliot's Prufrock to the unlikely heroes heralded by Saul Bellow, Ralph Ellison, William Faulkner, Carson McCullers, Kurt Vonnegut, Nathaniel West, Robert Frost, Richard Brautigan, William Carlos Williams, Zora Neale Hurston, and many others, to celebrate their lives and understanding of relationships: heroes who ranged from in-bred country hicks, to young children, to holocaust survivors, to ghetto dwellers, to naked poets dancing in their mirrors, to potential terrorists, to a thirty-three year old mentally "retarded" outcast named Benjy Compson (whom Faulkner labels an idiot)—a post-modern avatar of how the philosophical Naturalist sees Jesus.

The pattern culled out by Strandberg in contemporary fiction arose from his insights that **Jesus in his earthly ministry always seemed to choose the least likely person to be his man or woman for the hour. That should encourage all of us. You could be next.** Not only was that the pattern for choosing a reluctant leader to save the tribes of Israel in the *Old Testament*, but the pattern continued with those whom he chose to be his disciples and followers in the *New Testament*:

Mary, a teenaged virgin
David, an impulsive teenaged shepherd
Ehud, a disabled loner
Moses, a stammering murderer
Matthew, a despised tax collector
Isaiah, a man of unclean lips
Ruth, a widowed 20-year old
Simon and Andrew, ceremonially unclean fishermen
Paul, a persecutor of Christians
Jacob, a homeless wanderer
Rahab, a teen-aged prostitute
Ester a teenager who saved her nation
Joseph, at 17, a victim of human trafficking by his brothers
Jude, a violent Jewish nationalist
Jonah, a reluctant missionary
An unnamed thief on a cross, and many more.

Oh, there have been the esteemed theologians and champions of the faith in the past ranging from St. Augustine to Martin Luther to John Wesley to Billy Sunday to Thomas Aquinas to John Calvin to Charles R. Fuller to Billy Graham, but for the most part, **our Lord, what a risk taker, has decided to rely on you and me—what unlikely sources—to tell his**

story, to proclaim his kingdom, with our lives and personal witness to his mercy: totally unworthy inverted heroes.

The plots of our stories differ tremendously, but collectively they form the multiplicity of the individual subplots of the modern opus of faith. We have all been born as characters into God's great story, the metanarrative of which begins with Creation, moves into the disappointing Fall, demonstrates God's great personal and national Redemption, and culminates in the earth's Restoration.

> I am the alpha and the omega, the first and the last, the beginning and the end (ASV, Revelation 22:13).

Are you fulfilling your role? How are you preparing yourself for your role? This is the practical apologetic we have just begun to explore. The most mundane experiences often have a rich inverted theological significance which help us to mature as Christians and can have life-changing implications for others: "So whether you eat or drink or whatever you do, do it all for the glory of God." (NIV, 1 Corinthians 10:31).

> "Honour all men. Love the brotherhood. Fear God. Honour the king."
> (NKJV, 1 Peter 2:17)

CHAPTER X

In the Beginning...

Where else would you expect me to start? It's about time, right? Thanks for hanging in there. Think of the previous nine chapters as stretching before the exercise gets too vigorous. Many of the inquiries Christians get from unbelievers and skeptics have their origins here. Science has for centuries poo-pooed the notion of a first cause or some variety of divinity launching our universe into existence—what is a staple for a well-defined Christian apologetic. Despite Einstein's off-handed comment that "God does not play dice with the universe," or even the admitted atheist Louis Pasteur's deeper reflection that **"a little science estranges man from God, but much science drives him back,"** those of us who believe in a created universe have been told for centuries to stop believing in silly superstitions and legends and to go sit in the corner with the other village idiots. Just intimate that the universe might have been created by a divine force, let alone that it might have occurred in six, twenty-four hour days and get ready for ridicule in the public square, and maybe even from your pastor or priest, not to mention when your own kids come home from their high school science class with the brilliant insight that chickens evolved from T-rexes; sounds more like devolution than evolution to me, but that is their conundrum not mine.

Isn't it remarkable that philosophical Naturalists and all those who trust in evolutionary theory believe that natural selection implicitly yields increased levels of sophistication? According to their Naturalistic world view, man through chance and time has "evolved" into a much more sophisticated organism than pond scum, an amoeba, or even a tadpole. The more evolved we are the more sophisticated the organism. Yet these same scientists hold passionately to the second law of Thermodynamics—what we lay people refer to as entropy. What does entropy imply? Entropy is the scientific doctrine that all things tend toward randomness and disorder—death and eventually elimination. **So, one Naturalist pet theory tells us all things tend toward disorder and randomness, and their other favorite theory argues that primitive life forms evolve constantly toward increased sophistication and order. Talk about cognitive dissonance!** Raise that philosophical disconnect with your high school biology teacher and watch her begin to shake and drool as she gives you a D in her daily grade book and summons the principal.

Every so often when living our practical apologetic we may get a chance to try to persuade such theorists to consider a non-Naturalistic Biblical alternative, but those occasions are few and far between for most of us and can often cost Christians their personal relationships and their academic reputations. You certainly do not get published in "peer-reviewed" scholarly journals, as those who would dare to argue against human-caused climate change have been quick to discover in recent years. Chewing the wafer can do that, particularly when we chew with our mouths open. My own department chair, when I was teaching philosophy at the United States Military Academy, was quite frankly mortified when I publicly took on the philosophical Naturalist Milton Munitz (a colleague of Einstein's, the Chair of the Philosophy Department of NYU, and the world-renowned author of *Theories of the Universe From Babylonian Myth to Modern Science*), regarding the Genesis account of creation, when he was lecturing the West Point corps of cadets.

After Munitz's evening lecture on the Wittgensteinian View of Origins, that "did not allow of any external frame of reference" (you know this by now to be a Naturalistic intellectual position where the supernatural is irrelevant if not intellectually repugnant), the two of us informally debated origins—mine being an unintellectual Genesis-based view—that Munitz, a non-observant Jew, would have known intimately at one time in his youth and ultimately rejected as non-intellectual. Several students gathered around as we offered opposing arguments and debated one another for a mostly cordial but occasionally contentious hour in Grant Hall following his lecture. I suppose all that saved me from dismissal was Munitz's comment when he autographed my copy of his book with "To Colonel Bill Jeffries, a colleague who has encouraged me to rethink at least one possibility." Chewing the wafer is often considered impolite and not without consequences. Sometimes baby steps—merely outlining with honesty and integrity an alternative position—are the most you can take or encourage others to take at first. As my Cherokee buddy reminded us, we are the sum of our choices. Choose wisely.

Maybe this fictional example will confirm exactly how anti-intellectual I can be from time to time, as I look for apologetic premises in multiple arenas. One of my favorite movie lines comes from *Indiana Jones and the Last Crusade,* when Indiana has to cross a giant chasm to try to find Jesus' communion cup—the mythical Holy Grail—in order to try to save his father who has been mortally wounded by a NAZI sympathizer. Uncertain what he is going to do at first, Indiana is pressed by the movie's epitome of evil, Herr Doktor Walter Donovan, with the challenge, **"It's time to ask yourself, what do you believe?"** By the way, that is the challenge posed to each of us on a daily basis, by every skeptical Walter Donovan we confront.

Jones has to cross a vast chasm to reach his goal. At first uncertain of his steps, out of desperation he takes a tentative step out into what seems to be empty space (an apparent "leap of faith") and the faint outline of the first step of a stone bridge miraculously appears beneath his foot. Initially surprised by its existence and somewhat confused, he continues and with each tentative step, his path becomes clearer and the outline of a stone bridge more apparent. His faith grows, until he finally makes it all the way across. What at first seems mere empty space, a bridge invisible to the natural eye—a "leap of faith" to the Existential world view—once tested, becomes a confident step of increasing certainty and becomes clearer to him with each step he chooses to take. Looking back across the great gulf that he has just crossed, Jones sees the entire bridge with total clarity. When he finally crosses the wide chasm, he meets an ancient Knight Templar who has for years been charged with guarding Christ's communion chalice, just one cup nestled among dozens of possible chalices lined up along the wall that present themselves as options to Indiana. Think of the chosen chalice as the heart of one's world view. The old knight tells Indiana, just "as the true grail will bring you life, the false one will take it from you." Choice is important.

As Indiana is speaking with the aged guardian of the faith his antagonist, Dr. Donovan, who has a purely Naturalistic world view and understanding of Christ and his ministry, races across behind him and beats him to the punch, so to speak. He greedily selects the gaudiest, most pricey, and most ornate chalice—completely misunderstanding Jesus' ministry—to dip into the fount and drink. **His erroneous choice results in a rapid and hideous death. False religions and wrong world views tend to do that**. Indiana, recognizing the humility of Jesus' ministry, selects the most humble and unassuming communion chalice—a thoroughly inverted choice but one befitting a poor carpenter's son—drinks and lives, as does his father. As the guardian of the faith—the old Knight Templar—prepares to die, having fulfilled his mission on earth, he remarks to Indiana, "He chose poorly," and "You…have chosen… wisely." **The Christian world view is the only wise choice**.

Human and animal origins alike have only recently taken a swing toward a biblical understanding, and discoveries almost on a daily basis in all the sciences are gathering to support the Genesis account of creation. Every year another prominent scientist or two rejects the Naturalistic view of origins and the Darwinian theory of development and staggers reluctantly toward belief in a creator. As recently as 2018, the admittedly famous agnostic scientist Dr. David Thaler at the University of Basel, was compelled to admit, "I fought against it as hard as I could," but was nevertheless eventually forced to admit "that DNA Bar Codes of over 5 million animals from 100,000 different samples can all be traced back over 90% of the time to just two parents alive at roughly the same time, less than 250,000 years ago." His atheist research colleague, Dr. Mark Stoeckle at Rockefeller University, was forced to agree. This meager distance in years is quite different from the "billions and billions," to quote the late Carl Sagan (American astronomer, cosmologist, astrophysicist, astrobiologist, author, and science popularizer), of evolutionary years that have been crammed down our poorly evolved throats for decades (Ann Gauger in *Evolution News*, 12/5/18).

Their admission isn't necessarily a recognition of the historical validity of Noah's Ark or scholarly support for either a young earth theory of creation (YEC) or an old earth Christian theory (OEC), but the discovery has given pause to biologists and scientists of every ilk just now starting to try to reconcile their graduate school indoctrinations with the credibility of modern science (*Ever Ancient Ever New,* by Winfield Bevins). The scientific evidence leans more and more in favor of those of us who believe in a divinely created universe. It should, therefore, come as no surprise that 65% of Nobel Prize winning scientists are Christian and another 21% are Jewish Theists. The remaining 14% are "all others": agnostics, atheists, or New Agers (Freedom from Atheism Foundation). The point is that the majority of recent scientific discoveries have come from those espousing a Judeo-Christian ethic. You can stay up with many of these recent revelations regarding origins simply by following the YEC group on their musings in that respected "scientific journal," Facebook. Some of their observations are a little sketchy and there are some trolls that pop up there from time to time, but many of their member inputs will give you keen insights into recent scientific discoveries that will bolster your faith and help you in your apologetic discussions.

If you allow me to mix disciplines, I'll just remind you that it was the management guru and organizational theorist Dr. Deming who in order to debunk many of the myths of management practice and team development of the past century famously said, "**In God we trust, all others bring data.**" The scientific data being uncovered almost on a daily basis has begun to debunk the Naturalistic teachings on origins that have been blindly accepted by academia since the 19th century and, instead, to support the spontaneous creation of the universe by some force outside of it (just as the artist is always external to his masterpiece). In a recent debate I was having with two NASA scientists at the Houston Space Center, they asked me my biggest objection to their evolutionary theory of origins that NASA hoped to confirm with their Orion Mission to return to the moon in 2022 and upcoming Artemis trips to Mars. After receiving concessions from them that science was about observation and experimentation and the need for repeatability to verify results, I simply said that as soon as they could provide me an experiment where some scientist created something (anything) from nothing, I would pay attention to their theory. Until then, they might consider my world view. They were silent.

As the poet, Robert Frost puts it, "We [the critics] dance round in a ring and suppose, But the Secret [the artist] sits in the middle and knows." That is a non-Naturalistic approach to metaphysics and science that argues well for a purposeful Creator based on the complexity of the teleology alone. A theoretical and "purposeless random explosion of mystery matter as an explanation for intelligibility, truth, knowledge, natural laws, logic, the uniformity of cause and effect in nature, morality, and human values is just a bit of a stretch" says Peter Schutts, of the YEC Coalition. Again in 2019, reiterating an original survey in 2001, because of such discoveries as the incredible complexity of the genetic code, 1,000 prominent scientists issued a statement expressing skepticism about contemporary teachings regarding evolution (dissentfromDarwin.org).

What was once considered academic idiocy is now grudgingly accepted by a growing believing segment of the scientific community. With prominent scientists' acknowledgment of the veracity of Big Bang origins of the universe—not necessarily a Christian premise, but clearly a first cause of some magnitude—believers have begun to cast their silly dunce caps aside and move closer to the academic lectern. They haven't all been converted to non-Naturalistic deontological absolutists like me, but the momentum has begun to shift. **And who was there at that moment of creation, whenever it occurred? "In the beginning…God."** And what does that God do in his first interaction with human beings? He offers a choice regarding world views. Obey him or listen to Satan's lies. Most significantly, the word *Elohim*, translated as God in the first verse of the

Bible, is one of many used in Holy Scriptures to describe the nature of divinity.

We are told by the Psalmist, "And those who know thy name will put their trust in thee; for thou, O Lord, hast not forsaken those who seek thee" (KJV, Psalm 9:10). So, knowing the various names that God is referred to at different times, must have some significance. For some he revealed himself as El Elyon (The Most High God), and for others El Shaddai (The All-Sufficient One), El Olam (The Everlasting God), Adonai (Lord and Master), Jehovah-nissi (The Lord My Banner), Jehovah-raah (The Lord My Shepherd), Jehovah-sabaoth (The Lord is Peace), and many others—at least nineteen totally distinct ones by my unofficial count. My personal favorite was always *YHVH*, sometimes known as the Tetragrammaton (meaning four Letters), used over 7,000 times in the *Old Testament* and is the Hebrew word translated as Lord.

That particular one actually comes from the Hebrew, "to be," and is the one used by God when he tells Moses his name is "I am." **In other words, God is the origin of ontology—the very essence of being**, for those of you steeped in philosophy—the fundamental basis of every world view, and the essential premise of any practical apologetic. But in the first verse of Scripture, *Elohim* is of significance not only because it was the first name of the divinity introduced in scripture, but because as a plural noun it introduces us as early as in the Hebrew *Torah*, to the Christian theological concept of the Trinity—three Gods that are One. Yes, Christianity is monotheistic like Judaism and Islam, but a monotheism expressed in three persons. Sounds like a perfect team to me. "Let them praise the name of the LORD: for his name alone is excellent; his glory [is] above the earth and heaven" (NIV, Psalm 148:13).

The Trinity, then, is not just a *New Testament*, Christian, addition to Hebrew theology, but one apparently extant at the moment of creation. Not three aspects of one God, but three beings: Father, Son, and Holy Spirit—"three co-eternal, consubstantial persons, or hypostases"—three parts of one divine nature (Wikipedia). God the Father created the world *ex nihilo* through the Son (the Word) in the Holy Spirit. As we read further in the book of Genesis, we find each member of the triune Godhead had a distinctive role in that creation. The Apostle John echoes that in the introduction to his gospel ("In the beginning was the Word"), tying together both Testaments. It seems that there was a team present from the beginning. If we are made in the image of God (Hebrew: צֶלֶם אֱלֹהִים, *translit. Tzelem,* Elohim; or the Latin: *Imago Dei*), and his first revelation of himself to us is as a holy team, we might have reason to suspect that **teams are not only important, but a critical aspect of God's creation and how he might want us to function within his creation.** It follows, therefore, that we should probably learn more about them. That premise becomes one of the reasons why emphasizing Team Building to create exceptional organizational performance is fundamental to our business. As with all of our business consulting, training, and coaching, the approach to developing high performance teams, whether college and professional sports teams, business teams, or ministry teams is implicit in a Christian world view and has its origin in Genesis.

It was also a team that the Apostle Paul discussed in his first letter to the church in Corinth when he discussed the various gifts existing in the local church. This is God's ideal model for the local church.

> There are different kinds of gifts, but the same Spirit distributes them. There are different kinds of service, but the same Lord. There are different kinds of working, but in all of them and in everyone it is the same God at work. Now to each one the manifestation of the Spirit is given for the common good. To one there is given through the Spirit a message of wisdom, to another a message of knowledge by means of the same Spirit, to another faith by the same Spirit, to another gifts of healing by that one Spirit, to another miraculous powers, to another prophecy, to another distinguishing between spirits, to another speaking in different kinds of tongues, and to still another the interpretation of tongues. All these are the work of one and the same Spirit, and he distributes them to each one, just as he determines. Just as a body, though

one, has many parts, but all its many parts form one body,
so it is with Christ. For we were all baptized by one Spirit
so as to form one body—whether Jews or Gentiles, slave
or free—and we were all given the one Spirit to drink.
Even so the body is not made up of one part but of many.
(NIV, 1 Corinthians 12: 4-14)

Just as an NBA team composed of five outside shooters and no one willing to set a pick, or an NFL team with eleven QB's and no receiver to catch the passes they throw will never be winning teams, so the local church must have different people with different gifts. I know the Apostle Paul uses the body analogy, but I find the sports metaphors more in line with my background and expertise. Eleven noses or five ears is just a little too bizarre for me.

Belonging to a team is part of my history. Not only is Team Building at the heart of many of my books and a major part of the business for which we at ESI are internationally acclaimed, but it is rooted in my personal development as well. Growing up in South Jersey, I led a band of adolescents known as the Dragon Gang. We even had membership cards—how lower middle class was that! Okay, it was Ocean City, New Jersey, a Methodist retreat town that to this day is still a dry family-oriented beach resort on the Jersey Shore that as recently as 2019 reaffirmed the city's ban on all uses of cannabis—hardly the genesis of the *Real Housewives of New Jersey*—so the word "gang" is probably somewhat misleading. We aren't talking about MS-13 or some group of heavily tatted and variously pierced amoral thugs ravaging Chicago's south side or isolated Long Island communities on weekends with which the DOJ should be concerned.

Our motives were more rooted in rescuing adolescent damsels in distress (Thelma, Ellen, Beth, Diane, Nancy, Jeannie and others in our grade school classes) from imaginary villains, as we rampaged through the tall weeds behind the A&P supermarket on West Avenue and Mazzitelli's Plumbing, seeking out Redskins—yes, that is what we called them—or other bad guys with our plastic weapons and homemade slingshots and housefly slaughtering guns made out of rubber bands, wooden clothespins, and plastic rulers (that's plastic not plastique). It was my gang, and I was proud of it. I certainly didn't give any thought to God's intended purpose for teams. But there we were, and I was in charge. Teams were there in my beginnings. It just seemed natural.

In my beginning, in those adolescent years, we didn't spend time defining our Purpose, outlining our Core Values, articulating a Vision of what success looked like, formulating a Mission Statement, agreeing on Operating Principles or Norms, or defining the Metrics we would use to prove our success. Although we did have defined Roles; I was the leader, and the others were my scouts. It just seemed natural. But these trite adolescent experiences later affirmed the origins of my world view. Life back then was far less complicated. Even though these are the key elements outlining an exceptional team's performance that I discuss in *Hannibal, Hummers, and Hot Air Balloons: High Performing Strategies for Tough Times, Culture and High Performance,* and more recently in *Inliers: The Curse of Polarity Thinking,* we just pretended and acted out TV scripts similar to those we watched on *Wild Bill Hickok, The Roy Rogers Show, Starsky and Hutch, Miami Vice, The Cisco Kid,* and years later, *The A-Team.* These and other "educational" shows featuring intellectual giants in Hollywood served as our team building mentors on the black and white family television. Teams just seemed like the normal way of working together. What a team was and why we should work together for success began to be ingrained at an early age.

Because I always had the biggest guns (a cap-popping six-shooter in a fringed hip holster) and, most importantly, a plastic pump gun that fired ping pong balls at the rate of almost fifteen per minute—no bump stock required—just a well-developed bicep, it followed that I should be in charge, and I usually was. Butch, Jerry, Gary, Frank, and a few others just acquiesced to my leadership. High school found me quarterbacking our Cape Atlantic League Red Raiders football team, captaining our church bowling team, playing third base at the hot corner and co-captaining the New Jersey Natural Gas Company fast pitch softball team, organizing our church basketball team at the Atlantic City YMCA, being a discus and javelin hurling member of our Ocean City high school track team, and serving as the leader of our church high school youth group. It seemed early on that teams were going to be in my future, a team future that began in earnest as I was accepted at and matriculated at West Point and began to learn what teams were really all about. But we'll get to that. **World views take time to develop.**

CHAPTER XI

My Heritage

Like some of you, I was named after my father. Being a "junior" always seemed a bit of an administrative nuisance to me, so I dropped the Jr. after graduating from West Point, but the more I reflect on the learnings that he passed on to me, the prouder I become to bear his complete name. I will be forever his junior and never quite as clear a witness to our faith as he. He lived a practical apologetic for all to see and set that example for me before I ever knew what the words meant. God blessed me with two wonderful Christian parents who tried to raise me and my sister in what they would always tell us was "the nurture and admonition of the Lord." For them that meant the basis of a Christian world view. I fought them, of course. I was just a cocky, ignorant, and brash little "head full of mush," as one popular conservative radio commentator likes to call present-day Gen-Nexters. I may not have always listened, but I watched and learned.

My first memories of our family were while I was growing up in Haddon Heights, New Jersey. After being born in Camden, NJ, I lived at number 11, 11th avenue for the first five years. I never thought about it before, but upon reflection it is probably not just a coincidence that the number on the back of my football jerseys years later while quarterbacking the Ocean City High School Red Raiders and still later quarterbacking and playing safety on the West Point Sprint football team, which at the time was just called the 150's or lightweight football, was also number 11. I even got issued the number 11 jersey as the plebe quarterback of our company's intramural football team during my first year at the Academy. As NCIS Special Agent Leroy Jethro Gibbs, on the TV show *NCIS*, often counsels his team, "there are no coincidences in life"—Rule # 39. All Christians should agree with that shibboleth.

My memory clouds over those times in Haddon Heights, but I know that on the left side of our house lived the Utze family, and next to them the Gabriels. I was friends with Betsy Utze, who was my same age, and my sister, Jean, was a BFF with the youngest daughter of the Gabriel family, two doors away. I never saw Betsy again after we left Haddon Heights at the age of five, but Jean, more of a people person than I, apparently stayed in touch with the Gabriels all through college.

On the other side of us lived the Knapps. They were an older German couple who spoke broken English; their house always smelled of spices, anise, and ginger. The wife seemed to bake every day and always waved me over to lick out her mixing bowls and sample the gallimaufry of treats spilling out of their kitchen. Anise-laced springerles were her specialty, as are, not so surprisingly, mine today every Christmas. Each year for us it becomes an act of love and family tradition to press out individual cookies from hand carved wooden German and Swiss molds with shapes of Nutcrackers (which Cheryl and I have collected now for over 25 years): angels, Father Christmas, *jägermeisters*, candles, manger scenes, and Christmas trees. Since World War II with the Germans had only recently ended, a couple years before I was born, nerves were still pretty raw in Haddon Heights, and most everyone avoided the Knapps, or sometimes cast a suspicious eye their way. I was never aware of any outward aggression directed towards them, but, except by my family, they were generally ostracized by the neighborhood. Not me though. No spy could ever cook like she did, and I was a perpetual official taster in their aromatic kitchen bedecked with numerous hand-carved wooden crosses on the wall and bunches of dried herbs dangling from the ceiling.

Aside from chasing Betsy around the floor on our hands and knees under our dining room table when the neighbors visited, my favorite memories were of the frequent visitors my Mom and Dad had in the house. Mom was very reserved and introverted, a real ISTJ if you know your MBTI® technology, and Dad was a very sociable ESFJ. He loved people and loved sharing his Christian faith with them. The visitors I remember most prominently were all the major players from the then fledgling Billy Graham Evangelistic Crusades. They seemed to live at our house.

Before I was born, Dad had been the advance man for the Fuller Evangelistic Crusades—kind of an early twentieth century Billy Graham—holding large tent meetings mostly in the northeast part of the USA. It was Dad's job to arrive in a city well in advance of the crusades and coordinate the efforts of all the local churches who were willing to participate. Without any college degree, Dad had been ordained as a Methodist minister and preached in churches all around the east coast, mostly in New Jersey, New York, and the New England states. I still remember his speaking at mostly all black baptisms held at the many lakes in the woods and pine barrens of South Jersey. As those baptized in the creek rose up out of the water, they would shout "hallelujahs" and "praise Jesus" as they raised their hands in celebration of their new births and following Jesus' commandment to be baptized, while running barefoot excitedly through the pine barrens praising their redeemer. The picture of dozens of white robed black men and women running through the woods, celebrating their faith and obedience to Christ is still rich in my memory. There was always an exuberance in their expression of faith that seemed to be missing in more conventional denominational gatherings and ministries.

During the thirties, the Methodist denomination appeared to lose all interest in being a *Bible* believing church and embraced the social gospel of the day—far easier and more socially acceptable to serve a hot meal than try to get a sinner to repent. Religious tracts were embarrassing, but doughnuts were quite acceptable. They left Jesus, the embarrassing bloody cross, the idea of unexplained miracles, the "fairy tale" of the Garden of Eden, the divine separating of the waters of the Red Sea, the "obviously" mythical hell, and all those overly emoting elders shouting frequent "a-mens" from the front benches of the church in the dust and adopted a more respectable theology of salvation by good works. Justification by faith alone was purged from most of their churches along with the "old-fashioned" intellectually embarrassing theory of dispensationalism. In its place was substituted a Humanistic sanctification by which parishioners would earn their own salvation by being socially responsible. The 2019 fracturing of the denomination along the unbiblical LGBTQ fissure had its first cracks appear in the 1940's. I would call them secular Humanists, but that opprobrium gives some of them far too much intellectual credibility. They just tossed the *Bible* into the dustbin and struck out on their own.

Their religion had morphed into a lukewarm Neo-orthodox theology that would grudgingly grant that the *Bible* might "contain" the word of God but surely was not the literal inspired word of God. They eventually told my dad that he could not preach salvation by Christ alone, and that he had to stop speaking at Youth for Christ meetings and other such embarrassing fundamentalist gatherings. That did it, and Dad never preached in a Methodist church again. The Baptist church, several Bible Churches, and non-denominational fellowships throughout South Jersey became our new church homes wherever we lived.

When he was a young minister, before I was born, Dad's young wife, his piano player and organist of all things, had an affair with some reprobate in his church and ran off with him—sounds like an Updike novel, doesn't it? Talk about a real-life *Month of Sundays*! My dad and she were subsequently divorced, and because of that, the Baptist Church never allowed him to be an elder in the churches we attended. They would allow him to preach from their pulpits, be a deacon, serve communion, teach the men's Bible fellowship, witness to neighbors in outreach meetings, preach at Salvation Army meetings on the Atlantic City boardwalk, be their representative at numerous missions in the South Jersey area, and generally run the Ocean City Baptist Church Summer Bible Conferences each year, but not serve as an elder. To have been divorced was a permanent stigma, a scarlet letter, for the GARB (General Association of Regular Baptists) churches in South Jersey who believed that an elder needs to be "the husband of one wife" (1 Tim. 3:2, Titus 1:6), instructions given to the local Church when many in the tribes of Israel and some in the fledgling first century assemblies of new believers in Galatia, Ephesus, Corinth, Thessalonica, had more than one wife—polygamists in our jargon. That was their fledgling first century syncretistic church culture that Paul was addressing and trying to rectify in his epistles; not divorce, but multiple wives.

You of course will have been indoctrinated by your own seminary, denomination, *Bible* study, small group, or tradition, regarding this principle, but I find nothing in the inspired writings by the Apostle Paul, who was trying to correct the new believers' concept of marriage, indicating that divorce alone disqualifies a man as an elder; indeed, the Greek simply means that an elder must be faithful to the woman to which he is married (in Greek, "a one-woman man"). That aspect of marriage itself was a significant challenge for the 1st century church. That literal interpretation was dismissed in South Jersey and, sadly I readily admit, in the majority of evangelical fellowships today. Most of the churches we have attended over the years cling to the same principle that divorce disqualifies one for the position of an elder.

As an INTJ, I have done my homework in English and the Greek regarding Paul's admonition and am more than willing to debate such a Procrustean line of thought. You will have to exegete that requirement for yourself and speak with those whom you trust, but I believe them to be wrong on this important theological principle. Curiously, the same criteria described for an elder in 1 Timothy 3:2 (the husband of one wife) is identical in the Greek to the criteria for a deacon in 1 Timothy 3:12 (the husband of one wife). Ask your spiritual mentors to explain that one. Dad could always be a deacon but never an elder. Go figure. I'm quite sure that is not the only point of interpretation upon which we will disagree—just give me time. We can still worship together. Dad accepted their interpretation without question—a good faithful ESFJ will tend to do that. I watched those church leaders sideline a great spiritual warrior for years and break his spirit again and again.

The timeline for all this is very hazy. All I know is that by the time I came along, my dad's affiliation with evangelistic crusades created exciting evenings in our home in Haddon Heights. Any given night might have Billy Graham, Cliff Barrows (Billy's crusade song leader), or George Beverly Shea (his chief soloist) over to our small house for dinner and informal prayer and song sessions. These great expositors of scripture, along with my parents, laid the theological foundation for my world view. Bev Shea would light up the house with his great voice, and soon Cliff would have my family and all the youth from the Haddon Heights Baptist Church, who seemed to live at our home after church services on Wednesday and Sunday evenings, singing gospel songs late into the night. Our neighbors, including the Gabriels and the German Knapps, would gather on blankets on our front lawn as Ethel Waters, a huge black lady and famous singer and movie star who joined the Crusades later in her life, would belt out "Amazing Grace," "How Great Thou Art," or the song she made famous, "His Eye is on the Sparrow," from our small and very crowded front porch. My dad had a great bass voice as well—one he neglected to pass on to me—and he reveled in singing gospel songs that seem to embarrass most church attendees today—"Just as I am," "The Old Rugged Cross," "In the Garden," "At Calvary," "I Love to Tell the Story," "Onward Christian Soldiers," and other great missionary songs that were ingrained in me as a young child as my world view began to take shape. I frankly miss that music in our current guitar, keyboard, and drum obsessed music programs. Hillsong, Mercy Me, Casting Crowns, and any number of contemporary young Christian groups produce great music, and our music director has us learn a new one almost every week, but would it kill'em to have us sing a song from time to time, without modernizing the tune or changing the words, that those over fifty might actually recognize? Even Kanye West, these days known as "Christian Genius Billionaire Kanye West," goes traditional occasionally. Sorry, my bias, not yours. Clearly the Christian world view is not monolithic and can appeal to any generational grouping.

Serving as a denominationally unaffiliated itinerant preacher in those days paid no bills, so my dad took a series of different jobs. He had been a bank teller as well as a roofing and asbestos siding salesman. Later he opened a small store in Haddon Heights called Jeff's Style Center (a great name for an ESFJ's business, by the way), that was essentially a Florsheim shoe store. My mom ran a homemade candy store out of our home and took in laundry and ironing from the neighbors to earn some extra money; the smells of hot dipped chocolates, fresh butter creams, and fudge drift through my memories of those times. No doubt my family's passion for whipping up batches of fudge every Christmas arises from this sweet genetic memory. Cheryl would cook the batch of boiling crackling candy and then pour it into a large pan full of Ghirardelli or Nestle chocolate chips, and then I, Paul, and Austin would take turns whipping it until our arms tired. Rather ironically, when we eventually compared notes, my wife's grandmother and my grandmother both had written out recipes in cursive for fudge that turned out to be identical in ingredients and amounts. Somewhere in Gramma Crawford's Polish background and my Grandmother Amelia's German background, homemade fudge was produced in identical ways. Gotta love those European ancestors! Maybe they swapped notes while waiting to be processed through Ellis Island.

Everybody seemed to know my dad in Haddon Heights. When I was four, I got a new toy pistol for a birthday present. No concealed carry permit was necessary then for a cap pistol (just give the politicians time), so I carried it everywhere I went in a *faux* leather holster hanging off my hip. That was my Second Amendment right, right? It went very well with my cowboy chaps, leather boots, and ten-gallon hat that I enjoyed sporting all around Haddon Heights, Barrington, and Haddonfield neighborhoods. The curious fact that our youngest daughter, Ainsley, has saddled all her kids with western names (Dylan, Wyatt, Cody, Annie, and Millie) must have some unconscious genetic link here. Yee-haw! Wasn't it the wise King Solomon, whom the Hebrew *Bible* also calls Jedidiah (a good western name), who tells us that, "Grandchildren are the crown of the aged"? (ESV, Proverbs 17:6)? Genes rule! With prayer and good teaching, world views just might transfer as well.

One day, a good friend of Dad's, the local beat cop who patrolled Station Avenue in front of his store, asked to see my new pistol. As I proudly presented it to him, he decided to show me how a real pro would load it, so he took the barrel in one hand and the *faux* pearl handle in the other and with savvy expertise bent them together to show me how to open a revolver for cleaning. Sadly there was no hinge, the pistol was once a solid piece of plastic not meant to be opened, and never had been until Sgt Gray snapped it in half. I was heartbroken as only a cowboy can be when he has lost his piece, and Gray was mortified. I remember his apologizing profusely to my dad when he took me into the Style Center to show him what he had done. That afternoon, Sgt. Gray drove me to Murphy's 5 and 10 Cent Store in Barrington, New Jersey, to buy me a new pistol. I had bad guys to catch and Injuns to kill, after all. Yes, I actually said that. These days our culture's concern for language seems to trump more important core values—always an outshoot of a Naturalistic world view. Between chasing Betsy under the dining room table, tracking down "Redskins," and toting an unregistered six-shooter with no serial number or open carry permit at the age of four, I guess I can never become a Supreme Court Justice. I'm just not "woke" enough, and totally unconcerned with triggers, safe places, micro aggressions, and preferred pronouns. The nation's loss.

When I was four or five, my dad had taken on a partner in the Style Center business, I'll call him Horace, a man my dad thought was a good "Christian" friend. After all, he was a never-divorced elder—the husband of one woman—in the Haddon Heights Baptist Church. Horace turned out to be a thief and ran up a series of large unpaid bills without telling Dad, took out a number of personal loans, emptied out the business bank account, and absconded to Florida one night with his wife, leaving my parents with over a hundred thousand dollars in debts. That was more than a small fortune in 1951. We were flat broke, and my parents lost their store and our home and consequently had to declare bankruptcy. While he and mom did not have to do so legally, they promised all their creditors that they would pay back every dollar that they had owed with interest. That was their Christian obligation—**their world view demanded it**.

> Pay to all what is owed to them: taxes to whom taxes are owed, revenue to whom revenue is owed, respect to whom respect is owed, honor to whom honor is owed. Owe no one anything, except to love each other, for the one who loves another has fulfilled the law (ESV, Romans 13:7-8).

Fulfilling that commitment to their world view took sixteen years of maybe one or two meals a day and abject poverty for us as a family. French's yellow mustard and white bread sandwiches and an occasional stalk of cream cheese-filled celery for supper during most of grade school and high school were not out of the ordinary, but my parents eventually made their word good. That was part of their practical apologetic—putting their world view into action. What an example for a young man to have for parents! *Trap Door to the Dark Side* includes a brief vignette of the time I tracked Horace down in his posh little Florida condo upon my return from one of my tours in Vietnam. I did my best to change his life forever, with "kindness and reverence," of course.

CHAPTER XII

Haddon Heights in the Rearview Mirror

I find it interesting that so often these days the newest movies coming out provide the "back stories" for superheroes who have already starred in the movies for the last ten years. Either Hollywood has run out of ideas—always the most likely possibility in that fetid immoral swamp—or somehow the importance of those back stories has gained resonances if we really want to understand why our favorite heroes developed as they did. Back stories often provide the philosophical premises for our world views. The earlier plots have jumped ahead to the end and are now filling in the developmental steps that assisted in developing their various world views. Sound familiar? While certainly no superhero, I need to relate a few more homely stories regarding how my Christian world view developed. Who knows, yours might take a similar path. **Don't give up, parents. Some of us are just slow learners.**

When I was five, since there was nothing further holding us in Haddon Heights, we packed up our gray Hudson Hornet—as I recall, all Hudson Hornets were gray in those days—and moved to the seashore in South Jersey to give us a fresh start. For several years, just to pay the bills, Dad would take the train each week from Ocean City to South Philly (about a 6-hour commute by train each way in those days), where he worked as a bank teller during the day and preached in South Philly missions in the evenings. His biggest claim to fame was the year that the bank wanted to introduce the "new-fangled technology" of adding machines for the first time. Dad thought that investment was an unnecessary and very slow expense for the bank, as long as they hired qualified clerks and tellers, so he challenged the machine operators to a formal competition of rapidly adding and subtracting large sums accurately. The calculators proved too slow, Dad won, and the bank cancelled orders for the new machines for another two years until he quit his job in order to be closer to home during the week. Ocean City became home for us, until I left for West Point eleven years later. What I had for all that time was the model of a mom and dad with deep faith in Christ and an unimpeachable record of personal and professional integrity, and two parents who vowed to ensure that every aspect of their lives reflected a Christian world view. Such small often insignificant actions are part of living a practical apologetic. Sorry to quibble with Bush 43's comment about his dad in his funeral oration for Bush 41 in 2018, but my dad was the greatest father a boy could ever have. I watched his world view in action every day.

In their unassuming way their faith and world view impacted everything they did, and everyone they knew. I have related this story before in my book *Culture and High Performance,* but it bears retelling here. In one of his many sales jobs after leaving the bank, it was my dad's duty to make frequent calls to homes in the South Jersey area providing estimates for refinishing furniture or reupholstering chairs and sofas. The economy was soft, and it was a rather low margin business even in good times. Often, he would have to lug two or three heavy sample bags of upholstery material up several floors of stairs in older tenement buildings in Atlantic City, Ventnor, Long Port, Millville, or Margate, New Jersey, often with no financial return. During vacations and summers while in high school, I would travel with him to help him carry all the heavy bags.

On one such sales call, Dad had been asked by an elderly couple to come to give an estimate for reupholstering a well-worn over-stuffed chair where the disabled husband spent most of his day. We really needed the money, so Dad had cut the price to the bare bones to try to get the business. As Dad explained the costs associated with the job, I recall watching the expressions on the couple's faces cloud over as they realized it would still be far too expensive for their limited funds. They thanked my dad for coming but said they would have to wait for a while to get the chair reupholstered. Dad understood the real reason and out of the blue, asked if he could pray with them before we left. They were very surprised but agreed and Dad prayed. They thanked him for his understanding and compassion, and we left. On the way out the door, I watched Dad reach into his pocket and take out his last ten dollar bill and leave it on the small wooden table by the door. I knew that was all we ourselves had for the rest of the week, and Dad saw the concerned look on my face. **He smiled and just said, "God will provide." And…He always did.** It was his actions, not just words, that rooted my world view. He lived a practical apologetic.

On weekends, Dad would frequently preach at street meetings or on the Atlantic City boardwalk at Salvation Army Meetings. He would also speak at various missions in the South Jersey area well known for helping Ex-cons, alcoholics, and other addicts get back on their feet. He personally employed two of the men whom he would pick up each morning from the mission where they often slept, sober them up with black coffee, drive them the twenty miles to his small furniture plant in Somers Point, and then drop them back off in the evenings. Not unusually, he would from time to time buy a small bag of groceries and drop them off with their "common law wives"—a phrase I never hear used anymore, since such relationships have unfortunately become almost the unspoken norm in our current thoroughly secularized culture—and several children, who lived in what was then referred to as the "colored section" along Baltic Avenue in Atlantic City.

Often, he would make me go with him and play the trumpet to help him lead the singing at these boardwalk meetings. I was the first trumpet in the Ocean City High School band but mortified every time I had to play on the boardwalk to the jeers and laughter of the passersby. It clearly wasn't something I enjoyed, but it was a chance to be with him for a few hours—times I really miss. One trumpet could really light up the boardwalk crowds with "Onward Christian Soldiers," "Blessed Assurance," or "What a Friend We Have in Jesus." From time to time, when I traveled with him on summer vacations as he made sales calls, we'd be having lunch in a local diner—establishments for which New Jersey is infamous—and there would be a couple of uniformed Salvation Army folks eating there as well. Dad would always use his meager paper money when we checked out, without telling them, to pay as much of their tabs as possible. **Talk about chewing the wafer! He was in every way a model for taking your world view to work**.

I told that story to all of our kids at different times not really thinking about the long-term consequences, but just wanting them to know about their grandfather whom none of them, except Tiffany and Ainsley when they were very small, had ever met. Once when traveling out to Park City, Utah to ski, as we hustled to our connecting flight through the airport in Phoenix, I saw our son Paul stop at a small open café where two uniformed soldiers were sitting on stools. He reached back in his wallet for his meager funds he had saved for the trip and paid the tab for both of the very surprised army privates from the 10th Mountain Division sitting there, as he thanked them for serving our country. On another trip, Cheryl and I had used our frequent flier points to book first-class seats on a Delta flight from Newark to Denver. Paul, a high school freshman at the time, was sitting across the aisle. We saw him speak to the flight attendant and then get up, give us a thumbs up sign, and move to the rear of the plane. A few minutes later a very surprised uniformed army specialist came up and took his seat. Long before it had become almost *de rigueur* for Americans to say perfunctorily, "Thank-you for your service," to members of our military, Paul had put such thoughts into practical application once again and had given up his first class seat for the young soldier's center seat in the rear of coach. An ESFJ himself, he is every bit the grandfather he never met, but will one day in Glory. World views tend to be contagious.

To be honest, I wasn't a fan of my parents' upbringing at the time. Their world view seemed cumbersome and at times embarrassing. Prayer at every meal, even in restaurants where they would simply bow their heads in thanks; none of these made up prefab prayers like "Now I lay me down to sleep…", nothing to read or simply memorize, no I was expected to extemporize. Frequent family devotions, scripture reading and prayers, most nights before bed—I would always have to be the one to read, so I would purposely mispronounce words and names I knew how to pronounce, just to get back at him for making me do it. If there was an *Old Testament* name with three or four syllables, I could easily morph them into six. My dad would just patiently stop me and give me the correct pronunciation. I was your basic teenaged wise guy. Church every Sunday morning and Sunday evening, prayer meetings Wednesday nights, and youth group meetings on Friday evenings. The church was our second home. And…if there were guest speakers or a missionary conference during the week, we would all have to attend, and frequently have the speaker over for supper in our home, unless I could feign too much homework.

A few years after moving to Ocean City, my dad went to work for Dura Finish, a furniture refinishing business in Somers Point. Dad eventually bought the business and ran it until the local union bosses drove him out of business several years later. I actually got my first 16-gauge pump gun when I was a high school freshman to help my dad defend our home in case the union thugs came a calling after they had already twice set fires in his building because his employees had refused to vote to unionize. He had nothing against unions; it's just that the workers Dad hired could not afford the dues. I didn't realize it at the time, but he hired only disabled workers who had been injured in motorcycle accidents—Harry, who had lost a lung from several bullet wounds in the Korean War and had a left arm permanently injured when he wrecked his bike going to night school, Guido, an Italian cabinet maker who had only recently arrived from Genoa and barely spoke English and lost several fingers when he crashed his Harley on the ninth street bridge, Alphonso—the blackest man I ever met—who had broken his hip when his bike flipped one evening when he was drunk, and a few others whose names I have long ago forgotten. It was his not so subtle suggestion to me that I should never buy a motorcycle. He never said a word but just surrounded me with examples to see.

They were good workers and Dad always paid them more than I thought he should, but that was Dad. My parents rarely "preached" to me; they just lived lives that reflected their sincere Christian world view: But when you host a banquet, invite the poor, the crippled, the lame, and the blind"

(Luke 14:13). About the same time, my mom went to work for Stainton's Department Store on Asbury Avenue where she worked in the flower shop and as a retail salesclerk until she eventually worked her way up to become the credit manager for the store. At supper each night we would have to include in our prayers those customers whom my mother knew needed assistance to pay their accounts. Most of my school days were spent playing football or running track and then walking or hitchhiking the three or four miles from school to Stainton's Department Store on Asbury Avenue after practice so, my dad could pick up my mom and me at 6:30 and drive us home. I relate these stories, reluctantly, not wanting to focus at all on me but to encourage all of you who are parents to know that before you speak a word, the way you simply live your Christian world view is speaking volumes to those whom you raise. **Children do not learn their world view from a high school textbook but from the examples surrounding them**.

On days I didn't have football or track practice, I would take the school bus home and then prepare supper for the family. We were fortunate to have my grandmother, Amelia, living with us as well, but she was too infirm to do any of the chores, so with two working parents, such duties fell to me. I made a mean hotdog casserole, when we could afford the meat. When such funds were not available, there were far more of these times than I care to remember, I would stop on the way home from school at the docks down by the bay as the commercial fishing boats came in at the end of the day and beg the skippers for the unwanted and more or less worthless eels that had been accidentally snagged in their nets. Often there were three or four of us at Montagna's or Chris's by the ninth street bridge for the same reason, so I would occasionally have to do battle with the other boys to get enough eels for our family. The first time my nose was broken was by Jerry, whose family that day apparently needed the eels more than mine. If you ever read *Trap Door to the Dark Side*, you will meet Jerry again, when eight years later, much to my surprise, I had to carry him legless out of a firefight in Vietnam, when his army unit had been overrun by the Vietcong. I hated the greasy taste of eels, and they would eerily rise out of the boiling water screeching at us as they were cooked, but they were food—just another reason, I suppose, why I do not eat *Unagi* sushi, today.

We may have lived in other places in Ocean City as well, but I distinctly remember living at 328 Asbury Avenue (two blocks away from the "colored section" of town, where Jerry lived) in a small upstairs apartment and later living on Wesley Avenue, in a three-room house right across the street from Wesley Avenue Elementary School, which later became the Ocean City Museum, and close enough so we could walk the eight blocks to our church on 10th Street to save on gas money. It was me, my dad, my mom, and my sister, Jean. I never really got to know Jean, because she was several years older and ran with a different set of friends. I can't recall a single thing we ever did together. She eventually went to Bob Jones University, an ultra-fundamentalist university in Greenville, South Carolina, infamous for their "date line." Dancing, card playing, drinking alcohol, and attending movies were not allowed at this school, so for a good date, couples were merely allowed to walk around campus in designated walkways called the dateline, at least six inches apart to ensure sexual purity. Jean went home to be with the Lord in 2010. We actually talked more in her last ten years while she and her husband, Allen, lived in Ohio and Cheryl and I lived in Zionsville, Indiana—and that was few and far between—than we ever did when I was growing up. Jean had also learned well from our parents to be a wafer chewing believer and spent her last twenty-five years as the headmaster of a Christian school near Dayton.

We eventually moved to Arkansas Avenue on the 19th street lagoon in Ocean City, when Howard Stainton, my mom's boss, bought a tract of mosquito-infested marsh land and threw up several small prefab homes which he offered to his most trusted employees for very low rates. Thanks to Mr. Stainton's largess, we lived in a small waterfront house for most of my high school years. We occupied a first-floor apartment that flooded in every hurricane when the ocean and bay would meet in our utility room and short out our oil heater, and during the summers rented out our dock space to well-to-do families from Pennsylvania, to help pay our bills. One family, the Sandstroms from New Hope Pennsylvania, owned a large Chris Craft cabin cruiser that docked in front of our house during August each summer; they seemed to fish out in the ocean every day. To help with expenses, I would net soft shell crabs off the bulkhead pilings in the spring and go door to door to sell them to neighbors and filet the fish our tenants brought home after each trip. If I did a really good job fileting their flounders or king fish, they would occasionally give me a small flounder or two to take to the family for dinner. Those were the days!

Kurt Loder, the well-known writer and columnist who famously ran the MTB network on television for several years, and later became the editor of *Rolling Stone,* was a year older than I and lived in a large house across the street from us. When I was in high school, his younger brother drowned in the lagoon right in front of our house. One day he just turned up missing, and the police found his body floating out in the lagoon near our small rowboat. The assumption was that he must have just run over the bulkhead while playing, fell in, and drowned. I remember Dad immediately going over to their house after the ambulance and police cars left and praying with their family. It wasn't something they wanted to do, but Dad would not be deterred.

Several years later when I was a cadet at West Point, my parents moved to 11 Village Drive in Somers Point, NJ, right across the bridges from Ocean City. That's right, another # 11 entering my life: Rule 39. My one memory of that house was when I was home on Christmas break my Yearling year (West Point's jargon for a sophomore cadet). A squirrel had apparently come down the chimney and when Mom opened the glass door to the fireplace to start a coal fire to warm the living room for a neighborhood *Bible* study that evening, that very adventurous squirrel used the opportunity to race around the house knocking over candles and picture frames until I was finally able to usher it out the back door with a broom.

While I was serving in Vietnam, my parents, whose health had gradually deteriorated, moved to New Port Richey, Florida. I would say retired to Florida, but they never really did. That would be too cliched. They just tried to escape the snow and ice of the New Jersey winters because Dad couldn't shovel snow anymore. Their faith remained fiercely active, however, and they became unofficial chaplains for the neighborhood. Age need not impact the out-workings of our world view. Their residential area was one of mostly older couples, many of whom had retired to Florida for health reasons, so ambulances racing through the neighborhood with sirens screaming was not out of the norm. Mom and Dad would spend their time comforting spouses who had suddenly lost their partners to heart attacks and strokes. I found that whole scenario very depressing when visiting them, but they saw it as their calling. The spiritual help they provided their neighbors all too soon became the same kind of help they themselves needed.

CHAPTER XIII

The Music is Extraordinary!

Not many years later when I was teaching ethics and philosophy at West Point, my dad grew ill and within a very short time, passed away in their New Port Richey home. He had been in the hospital for a few days for complications from emphysema, no doubt caused by several years of sand blasting old lead-based paint off furniture and spray painting lacquer without a mask—who knew back then—for his furniture refinishing business, and he wasn't doing very well. As he lay in his hospital bed, with heart and kidneys failing, he would read his *Bible* and sing songs of praise to his savior. "It is Well with My Soul," was his favorite. For those of you from younger generational groupings who may not be familiar with this old hymn—it doesn't go that well when accompanied by bongos and electric guitars in your mega-churches—the words go as follows:

When peace like a river attendeth my way,
    When sorrows like sea billows roll;
Whatever my lot Thou hast taught me to say,
    "It is well, it is well with my soul!"

It is well with my soul!
    It is well, it is well with my soul!

Though Satan should buffet, though trials should come,
    Let this blest assurance control,
That Christ hath regarded my helpless estate,
    And hath shed His own blood for my soul.

My sin—oh, the bliss of this glorious thought—
    My sin, not in part, but the whole,
Is nailed to His Cross, and I bear it no more;
    Praise the Lord, praise the Lord, O my soul!

For me, be it Christ, be it Christ hence to live;
    If dark hours about me shall roll,
No pang shall be mine, for in death as in life
    Thou wilt whisper Thy peace to my soul.

A businessman named Horatio Stafford penned these lines (based on 3 John 2) in 1873. Disaster seemed to plague his life. His youngest son died suddenly, and Horatio had lost his business and gone bankrupt in the great Chicago Fire of 1871. His wife and four daughters were returning to Europe when the *SS Ville Du Havre* on which they were sailing struck another ship and sank. All four of his daughters drowned, and the brief telegram he received from his wife simply said, "Saved alone." Later, as Stafford himself was sailing over the Atlantic Ocean to be with his still grieving wife, he penned the words of this hymn of affirmation of his Christian world view as his ship passed over the very site in the ocean where his daughters had died. What trauma are you facing? **Does your world view make sense of your experience? Is it well with your soul? Would anyone know it?**

Because Dad was singing gospel songs while so ill, his unbelieving attending physician in the Brooksville, Florida hospital called in the hospital shrink to do a psychiatric evaluation. In their view, Dad had to be nuts to be so ill and still rejoicing in his Redeemer; reminds me of Tyler Trent in so many ways. When I arrived on the scene, I physically had to usher the shrink out of his hospital room and refuse to pay the huge fee he tried to charge for his unnecessary and intrusive Naturalistic consult. Dad was eventually discharged and sent home, with the hospital telling us there was nothing more they could do.

Dad was home for a couple weeks becoming more and more unresponsive. I flew down to Florida from West Point, again, to be with him for what became his last few days. The day before he died, after having been in a coma and unresponsive for several days, he suddenly woke up and turned to all those around his bed and said that an angel had just come to him and told him she would be back the next day at noon to take him home (Luke 16:22; Hebrews 1:14). He had a great smile on his face and a remarkable sense of peace entered the room. Then he shut his eyes and drifted off into a coma or sleep again. The next day, precisely at noon, he awoke with a great smile and sense of peace and exclaimed, "Emily, do you hear it?" My mom asked him what he heard. He said, **"The music, the music, it is extraordinary. She has come back as she promised, and the music is incredible!"** He died to this world at that moment, and the Lord took him home. The *Bible* leads us to assume that angels are genderless (Mark 12:25; Matthew 22:30). This one apparently belied that exegesis. What a way to go! Yes, he was the real deal!

After he went home to be with the Lord, my mom wanted to stay in her home in New Port Richey, Florida. It was all she really knew. Within a year or two, however, it became clear to me that she was not doing well living by herself far away from anyone who loved her. She had a few friends but was apparently desperately lonely. On one visit to Florida, I found some notes she had written discussing how much she hated being alone and expressing her desire to die and be reunited with Dad, so I persuaded her to come live with me in Virginia Beach, Virginia, where I was teaching at a branch of the War College in neighboring Norfolk. I knew what a blessing it had been to have my grandmother live with us for so many years and, in addition to not wanting her to have to be alone, wanted my kids to have the same experience with their godly grandmother. Mom became a great role model for my daughters Tiffany and Ainsley, one I hope they remember.

Within a short time, she developed melanoma cancer, probably because of the years gardening in the intense Florida sun, and became progressively worse. When it became clear that she didn't have much time left with us, we arranged with Hospice to assist us with last minute arrangements. For her last few weeks, they were a very caring and supportive organization. They informed me that when Mom eventually passed, I would just have to call one phone number which they provided us, and an EMT or police officer would be sent to the house to pronounce death, and the funeral hall would be notified, in accordance with our wishes. They would take it from there. A car would then be quietly sent to the house to take her to the funeral home, and they would begin preparations for her burial. It would all be handled quietly, discretely, and respectfully.

Very early in the morning of June 15, 1985, Mom went home to be with the Lord. She died peacefully in her sleep. I called the number I had been given by Hospice and a few minutes later, several fire engines and police cars came screaming up to the house with sirens blaring. Almost simultaneously, the local SWAT team arrived in an armored car and with weapons drawn, surrounded the house pounding on the door, and bursting into the living room. Apparently, someone, at some switchboard, had entered the wrong code and the drama began. Suddenly, the entire peaceful Virginia Beach neighborhood turned out for what looked like some kind of bizarre criminal enterprise. At the time, I didn't even have a ponytail or mustache. Go figure. My neighbor across the street, a rather notorious commander of SEAL Team 6 and author of several books on SEAL activities, such as *Rogue Warrior* and *Red Cell*, yep, he's the guy, came running over to help, holding a Glock in one hand and a Sig in the other. The only thing missing were helicopter gunships from Dam Neck Naval Base and army rangers from Fort Story fast roping out of helicopters onto our roof, as reporters swarmed the yard snapping pictures for the evening news. Film at 6. What a sendoff! My mom, demure introverted ISTJ that she was, even reluctantly drew a crowd at her passing. No angels appeared at her death, that I am aware of, but I'm sure she had a great laugh as Dad welcomed her soul home into Paradise.

One of our neighbors named Richard, a kind and very well-intentioned, but atheist psychiatrist, came over to try to help. His daughter Tara and my daughter Ainsley had become good friends. He walked up to Ainsley, who was just seven years old at the time, and knowing her grandmother had been ill and rightly surmising that the commotion was about her, bent down and asked her kindly, "Is your grandmother okay, Ainsley?" Ainsley smiled and said, **"Oh, she is fine, now. She died this morning."** That was the surprising, impolitic, but appropriate response for a young Christian dealing with death. In our frequent conversations, Richard, a well-educated philosophical Naturalist, always told me that he thought it was pure folly to believe in anything sacred or "Other" as he phrased it and was thoroughly convinced that no one under the age of ten was capable of even holding a concept such as God or the afterlife. At the age of seven, Ainsley blew him away. She knew her grandmother had been sick for weeks and in frequent pain, but NOW she was fine. She had finally been called home and healed by the Great Physician.

As my parents taught me, and I am sure some of your parents told you growing up, borrowing from Ralph Waldo Emerson's nineteenth century essays, "Your actions speak so loudly, I can't hear a word you say." That framework is the basis for living a practical apologetic. Christian faith, my early upbringing had demonstrated, was not something simply to believe in privately and to keep out of the marketplace. It was meant to engage the world—**chew the wafer**.

> But Jesus said, Suffer little children, and forbid them not, to come unto me: for of such is the kingdom of heaven (KJV, Matthew 19:14).

> The wolf shall dwell with the lamb, and the leopard shall lie down with the young goat, and the calf and the lion and the fattened calf together; and **a little child shall lead them** (ESV, Isaiah 11:6).

CHAPTER XIV

Goose Hunting and College Shopping

As I assume has become clear, while growing up, I never had very much, but I never went without. Oh, we were poor, alright, no doubt there, but I never really knew it. But while monetarily challenged, we were spiritually rich. **Financial status does not determine one's world view. Wafers cost very little**. As I have related, my dad went from job to job, minister, evangelist, shoe salesman, bank teller, roofing salesman, upholsterer, and finally furniture refinisher running a small business. Each new job was an opportunity to show his world view. He was never a tentmaker like the Apostle Paul, but he did just about everything else to support his personal ministry and our family. My mom was his partner in everything and worked in retail stores as a clerk all my growing up years.

While I had glimpses of our finances from time to time, I was never aware just how tight money really was. During our various church attendances, Dad would always hand me a few dollars to put into the inevitable offering plate for our family as it was passed in order to establish a habit of giving for me. I just knew that my mom kept several mason jars on the kitchen counter: one for church, one for utilities, one for rent, one for gas, and one for food—that was the last one used when the others held enough. Somehow a jar for entertainment or other frills didn't exist. I never saw a commercial movie until I snuck into the Village theater on the Ocean City boardwalk when I was a high school senior to watch *Lawrence of Arabia*. Life was pretty simple in those days. When my dad, mom, sister Jean, or I made any money by shoveling snow, cutting grass, cleaning fish, taking in laundry, ironing neighbors' clothes, or babysitting we gave the money to Mom, our financial manager, and she put it in the appropriate jar as needed.

One particularly very spartan year when I was in high school, as we approached Thanksgiving, I became aware that we had no money for a special meal. That wasn't particularly rare for us, but it was the Thanksgiving season, and as I heard friends in school talking about having turkey and all the "fixings" I'll confess I was rather envious. I could tell that my parents felt particularly guilty this season at not being able to provide for us as they wanted. We even had to give away my dog, Mixie, because food for her had become an unnecessary expense. A few days before the holiday, Dad and I were working out in the yard doing some chores together, clearing branches and old lumber that had washed up against our fence during the previous nor'easter when a large goose alit on the driveway. Unlike human beings (regrettably), geese always mate for life and travel in pairs, so we knew that this one had lost its partner somehow. Dad excused himself and went inside and procured some Cheerios, I thought to feed the goose. When he came back outside, he told me to go inside and help my mother with some chores.

Once I was in the house, he apparently laid an enticing trail of cereal from the goose to just inside the garage. He waited as the hungry goose eagerly pecked at the cereal moving closer and closer to the garage. Once he was inside, Dad pulled the door down and trapped the hapless bird. When Dad entered the garage from the side door, there was a horrendous honking and squealing from the goose (as well as from my dad, I'm sure) for several minutes until he emerged bruised and bloodied, pecked about the head and shoulders, but with a Thanksgiving meal for us. That year we had goose for a Thanksgiving feast. Growing up was often like living in a Dickens novel. As Dad would frequently remind us, "God will provide." It wasn't manna from Heaven, but I am quite sure it was much more delicious than grain found lying in the morning dew. I haven't missed turkey on Thanksgiving one year since, even when living in Southeast Asia or Europe. For what it is worth, arranging to have a live turkey flown to Vientiane, Laos from Singapore during a war is rather costly. As I recall it cost about a month's salary including combat bonus pay, but you do what you need to do.

I have very few physical things today that belonged to my parents: my mom's favorite red vase (one I had bought for her one Mother's Day with some lawn mowing money that I had squirreled away), a cheap little gold painted metal lady that sat on her bureau, a set of fireplace andirons forged by my dad's father who was a blacksmith in Seaville, New Jersey, a Civil War sword that belonged to my great grandfather, that my Dad always cherished, and a Colt six shooter, that Dad carried for self-defense when he traveled as a salesman, and when he was, oh, I almost forgot, a deputy sheriff in Barrington, N. J. several years before I was around. I also have a letter my mom wrote to me when I got accepted at West Point that I look at every year or two. I had never seen two parents so proud as when I was accepted at that school. What happened to everything else when they went home to be with the Lord, I have no idea. Like I said, we didn't have much, but what they had must have gone to someone else. They probably needed it far more than I.

They were the physical things. The other things I inherited were the most important: a firm biblical understanding—we read it together every night before bed—an enduring confidence in my Savior to care for me regardless of what difficulties life threw at me, absolute confidence in our Lord's Pre-Tribulation, Pre-Millennial return to take me home for all eternity, and a model of how a husband and wife are commanded—in a Christian world view—to work together with love and respect in a covenantal relationship with one another. They modeled in every way possible Christ's relationship with the Church. **Their legacy was that our faith was not just some private concern but should be a way to engage the world** (KJV, 1 Peter 3:15). **Chew the wafer.**

As I trust has become clear by now, I saw a Christian world view expressed in behavior every day by my parents. I thought of my dad as the kindest man I knew and my mom the epitome of responsibility. Their practical apologetic leaped into. view every day, but all that is just tangential to my story. I found out years later that they had paid the tuition and all expenses for a young girl from their church to go to a four-year college because her parents had booted her out of their home when she became a Christian, and she had no one else to help. I eventually learned that she had graduated from Wheaton University as a registered nurse and became a medical missionary in Ecuador. As far as I know, she never contacted my parents to say thank-you or in any way acknowledge their kindness. Of course, they hadn't helped her for that reason. They just did it because of who they were and the Savior they wanted to honor. She probably never even knew who it was that had been paying her tuition and living expenses for the four years she was in college. **Sometimes chewing the wafer can go unnoticed by those closest to us**.

Because they had spent so much of their money paying for her education, there was little left for my sister, whom my parents wanted desperately to go to college. Neither of them had; indeed, as I have previously mentioned, my father never even graduated from high school—after all there were bills to be paid and his family needed his hands in the blacksmith shop at an early age to make ends meet. Ensuring that my sister Jean got a college education I suppose was their way of ensuring that she would be taken care of when they were gone. So they scrimped and saved and sacrificed for several years to put her through college, thereby enabling her to become a schoolteacher. What that meant, though, was that I would be on my own to pay my way, if I decided to go to college. That was just a fact of life in those days, so I went to work to become the best student and athlete I could become to try to earn the necessary scholarships.

For me that would mean excelling at football, becoming President of the National Honor Society, becoming an officer on the high school student council, throwing the Javelin on the track team, and generally ensuring that I excelled athletically and academically to make myself as attractive as possible to the best schools I knew about. During my junior year of high school I was one of two students from New Jersey picked as the best math and science students in the country (two were chosen from each state that year) to attend the first National Youth Conference on the Atom in

Chicago. The trip from New Jersey to Chicago on the Great Northern Railroad with just one other student and an academic sponsor was exciting enough—one of my few times ever out of New Jersey at the time—but being able to play, they called it experiment, with the nuclear accelerator, the cyclotron, at the Fermi National Accelerator Lab at the University of Chicago at the age of sixteen with 95 other STEM whizzes from across the country for several days, whet my appetite for science and my appreciation for all things nuclear. This foundation in logic and the STEM fields would come in handy years later in the military and later when having to defend the science of creation and other apologetic concerns.

I wound up finishing 3rd in my large high school class and being chosen as one of the graduation speakers for our class, speaking on why the American U-2 pilot Gary Powers, who had been shot down by the Russians in 1960 and too readily admitted to them to be spying for the CIA, should have been executed by the US for treason when he was returned stateside. That speech may have presaged much of my future, but shocked most of the clergy, parents, and friends in the Ocean City Music Pier who had come to celebrate their children's joyful graduation not to ponder the execution of a traitor. I was able to earn Rotary Club, Lion's Club, American Legion, Jaycees, and other city and state scholarships for academic achievement as well as getting offers to play football at Rutgers, Duke, Lafayette, Lehigh, the University of Maryland, and others.

One of the weekly shows I watched on our frequently malfunctioning 8" black and white Capehart television was the *West Point Story*. Week in and week out I watched sharp looking athletically fit cadets struggle with some leadership or moral dilemma and solve it in less than an hour. Their obvious passion for honor and integrity really impressed me. Admittedly, though, what I mainly found attractive was that they always seemed to date the best looking girls, drive the coolest cars, wear sharp looking uniforms, and march in parades. What the army was and how those cadets would have to assume their leadership roles in that service upon graduation, I had no clue. I was even mostly oblivious to the rumblings of the disturbances that had begun in South Vietnam to where these cadets would no doubt be heading as young lieutenant combat leaders upon graduation. When I asked our high school guidance counsellor about going to West Point, he informed me that it was a free college education calculated to be worth about $ 250,000.00 and that it was far too difficult to get in. He further advised me that ninety-five percent of all the applicants failed to gain admission, that most applicants probably needed to have some political clout to get a nomination, and that consequently no graduate had ever gotten in from our Ocean City high school. I suppose that was just the challenge I needed.

Early in my sophomore year of high school, I wrote to Representative Glenn—not the famous John Glenn who had been an astronaut; he was from Ohio. Our John Glenn was a relative light weight representing the cranberry bogs in Ocean and Cape May counties in South Jersey that few had ever heard about. What I told him was that while he didn't know me and certainly didn't know my parents, when I graduated from high school in three years he would want to have known me and he would want to appoint me to West Point, because I would make him incredibly proud. INTJ arrogance admittedly begins relatively early in life. I heard nothing from Representative Glenn's office for a year, and then out of the blue I got a letter telling me that Congressman Glenn was holding a service academy qualifying test on an upcoming Saturday to look at the potential of possible nominees to the academies and inviting me to attend. I showed up with about a hundred and fifty other high school juniors and seniors from the South Jersey and took a test that greatly resembled a math and science heavy PSAT and SAT but was solely used to help senators and representatives sort out those students most academically qualified for the academies. I must have done passably well, because a couple months later I was asked to go to Fort Dix, New Jersey to take a service academy physical aptitude test: pullups, sit-ups, a two-mile run, a dodge run and jump, standing broad jump, and throwing a medicine ball and also undergo a medical exam. Since I was in great physical shape from all the sports I played, they were a piece of cake.

I will readily admit to thinking the whole thing was a lark, that I probably didn't have a chance. Unbeknownst to me, though, my parents had been praying diligently for years that God would somehow enable me to matriculate at the best college possible. They also always encouraged me to pray that God would close some doors and open the right door to work his will in my life. While admittedly remiss in several aspects of my Christian walk, I doggedly attended to that one. My senior year arrived, and sometime in December I was notified that I had received primary nominations from Congressman Glenn to the Air Force Academy in Colorado Springs, the Coast Guard Academy in New London, and the Naval Academy in Annapolis. As his highest rated candidate for the service academies, I could take my pick. Apparently, he had no nominations for West Point available that year. Much to the surprise of his congressional staff and to the shock of our high school guidance counsellor, I turned them all down, having decided that if I were going to attend a service academy, it would be West Point or nothing. It was by far the most prestigious, had the finest legacy of academic excellence, and, after all, these other military schools didn't have its own television series.

Early in the spring, after visits to Rutgers, Lehigh, Lafayette, Duke, the University of Maryland, the University of Delaware, and The King's College (at my parents' and pastor's insistence), all of which, except King's—all King's required was my pastor's recommendation—showed interest in my very strong passing arm and near perfect SAT scores, I accepted admission and a mostly full ride to Lafayette to play football and study, I thought, engineering or prelaw. I was on my way to Easton, Pennsylvania in the fall. On June 10th I received a telegram—the first and only telegram I have ever received in my life—from the Superintendent of the US Military Academy at West Point—saying that I had been granted a "special academic appointment" to West Point as a Qualified Alternate Nominee. I had 48 hours to accept or decline.

I never heard of that possibility occurring either before or afterwards. Even more curious is the fact that years later while I was teaching at the Academy and sitting on the Admissions Board, I enquired from the admissions department Head and the Dean, General Jannarone, about my own previous admissions process years earlier and the "special academic appointment" that the telegram stated that I had received. No one in the admissions office had ever heard of such a possibility existing. Hmmm.

Twenty-one days after receiving the telegram, on a very hot and humid July 1ˢᵗ morning, I walked onto the grounds of West Point and nine hours later raised my hand and took the oath as a new cadet while overlooking the Hudson River at Trophy Point. I was inducted into the New Cadet Corps, and my life changed forever. Always trust God to come through and answer your prayers, but…here's the rub…on his terms and on his schedule, not necessarily yours. He has already written the storyline we are to follow. God promises to answer our prayers; scripture just doesn't always reveal how or when. **Christians should always be open to change and serendipity.**

I knew very little about the military. Dad had been a draftee in WWI and trained with a wooden stick at Fort Dix, New Jersey, in lieu of a real rifle—all the real ones were being used in Europe. Owing to the war's coming to an end before his basic training ended, he had never been deployed overseas, having been drafted just at the war's end, and soon after basic training was mustered out to save costs. My Uncle Bud had served on the *USS Nautilus*, America's first nuclear submarine, and had been a bosun's mate on that boat on its maiden trip under the Polar icecap. Another uncle named Ed Richards served on a diesel sub during WWII and was on the American sub that held the unhappy record for undergoing the longest sustained underwater bombardment by the Germans—three sailors on that boat actually died during the prolonged bombardment from oxygen deprivation because they could not surface for air—and my uncle Gene had served on a sub chaser in the North Atlantic in WWII. I remember seeing an old picture of him while standing watch on the deck with a long scruffy beard frozen to the steering mechanism, but that was about it for our family's military expertise—mostly navy, to that point. With such military ignorance in my wake, I arrived at West Point on July 1ˢᵗ with a tennis racket in hand and a bag of nine very cheap golf clubs over my shoulder, ready for what I thought would be a fun summer camp.

When I arrived and walked through the sally port on the east side of Central Area, the upper classmen that saw me knew instantaneously that they had a raw one in their midst—fresh fish as they called me. They apparently had decided on first glance that I was in the wrong place and they would drive me out and make me quit by the end of day one. I clearly didn't belong there. On that day, over 150 of my fellow fresh fish did just that and left before being sworn in at 6 pm that evening, to pursue other academic or professional pursuits. Once the upper-class cadets on the New Cadet Barracks detail had decided that I would be one of the exiting masses, I became equally certain there was no way in the world that would happen, and the battle was joined. Of the 1,150 young boys who arrived with me that morning, 706 men eventually tossed their hats into the air with me four years later. West Point was made for me, and I was clearly made for West Point. West Point and I would become fast mates. It would become a major contributor to my developing world view but ultimately, one of its greatest challenges.

Thank the Lord for the Baptist Student Union (BSU), The Fellowship of Christian Athletes (FCA), and the Officers Christian Fellowship (OCF) that became my spiritual retreats for the next four years. As one of my roommates put it, he "found Christ in a Coke bottle." Many cadets did just that. Years later, when owning a ski condo in Deer Valley Utah, my wife and I would often hear locals say that they had come to Deer Valley and Park City for the snow and great skiing in the winter but wound up buying a home and staying because of the mountains in the summer. I can't begin to recount the number of Plebes (West Point freshmen) who attended weekly BSU meetings for the free cookies and Coke and temporary refuge from the persistent harassment of the upperclassmen and then stayed for the *Bible* studies. The Oreos weren't wafers, but for some of us it was the only food we got during the day.

> Come now, you who say, "Today or tomorrow we will go into such and such a town and spend a year there and trade and make a profit"— yet you do not know what tomorrow will bring. What is your life? For you are a mist that appears for a little time and then vanishes. Instead you ought to say, "If the Lord wills, we will live and do this or that" (ESV, James 14: 13-15).

CHAPTER XV

The Man in The Red Sash

Most folks still remember the name Roger Staubach—Roger the Dodger—as he was nick-named. As a midshipman at the Naval Academy, Roger was named recipient of college football's top honor, The Heisman Trophy. Staubach graduated from the Naval Academy in 1965 and went on to serve four years of active duty service in the Navy before playing eleven years of professional football with the Dallas Cowboys under fellow believer, Tom Landry's, leadership, while leading them to two Super Bowl victories. He was elected into the Hall of Fame in 1985, in his first year of eligibility. While Roger was quarterbacking Navy, one of his teammates was my occasional substitute Sunday school teacher at our local church during his summer break from the Naval Academy in July or August. Occasionally after church, our high school youth group would meet on the sprawling grounds of the Methodist Tabernacle at 6th and Wesley Avenue in Ocean City, NJ and play flag football. He would always quarterback one team and, because I was the quarterback for the Ocean City Red Raiders, I would usually quarterback the other. We won't discuss win-loss records.

One of these Sundays, after our game, a group of us met at Jimmy's Sub shop where our famous midshipman Sunday school teacher bought us all milkshakes and Italian subs. During lunch, he said, "Jeffries, you really ought to go to a service academy." That was probably the very fertile seed planted that further encouraged me to make the attempt. He continued by saying that I should try to get a copy of the famous "Duty, Honor, Country speech" delivered to the West Point Corps of Cadets by General MacArthur upon his return to the States in 1962, after having been fired by President Truman for insubordination. He told us that Roger Staubach had posted it in Navy's varsity locker room and encouraged everyone on his football squad to read it.

Some of you may recall that at the end of the Korean War, President Truman had ordered American troops under MacArthur's command in Korea to stop at the 38th parallel. General MacArthur had publicly disagreed with the order and argued the political and military need to progress north and destroy North Korea's war fighting ability once and for all, knowing that county would become a perpetual menace to the world in the future and an eventual nuclear threat. His sense of duty and honor had demanded that he confront even his Commander and Chief, when he believed him to be wrong. I don't recall having heard the General's name before that time, but I tucked Staubach's comment away. After all, if some navy squid from Annapolis was recommending a speech by an army general, it must have some significance.

During my sophomore year of high school, I was doing some research in the library for an English paper for Walter Williams, who taught honors English. Incredibly bored by Harper Lee's *To Kill A Mockingbird*, I took a break to look at some articles on college football in our local newspaper, *The Sentinel Ledger*. On the Op Ed page, I stumbled across an article regarding the speech given by MacArthur to the Corps of Cadets in 1962. Remembering Staubach's vicarious encouragement, I looked it up and read the first paragraph.

> *Duty, Honor, Country* — *those three hallowed words reverently dictate what you ought to be, what you can be, what you will be.*

They are your rallying point to build courage when courage seems to fail, to regain faith when there seems to be little cause for faith, to create hope when hope becomes forlorn.

The words really engaged my attention, so I read on a bit farther.

Unhappily, I possess neither that eloquence of diction, that poetry of imagination, nor that brilliance of metaphor to tell you all that they mean. The unbelievers will say they are but words, but a slogan, but a flamboyant phrase. Every pedant, every demagogue, every cynic, every hypocrite, every troublemaker, and, I am sorry to say, some others of an entirely different character, will try to downgrade them even to the extent of mockery and ridicule.

Wow, this guy didn't sound like any soldier I had ever seen on TV or read about, and he was far more exciting than Harper Lee. To that point, my only familiarity with the army was the Civil War novel, *The Red Badge of Courage*, by Naturalistic/Deist writer Stephen Crane. The words were not biblical to be sure, but they had the same profundity and hints of the basics of the Christian world view found in C. S. Lewis's *Mere Christianity*, as well as the Apostle Paul's appreciation of the early Christians in the Roman colony of Philippi. I saw enough resonances, I suppose, that I kept reading. His passion for values and the clarity of his world view really resonated with me. General MacArthur was different; I needed to hear more.

But these are some of the things they do. They build your basic character. They mold you for your future role as the custodians of the nation's defense. They make you strong enough to know when you are weak, and brave enough to face yourself when you are afraid. They teach you to be proud and unbending in honest failure, but humble and gentle in success; not to substitute words for action; not to seek the path of comfort, but to face the stress and spur of difficulty and challenge; to learn to stand up in the storm, but to have compassion on those who fall; to master yourself before you seek to master others; to have a heart that is clean, a goal that is high; to learn to laugh, yet never forget how to weep; to reach into the future, yet never neglect the past; to be serious, yet never take yourself too seriously; to be modest so that you will remember the simplicity of true greatness, the open mind of true wisdom, the meekness of true strength.

They give you a temper of the will, a quality of the imagination, a vigor of the emotions, a freshness of the deep springs of life, a temperamental predominance of courage over timidity, an appetite for adventure over love of ease.

I was sold. Even reading those words again now I feel spurred to action; I want to get up and do something and put my Fitbit Blaze to work! I realize that in a different fashion MacArthur's words have always formed my basic Philosophy of Leadership and the premises for all my books on leadership as well as the foundations of all the principles I rely on as I coach others, both professional athletes as well as business executives, heads of state, and occasional church leaders. But where that philosophy led me is as important as the principles themselves.

There are many books describing a cadet's first year at West Point. While all are heavily anecdotal, most are fairly accurate. I'll just take you through my first few minutes because they go to the heart of my developing world view. The 4th time I had to report to the Man in the Red Sash, I got it mostly right and was sent off to procure my basic military equipment and uniforms.

Yes, the 4th time. If you have been in New Cadet Barracks yourself or had one of your youngens attend this rite of passage put those thoughts on hold. West Point has changed, not always for the good. We older graduates often moan that "The Corps has;" in other words, those matriculating today don't have it nearly as tough as we did—probably an inflated sense of self-importance, but I'll leave it at that. While my first day at West Point as a new cadet had a different purpose and tone than the first day in recent years, some traditions have stayed mostly the same. It is still challenging and difficult, but different. We called it Beast Barracks in those days. Officially known as Cadet Basic Training, Beast Barracks is a seven-week process that transforms young people accepted into West Point from civilians to cadets. It tests the commitment to your world view from the minute you arrive.

There are a number of new cadets in each entering class who have already spent several years at other universities; about a fourth of our class had prior university experience, a few were even college graduates, but they also have to begin again as Plebes (West Point freshmen) regardless of how many years of college they had under their belts already. There are also several new cadets in each class who have had prior military experience as enlisted soldiers, or even as sailors or Marines, before coming to the Academy; some have already served in combat for a year or more. They are required to go through Beast as well, because being a cadet and a future officer incur different values and obligations than serving as enlisted soldiers and sailors—even their oaths of office were markedly different at the time.

Cadets in their Cow (junior) and Firstie (senior) years are assigned to the leadership and training cadres during Beast, and together, they and their new cadet charges train in a number of military skills. There are two halves of Beast, the first of which teaches new cadets how to act, speak, and present themselves in a soldierly manner, while the second teaches new cadets elementary military tactics, the basic use of weapons systems, and other valuable military skills such as repelling, land navigation, hand to hand combat, and the use of gas masks and other protective gear. Both halves include at least two hours of physical conditioning from 5 am to 7 am every day, and classes of instruction in the cadet Honor Code: "A cadet will not lie, cheat, or steal or tolerate those who do."

Even though it persists, the term Beast Barracks is generally frowned upon these days by the military hierarchy as sounding a bit too barbaric, but it is still in unofficial use. Physical and mental hazing was also "officially" frowned upon in the past but, truth be known, was intrinsic to the new cadet and later Plebe experience, for those who made it that far, after the two and a half months of Beast initiation. If you have been through military basic training yourself, think of Beast as Marine Corps basic training on steroids, from 5 am till after midnight each day, with academic work thrown in as well. Day one, particularly for those with a fear of the unknown, unacquainted with the military experience, or not in good enough physical condition to endure it, can be a nightmare. Anyone worried about micro-aggressions or in need of safe places or crying closets should stay very far away. Of the group of aspiring New Cadets I arrived with, as I mentioned, over 150 quit the first day. One of my three Beast roommates actually jumped out of the 3rd floor window of New South Barracks onto the concrete below to evade upperclassmen and apparently tried to commit suicide before I even had a chance to get to learn his first name or know where he was from. We never saw him again.

Lest you think that the "hazing" was pointless or mere vindictiveness or retribution, not tied to leadership development, let me try to disabuse you of that common misconception. I certainly did not appreciate the harassment and psychological and physical "development" at the time, but some years removed began to recognize the importance of the learnings gained from bizarre activities such as "shower formations," "clothing formations," "submarine drills," "swimming the alcove rail," and their ilk, but my post Academy experiences were admittedly very different from many of my classmates. Most of them routinely served in regular army units with classmates and other West Point graduates during their post-graduation careers. My experiences were different, so with the notable exception of my time on the West Point faculty, I rarely served with classmates or other West Pointers. My associates were routinely more primitive and less well educated and usually spoke a different language. Today I recognize that some of these harassing Plebe experiences, which at the time seemed pointless and excessive, are probably responsible for my being alive today.

Some of you may recall the name Admiral Jim Stockdale. Before Jim became the Vice-Presidential running mate with Ross Perot, he had a distinguished Navy career and is the only three-star admiral in the history of the navy to wear both the wings of a navy aviator and the Medal of Honor, as well as the Prisoner of War Medal. I had the privilege of getting to know him and to work closely with him as his executive coach upon his return to the USA, after his having been the senior officer held captive as a Vietnam POW in the infamous Hoa Lo Prison, known colloquially as the Hanoi Hilton, for seven years. A few months before he was named the 15th President of The Citadel, in Charleston, South Carolina, the Admiral asked me to accompany him on a visit to his alma mater, the U. S. Naval Academy at Annapolis. As we were getting a tour of Bancroft Hall, the largest contiguous set of academic dormitories in the USA, the Superintendent was giving the admiral a glowing report of the great educational and humanitarian changes that had been implemented at the academy since Stockdale had been a midshipman.

At one point during our tour, the superintendent said words to the effect…"and you will be happy to know, Jim, that we have eliminated all the needless hazing like shower formations, clothing formations, and other pointless harassment that used to take place in the basement of Bancroft Hall and filled that location with a new computer center." Admiral Stockdale paused for a moment or two and shaking his head replied, "How sad, Admiral. If there was anything that kept me alive for seven years in that dehumanizing hole of the Hanoi Hilton, it was what I learned about myself from the shower formations, clothing formations, and other hazing we were forced to endure in the basement of Bancroft Hall, and if there is anything that thwarted our ability to prosecute the war effectively, it was Defense Secretary McNamara and his whiz kids poking away at their stupid computers, trying to manage the war electronically from Washington." Stockdale was no Luddite, but certainly recognized that tough training prepares you for the greater harshness and potential immorality of war. As many of us learned in Recondo training, Ranger School, Jump School, and Jungle Warfare School, and navy SEALs learn over and over again in BUDS, "The more you sweat in training, the less you bleed in battle." Hooah.

Where Stockdale and I would often clash in our conversations about what the "right thing" to do was regarding professional ethics, educational policy, military intervention, or politics arose from our vastly different world views. Jim was a Stoic by philosophy and world view, as his essay

"The World According to Epictetus" ably demonstrates, but where we agreed was that **one needed a coherent world view in order to live consistently within it when difficulties arose**—that is what allowed him to survive the horrors of Hoa Lo Prison—and to make sense of even random violence in life, something Jim was all too experienced in enduring. Since we both understood the other person's world view we were able to listen respectfully and offer sound arguments as to why the other's may have lacked credence. A few friends would often join us for informal gatherings on Jim's front porch overlooking Charleston Harbor, when he was President of the Citadel, and listen in on our sometimes heated discussions. We told stories and our stories revealed character and philosophical principles underlying our world views.

As I would often argue, the Christian world view is the only one that allows such correspondence between truth and reality. We are encouraged by many of those great pearls of wisdom in the book of Proverbs to seek such truth in practice. That familiar passage in Proverbs 27:17 KJV, "As iron sharpens iron, so one person sharpens another," is often cited as a reminder that part of our obligation in the body of Christ is to help one another grow in our faith. Part of my prayer is that the iron in this book will help to sharpen your iron and that of the local church, too often fearful of engaging the mind of antagonists to the faith. Let me dare to assert that this bit of Solomon's wisdom could also encourage us to be willing to engage those with vastly different world views in order to refine our own. Seek opportunities to scrape off the rust and hone your edge (KJV, Romans 12:2).

Would that our local churches would be that kind of demanding biblical training grounds as well for our young people to prepare them for the barbs, questions, and blatant attacks they will have to endure from roommates, atheist professors, and skeptical managers at their future colleges and subsequently in the workplace. Such training is more than possible, but rarely ever sponsored by the local church. Too often, after students leave high school youth groups, they have no real support from their local churches. Many churches become spiritual deserts for college age or newly employed young people and are left totally unprepared to engage in any rational approach to their theology. **It is time for our local churches to wake up.** This is one arena in which an apologetics ministry can be incredibly impactful.

After bidding a hasty farewell to my parents that humid July morning, I had ten hours to learn some of the basics of military decorum, marching, saluting, following orders, and all that comes with those basic skills, so that I could march to Trophy Point at 1800 hours, sorry at 6 pm, in a somewhat respectable parade formation, and take the oath of office in front of teary-eyed parents whom we would not see again until Christmas break. That knowledge alone was enough to anger the upperclassmen, because our incoming class would be the first in the history of West Point to be allowed to go home at Christmas for a few days, instead of waiting a full eleven months until the following June—as all previous classes had done—to reconnect with our homes and families. Separation from all that has been normal in the past was the necessary preparation for instilling new values and allegiances based on Duty, Honor, and Country. We were the "Christmas break class"—clearly getting off far too easy—and so we paid the price by receiving rather persistent "additional training" for an entire year.

Part of our preparation for that 1800 hours ceremony was to learn basic answers that would define my existence for a year: "Yes sir, No sir, No Excuse sir." Yes, they were all "sirs." Women were not admitted to the academy until 119 arrived in 1976, when I was on the teaching faculty. Any other words or answers were deemed irrelevant and inappropriate and would incur the wrath of upper classmen, who clearly were not there to coddle inefficiency, failure, or excuse making. Once we had our heads shaven, been taught how to salute, had unflattering side, front, and back naked posture pictures taken, passed a cursory physical exam, been fitted for uniforms (by that I mean, some civilian guy held up pants and shirts next to our sweating bodies and said, that looks about right and tossed them to us), and signed for a duffle bag of gear we would later see and learn how to use, we were instructed to report to the man in the red sash—a cadet officer—to be directed to the barracks to which we had been assigned for the first two months. We just had to report using a relatively simple phrase: "Sir, New Cadet Jeffries reports to the man in the red sash as ordered." Seems simple enough, hmmm. Only took me four times to get it right, with an hour or more of running, dropping for pushups twenty or thirty at a time depending on the whim of the upperclassman and the egregiousness of my offence, getting yelled at, and otherwise hearing about my lack of worth as ducrot, smackhead, scumbag, and other less civilized names in between. Being recognized as someone created in the image of God was not included in their vocabulary repertoire.

Once double timing up the six flights of stairs (84 steps) to my third floor barracks room it was time to meet my roommates, learn where we were each from, briefly share our experiences of getting there, and meet our assigned upper class squad leader who burst through the door about an hour later to assign us our tasks for the rest of the day: shining shoes, shining belt buckles, stowing our gear, making our bunks, and memorizing several pages of *Bugle Notes*, our new 100 page cadet handbook: "Schofield's Definition of Discipline," "The Code of Conduct," "The Definition of Leather," and "How's the Cow." The last thing our new squad leader ordered us to do was to begin to memorize General Douglass MacArthur's "Duty Honor Country speech," something I had already done on my own two years earlier before being nominated to West Point.

Day 1 had been a spiritual void until that moment, when I realized that God—and apparently, two Christian brothers, one named Roger Staubach—had been preparing me for that moment for several years.

"Duty, Honor, Country--Those three hallowed words reverently dictate what you ought to be, what you can be, what you will be."

Those words not only drove me to attend West Point and launched my military career but also, in order to live consistently within my Christian world view, demanded that I leave the military academy teaching faculty fifteen years later.

> Yet those who wait for the LORD will gain new strength;
> They will mount up with wings like eagles, they will run

and not get tired, they will walk and not become weary
(ASV, Isaiah 40:31).

How these experiences were crystalizing my Christian world view and were
assisting me to become a practical apologist at the time was far beyond my
understanding and totally in God's hands.

> And we know that all things work together for good to
> them that love God, to them who are the called according
> to his purpose (KJV, Romans 8:28).

CHAPTER XVI

Why Art?

The undeniable gulf between a creature and a Creator, between art and the artist is fundamental to the non-Naturalistic Christian world view. It just takes a little while for some of us to understand that fundamental absolute. My introduction to "fine art" came from watching the chalk talk artist in the summer Bible Conferences at the Ocean City Baptist Church. During revival meetings and the annual four-hour marathon known as the Good Friday service, the visiting evangelist would attempt to astound us with his legerdemain as he would weave a story for the congregation as we sat anticipatingly on the edge of the pew—at least that was the plan—while he spoke about the crucifixion, the resurrection, the burning bush, a snake raised on a pole during the wanderings of the Israelites, or Noah's ark while drawing a picture as he spoke. Always a winner was the sunrise (or was it a sunset?) after the Battle of Armageddon as believers were portrayed walking across a huge white cross into Heaven as Satan and his minions were tossed off the cross into the burning abyss below. While the evangelist spoke with his back to the congregation, he would draw a picture with multi-colored chalk, and without telling us, add key features in "magic" chalk that would only appear when suddenly illuminated later with black light.

As the crescendo of the sermon was reached, just before the ever-present invitation to come forward and dedicate our lives to Christ, the sanctuary lights would dim and the artist would flip a switch and miraculously another picture would appear on the canvas courtesy of black light—Christ with his arms outstretched, a burial chamber that was suddenly empty with a stone rolled away, angels ascending and descending, a dove returning to the window of the ark with a green sprig in its mouth—or some other picture that expressed the grandeur and provision of God. As the hitherto hidden picture was revealed, the congregation would all emote with sighs and expressions of wonder. A-mens and hallelujahs would echo off the rafters of the church, expressing the congregation's wonder at the power of the Creator and the quality of art and theology suddenly revealed. **As one's world view is being developed, it is not unlike that hidden picture that will reveal itself when the right illumination is applied.** I assume these chalk talk artists and ministers still make the rounds of some churches, but I couldn't verify that fact, since I have not personally seen one in a few decades.

My other source of art appreciation began in school. In high school we had to take an art or music course each semester. Ever since I had tried out for the Glee Club—that's where the really good looking girls hung out—and been rejected by Miss Kyle, the music teacher and the director of the club, who served as both Scylla and Charybdis to my admission, when she said, "That will be all, William," after just my fifth word of "My Country Tis of Thee," I was relegated instead to the art course. Mr. P taught the course, but let me just say it wasn't his forte either. My next step in fine art appreciation came with his directions always to draw the human head shaped like a vertical oval. After succeeding with a perfect oval, we were instructed to draw two straight lines that intersected in the center of the oval, put the eyes at opposite ends of the horizontal center line, and locate the ears on the sides of the oval centered on the horizontal line. There were no instructions given regarding the mouth. Guess that was left to our imaginations and moods. Mine always had a stupid grin, probably belying my thoughts about the art teacher's intelligence. There was nothing right brain about his approach to art at all. We just drew lines and followed the rules. The school called it Introduction to Art; it could have been named elementary geometry with smiley faces. Most of current day emojis on my I-Phone look far more human than my "people" in art class. I must have drawn the same figure fifty times and just put different hats on him or hair on her. All of them wore pants. Don't blame me for that sexist approach; it was his instruction. Uncovered legs were apparently deemed scandalous in South Jersey.

When our randy purveyor of *faux* art eventually got caught cavorting with another teacher's wife one weekend and got removed as art teacher and subsequently promoted to assistant school principal—my first experience with the Peter Principle—art under his replacement teacher flourished anew in the basement of the high school. My figures suddenly grew hair and sported shapely mouths with different expressions and noses of interesting shapes. Eventually I broadened my portfolio to the female figure. From the critical comments I received from the teacher, I apparently made them too realistic. Who knew? That kind of art was more than appropriate for the Renaissance but almost grounds for suspension back then in South Jersey. We were just amateurs; God was the real artist.

My parents with their limited education and funds never expressed an appreciation of art. It is not that they lacked appreciation for beautiful things, it was just that life was too hard and demanded one's nose to the grindstone every day, just to pay the bills. Art was a luxury they could not afford. My mother eventually graduated from the jar approach to paying bills and began to adopt the more advanced envelope method of allocating funds to pacify creditors. At the start of every month, she would take 8-10 white business envelopes and put them in a shoebox. As money came in from her ironing for the neighbors or my Dad's sales from roofing materials or asbestos siding, she would put $ 10 in the mortgage envelope, $ 7 in the natural gas envelope, $ 3 in the grocery store envelope, $ 4 in the church contribution envelope and so on. **The point that there was always an envelope for church, regardless of how poor we were, was not missed on me; it was an outshoot of their practical apologetic.** When I eventually got a job as stock boy at Stainton's Department Store after school each day and on weekends when I didn't have a football game or a track meet, I would add my earnings to the envelopes as well.

Every waking hour went to attending interminable meetings at church or paying bills. There was no time for art. When I eventually went to a bullfight in Mexico, years later while a second lieutenant attending classes learning to arm and disarm nuclear warheads at the Air Defense School at Fort Bliss, Texas, just over the Rio Grande border, I bought them a picture from a street vendor of a bullfighter comprised of garish oil paints dabbled on black velvet. That was high art for me, and they cherished it until they both passed on to the great museum in the sky. It probably fetched a dollar or two at some yard sale in Florida. I had no idea at the time the role that authentic art would play in rounding out my Christian world view.

Sometime during the two months of my New Cadet Barracks experience, to acquaint us with the history of the Academy, we were taken on walking tours of several of the stone buildings on the reservation. Each was adorned by statues and massive murals of battles as well as portraits of great generals and famous battlefields from the past. Our Plebe escape of Cullum Hall, officially known as the Fourth Class Club, was the most impressive of all and seemed to exist primarily to house huge elegant murals and frescos as well as stone sculptures honoring the great warriors and philosophers of the past. To the extent that the military ethic grew out of a defined philosophical world view, this building encapsulated it. As Plebes, we were forced to memorize data associated with all of them, even down to the number of lights in some of the more historic buildings as well and the number of gallons of water in Lusk reservoir across the street from Michie Stadium, the varsity football field.

The best of the art however seemed reserved for the Cadet Chapel—an impressive neo-gothic revival cathedral patterned roughly after classic European churches, that stands atop a high hill presiding over the entire West Point campus. Chapel services were still mandatory when I was a cadet, before the ACLU got involved. Upon arrival, a cadet could pick between Protestant, Catholic, or Jewish, but you would attend chapel services; that was a given. Mandatory attendance at weekly religious services was justified as part of our ethics and leadership development. One of my early roommates was the first Buddhist I had ever met. With my encouragement, he chose Protestant. Every Sunday morning, rain or shine, we Protestants would form up at O dark hundred hours (6:00 am) and march in company formations for twenty minutes up the very steep hill to the Cadet Chapel. Once inside, I was overwhelmed by the magnificent stained-glass windows adorning the walls of the nave. It was my first real exposure to "high art."

I eventually learned that almost every graduating class as far back as the Class of 1802 had a stained glass window in the chapel dedicated to them with a scene from holy scripture that the class had selected to represent them. In 1910, Willet Studios in Philadelphia beat out the Tiffany company in New York City for the right to create these magnificent expressions of God's glory. The Willet Company, to honor the sacrifice of West Point graduates over the years, set the price at just $ 300 for crafting the first window and honored that price in perpetuity until the last window was finished in 1976. Our class paid just $ 300 for a magnificent eighteen-foot-high stained-glass window portraying the Visions of Abraham, in Genesis chapter 17.

As one enters the chapel from the main door, if you look up to the left, the first window you will see in section one of the nave is my class's memorial window. God initially visits Abram promising to make him the father of a great nation:

> When Abram was ninety-nine years old the Lord appeared to Abram and said to him, "I am God Almighty; **walk before me, and be blameless**, that I may make my covenant between me and you and may multiply you greatly." Then Abram fell on his face. And God said to him, "Behold, my covenant is with you, and you shall be the father of a multitude of nations…. I will make you exceedingly fruitful, and I will make you into nations, and kings shall come from you. And I will establish my covenant between me and you and your offspring after you throughout their generations for an everlasting covenant, to be God to you and to your offspring after you" (ESV, Gen 11:1-8).

Later in that same chapter there is another vision that may have been the Lord's coming in a preincarnate theophany with two of his angels or a more prosaic visitation by three angels. *Bible* scholars can't quite agree. The Hebrew *Peshat,* following modern literary criticism, expresses the moment as Abraham prostrates himself on the ground as a pre-incarnate Theophany. Based on my study of scripture, I would agree. All I know for certainty is that our West Point class recognized, as the first lines of the "Cadet Prayer" expresses, "Oh God our Father, Thou searcher of men's hearts, help us draw near to thee in sincerity and truth," that if we humbly chose to prostrate ourselves in the presence of God, we would be affirming that we would need God's presence and protection for our entire careers. That is why the class chapel window committee, that I served on as a cadet, selected the Genesis 17 visions for our class's window. As we are careful to point out to every client in our team building training, even for publicly held corporations and professional athletic teams, "Where there is no Vision, the people perish" (KJV, Proverbs 29:18).

I was delighted twenty-six years later that Cheryl and I could be married in that magnificent cathedral, and that as I waited for her to join me at the altar to exchange our wedding vows, she would begin her walk towards me as my bride from the foot of that very same window: "...**walk before me and be blameless**..." (Genesis 17:1). Several years later, my daughter Tiffany, who grew up at West Point, was also married in the same Cadet Chapel and began her walk toward her future husband, Lou, from the foot of that same window. Some traditions are marvelous!

When I returned to West Point to teach English, five years after graduation, we taught writing through an understanding of and appreciation for the great masters of world art. The Program Director before me had instituted that approach to elicit the most personal understandings possible for our students. We would hold up a painting by Degas, Picasso, a Dutch Master, or a picture of a window from the Cadet Chapel, and ask our cadets, "What do you see? What does it mean? Write about it." What the cadets did not know but our faculty eventually did, because I schooled them in the technology, was that the psychologist Carl Jung had taught us many years earlier that Perception (what we see and acknowledge as real) and

Judgment (decisions we make about that reality) are the heart of what it means to be a sentient human being made in the image of God. They are not only fundamental to art appreciation and analysis but also to the creation of a world view. These days we know this technology as the science of Psychological Type. That is the science underlying those letters I have mentioned several times already: INTJ, ESFJ, and ISTJ—more about them later.

To this day, I frequently meet former students of ours in several universities such as Georgia Tech, Carnegie Mellon, or the University of California at San Diego where I teach in their graduate business schools and departments of executive education or while instructing senior officers in the army, navy and air force War Colleges, who tell me that they had always sarcastically referred to Plebe English during those years as "Why Art?" Most importantly, from my standpoint, they were aware it was often well-regarded religious art that they were required to interpret and write about—whispers of a developing world view. I probably got the incentive from the Cadet Chapel and the Christian world view the windows declare. Now you know the rest of the story.

> But now, O Lord, you are our Father; we are the clay, and you are our potter; we are all the work of your hand (ESV, Isaiah 64:8).

CHAPTER XVII

Pick a Department

Before considering seriously enough the importance of living a practical apologetic to express clearly my Christian world view, I had other plans for my military career, but God is full of surprises. My selection to teach at West Point came out of the blue. I was about halfway through a thirteen-month combat tour of duty in Vietnam and at the time was out "in the green" working with a tribe of primitive Montagnards clearing our village's firing zones through the jungle in the Anna Cordillera mountains located along the Laotian border, when a shiny new headquarters helicopter landed in the field next to us. Out hopped a well-starched young butter bar (second lieutenant), apparently assigned to the personnel division of the 1st Aviation Brigade headquarters at Long Binh and none too happy to be out "in the field," who saluted nervously and handed me a very official looking letter. Saying, "It's important, Sir; it's from West Point," he jogged back to his slick (Huey helicopter), anxious to get out of harm's way as fast as he could, and literally dove back into it as the skids left the ground. The letter was simple and to the point. The gist of it was that the Academy, in coordination with my assignments officer at the personnel division at the Department of the Army in Arlington, Virginia, had reviewed my academic and military career records, and I was being considered for a teaching assignment at West Point, assuming I survived my current assignment. Always a fount of encouragement those folks.

I hadn't been fully aware of the fact at the time, but a natural career progression for a regular army officer would have been to spend two or three years while a captain or major as an instructor in a branch school (artillery, infantry, signal corps, etc.), Ranger School, Jump School, or as a PMS (Professor of Military Science), an ROTC instructor, at some university. The top 5% of the officer corps—based on their military records thus far—could also be considered for an assignment on the faculty at West Point. That was the potential assignment being offered to me. I wasn't particularly keen on teaching company tactics or communication skills to junior officers at Fort Bliss, Texas or marksmanship at the Infantry school at Fort Benning, Georgia for three years. I certainly didn't want to be assigned to teaching the assembly and disassembly of the M-60 machine gun or M-16 rifle to young enlisted soldiers at Fort Sill, Oklahoma, or mosquito and gator infested Fort Polk, Louisiana for three years, so the possibility of returning to my alma mater to teach was really intriguing. As an added benefit, the army would send me to graduate school to get an advanced degree and not only pay the tab but also continue to pay me my salary while there to boot.

Communications between soldiers deployed in South Vietnam and Washington, D.C., let alone with West Point, New York were very difficult in the early 1970's—certainly there was no internet, I-Pads, cell phones, or even short wave radio service without continuous, "over, over, over and outs," even if you could maintain the connection long enough without being cut off. If one were lucky, he might get one or two short wave calls a year from a base camp back to civilization, if one were stationed on one. That was not my experience, living out "in the green." I contacted a South Vietnamese army officer whom I knew was a chopper pilot with Air America—our unofficial CIA run air force based out of a non-existent air base in Long Tieng, Laos—and asked for his assistance. *Dai Uy* (Captain), Tranh, who had bailed me and my team out a few times in the past, said he would try to free up a chopper and get me a hop into Danang, where most of the general officers lived in trailers out of harm's way.

After one fierce unexpected two-hour fire fight along the Laotian border and two unmarked Air America chopper rides later, I arrived in Danang and managed to contact my assignment officer in the Pentagon from a telephone line in a sympathetic army general's trailer and said, "Got your letter, Sir. Sounds like a plan. Please sign me up." In my subsequent conversations with Academy officials, I was told to select an academic department or two in which I would want to teach and let them know my choice. They would circulate my academic and military records to those departments and see if anyone was interested in having me join their teaching faculty.

I had graduated from the academy with a BS degree in Engineering Management. It is a strange title but comes closest to a degree in mechanical engineering with a good dose of ballistics, barricade and bridge construction, and bomb disposal thrown into the hash. While stationed in West Germany for my first tour of duty out of the Academy, I had also attended a nuclear weapons pre-fire course at the NATO School in Oberammergau (famous for its *Passion Play* every ten years) and taken several courses in nuclear engineering through the University of Heidelberg, but I was frankly tired of such subject matter, so told the Academy I would like to teach in the Department of English. Since I had finished in the highest section of English at graduation, they said yes.

I was directed to apply to a graduate school—they suggested Duke, the University of Virginia, Harvard, the University of Pennsylvania, and the University of Indiana—get accepted, obtain my master's degree, and they would foot the bill for two years before returning me to West Point to join the English Department faculty. I applied to Duke, U. of P., and UVA, and decided to attend the first one that said yes. A few months later, Duke accepted me into their program. I said yes, and the dye was cast.

I often joke that I was trained at West Point but educated at Duke. That is probably a bit too glib and cynical, but the academic choices for a cadet at West Point in the 1960's were very few. During my four years as a cadet at West Point, we were allowed just three electives. The ones I selected were ORSA, Management, and Advanced German. The rest of our courses (24 credits per semester for four years) were all part of a STEM-based core curriculum. Needless to say, I suppose, when I had to compete with other students for their Master of Arts degrees and Doctorates in English at one of the finest graduate schools in the world, the task proved daunting. At first, just trying to stay up with my fellow graduate students at Duke, all of whom had arrived with sixty to ninety undergraduate credits in English and BA's in English in hand from Vanderbilt, Princeton, UVA, Emory, Harvard, Cambridge, and other prestigious institutions proved challenging. I had twelve credits in core English courses—mostly grammar and writing courses. I had never even heard of Virginia Woolf, John Updike, Auden, Browning, Donne, or a hundred other names with which my Duke classmates were very familiar. I just wanted to be able to write like MacArthur someday. Sleep was necessarily put on hold for a couple years. Not being able to sleep for the eight weeks of Ranger School (61 days long with 19.6 hours of scheduled training each day) almost prepared me for not sleeping for my first two years in grad school at Duke.

At any rate, after getting my master's degree in language, literature, and values (English) from Duke, I began a teaching assignment at West Point. Despite having found a good *Bible*-believing fellowship at the Chapel Hill Bible Church, the previous years had been a bit of a spiritual void— there was in my mind, just not enough time— I was looking forward to becoming engaged once again with the Officers Christian Fellowship while on the USMA faculty. The OCF, as well as the Baptist Student Union, was a powerful support network during my time as a cadet, much as it was for President Trump's Secretary of State, Mike Pompeo, who says he "found Christ" in a small cadet run *Bible* study while at West Point. I looked forward to helping out with the organization's leadership once on the faculty.

Within a year, I was on the Chapel Board of the Cadet Chapel—the West Point version of a board of elders—and by the next year was the Board's President.

The following year, I was leading the weekly West Point faculty *Bible* study sponsored by the Cadet Chaplain's office, and had organized another much smaller interfaith *Bible* study comprised of the Cadet Chaplain, an American Baptist by denomination, Father John McCarthy (a Jesuit priest who headed up the Catholic diocese on post), Rabbi Abram Soltes (who led the post Jewish community), and me. It was a fabulous learning experience and a powerful network of the post's spiritual leaders all of whom shared a common world view but approached the scriptures from vastly different points of view. We would normally meet Wednesday mornings before academic classes began and spend an hour sharing our diverse understanding of passages of the scriptures, both Christian and Jewish, and exploring the texts in the original Greek, Hebrew, and Aramaic.

My Department Head, a bright, urbane, and dedicated Episcopalian, at first seemed pleased by my involvement on the Cadet Chapel board. He and his wife were usually faithful attendees at Sunday morning services in the Cadet Chapel, believing as did I that the faculty should set the model by worshipping publicly with the cadets not at the separate Post Chapel that most of the church-going faculty attended. The Sunday services at the Cadet Chapel, following long standing military academy traditions, despite what the denominational bent of the head cadet chaplain at any one time might be, were mostly a high church (with strong Episcopalian influence) approach to theology, so my boss was at home there. As time went by, however, he had increasing privately expressed misgivings about my more extensive participation in the West Point ministries. He was okay with my involvement, as long as it didn't appear to "impact" my teaching. That was soon to change.

> ...let your light shine before others, so that they may see
> your good works and give glory to your Father who is in
> heaven (ESV, Matthew 5:16).

CHAPTER XVIII

Stars Deferred

The normal teaching tour of duty at the Academy is three years. My plan was to teach in the Department of English for those three years and then return to a regular army unit in Korea, NATO, or wherever current hostilities might need my particular expertise. The most cherished assignments for a career army captain and major are command assignments, leading companies, batteries, squadrons, or battalions of 150-800 soldiers at a time. Most of my peers in my same year group would have been fortunate to have secured one command assignment to that point in their careers—I already had three such commands in NATO and Vietnam and excelled in each. In my mind, I was destined for stars. After three years teaching at West Point I would no doubt be headed back to a division or corps somewhere in the world to command a battalion and later, I hoped, larger units of soldiers. A follow-on assignment in the Pentagon or the joint staff was not something I wanted but was also a possibility, because I had a secondary specialty of Public Affairs and had been assigned as a spokesperson for our Iranian Embassy hostages when they returned to the States and been sequestered at the Hotel Thayer on the West Point reservation. I was accustomed to dealing with the national media and high ranking leaders far more senior than I. At the time, to spend any longer than the basic three years in a teaching assignment was probably a death knell to wearing stars one day, because a future general officer was meant to have spent time commanding and leading troops in the field—something I loved to do—not just teaching.

During my third year on the faculty, as I was preparing for a follow-on assignment with the Joint Chiefs of Staff in the Pentagon for which I had received alert orders, a position became available for a Permanent Associate Professorship (PAP) in the Department of English—West Point's version of a career-long tenured position. At the time, the position called for someone with an exemplary military career with unit command time, combat experience, and possessing the rank of lieutenant colonel or full colonel who, upon selection, would be returned to graduate school again to attain a Ph.D and then return to West Point to serve on the teaching faculty until retirement after thirty years. I prayed very hard regarding my next choice. I had always wanted to wear stars someday, why else spend a career in the army? Despite the fact that at the time I was just a relatively junior army major, I felt led to apply for the tenured position. I believed that I would have very little chance of success, because I would be competing with dozens of lieutenant colonels and full colonels who had already been on the faculty at one time or another in the past and would most likely have the inside track with those senior officers and civilian professors on the selection committee. I interviewed with the selection board and to my surprise, was almost immediately selected for the appointment. West Point lived up to its end of the bargain and returned me to Duke University for another two years to complete my doctoral course studies. Always trust God to answer prayers, just not always in the ways we intend.

With two more years of graduate school studies under my belt, I returned to West Point. I was then one of just six tenured faculty members in the department. The other thirty-five instructors came and went on three-year tours and reported to us. It was our job to provide academic leadership and continuity for the entire department. There was the Department Chairman, the Deputy Department Head (who since he was not the Head of the Department bore the unofficial title of the "Not-head," a title more befitting of some of them than others), and four of us tenured PAP's (Permanent Associate Professors) who directed the major programs. We also taught most of the upper level electives in literature and culture. One of the most popular of them was my advanced English elective entitled Faith and Modern American Fiction that explored the world views of several modern and post-modern American authors.

As only natural, in my mind, I also reassumed my role as Head of the Cadet Chapel board. The Academy saw such a position as largely responsible for the Chapel itself: upgrading the world's largest pipe organ, ensuring the physical plant was well maintained, advising on budgetary expenditures, advertising programs, and advising the Cadet Chaplain—who at the time by tradition ever since 1826 was always a civilian—on issues regarding the Corps of Cadets. I saw it more as a way of helping to coordinate all cadet ministries on post, act as a liaison between the Corps of Cadets and the Chaplain's Office, and to be a support network for the several denominationally diverse chaplains assigned to the Cadet and other post chapels. To the extent the Protestant Cadet Chapel had a board of elders to provide spiritual leadership, myself and three other tenured professors (one, the Not-head from the Department of History, one a senior Regimental Tactical Officer, and one the Not-head in the Department of Physics) were it. That was part of being responsible to fulfilling my obligations to "Duty, Honor, and Country," those three hallowed words that ideally should reverently dictate my actions.

Over the previous two years in grad school, because of my constant involvement with university intellectuals and skeptical professors and graduate students—that is a kind description of their attitudes toward faith and a Christian world view, even at a United Methodist denomination affiliated university like Duke—I had been bombarded with difficult, probing questions by my fellow doctoral candidates and several professors, questions that I had tried to answer thoughtfully out of my Christian frame of reference. I had grown passionate about being able to respond to their skepticism with honest and biblical integrity and had grown in my appreciation of the value of taking an apologetics approach to personal ministry.

On weekends I had the support of a Christian fellowship in Durham, NC called simply enough, The Assembly, an unconventional non-denominational church with a passion for growing traditional Christians. My close friendship with the lead *Bible* teacher, a wonderful man named Welcome Detweiler, enabled me to preach at the church on several occasions and to grow spiritually as well as intellectually while pursuing graduate studies at Duke. I also spent time volunteering with the Campus Crusade for Christ group, based out of the Chapel Hill Bible Church.

Along the way, I had devoured everything written by Origen, Tertullian, Zwingli, Pascal, Anscombe, Chesterton, C. S. Lewis, Os Guinness, Francis Schaeffer, and many other less well-known Christian apologists. While at Duke the second time, I had not only completed all the course work for my doctorate, passed the four hour Ph.D written exam, passed both my language fluency exams in German and Spanish, passed my three-hour doctoral Orals, but had also managed to take several courses in the Duke Divinity School and Department of Religion where I could acquaint myself with more liberal writers such as Barth, Bultmann, Kierkegaard, Brunner, Niebuhr, and others from the Existentialist and Neo-Orthodox strain. As the military had taught me, always know your enemy and their tactics better than they do, themselves. Each expanded my ultimate Christian world view by forcing me to ferret out the truth often buried among competing hermeneutics and theologies. During that time, my relationship with Francis Schaeffer had developed into a friendship, and I sought a way to bring his Christian analysis of western culture to the West Point Community when I returned.

After I was on the tenured faculty for a couple years, West Point received the mandate from the Department of the Army to begin its first courses in Ethics and Philosophy that I have previously discussed. In addition to the tutorial in which I was able to participate, the Academy hired Dr. Bob Gurland to be the visiting professor of Ethics for more than a year to continue to mentor the philosophy faculty in the subject matter, once the program was launched. I was assigned as his faculty sponsor and spent untold hours with Bob in his office and quarters probing his mind for the best approaches to understanding and teaching philosophy and ethics, and arguing competing world views, often having my Christian world view challenged, if not impugned. Because of my obvious interest in the subject, our Department Head also asked me to launch and edit a journal we named *Ethics and the Military Profession*, that became a quarterly publication of the Military Academy for several years, to support the new program of instruction and to establish our academic bonafides in the subject. I wound up personally writing all of the first several editions of that Academy journal (*War and Morality*, *The Military Ethic*, *Professional Ethics*, etc.), a publication that, unfortunately, ceased publication once I left the faculty.

All this was preparatory for my forthcoming denouement at West Point. Dr. Francis Schaeffer had about the same time produced his ten-hour series based on his book, *How Should We Then Live*, his masterful study of the Rise and Fall of western culture from a Christian perspective. This is the book that Chuck Colson, for example (Founder of the Prison Ministry), said had awakened him to how biblical truths affected all of life. I agreed and used it and other related texts to teach several groups of cadets who would meet in the basement of the Cadet Chapel on weekends, through the ministry of the Chapel Board and the BSU. It is, at one level, a systematic cross disciplinary analysis of the origins of the Christian world view. When their schedule finally permitted, under the auspices of the Cadet Chapel ministry, Dr. Schaeffer's team agreed to come to West Point to present his ten-hour series over two and a half days. I naturally assumed the role as the faculty sponsor of the program and introduced each of the ten segments to the West Point community.

All the sessions were held on the weekends and everything was paid for by donations through the Cadet Chapel Fund. The evangelical Christian community on base was thrilled to have Fran's team come, and hundreds of cadets and post families attended their presentations, raising many of the same questions we had wrestled with at the Swiss L'Abri. Minds and hearts were changed, many faculty members holding Naturalistic world views were challenged with the truth, and Christians were empowered to express their faith in their lives and careers in renewed ways. So successful was the program that we asked them to come back a second time the following year. My Department Chair, however, seemed less than pleased with my involvement and was apparently concerned that my growing interest in Christian apologetics and obvious Christian world view could possibly adversely impact my teaching of philosophy and ethics. Later that year, I was reassigned from the ethics and philosophy group and instead directed to reassume the role of Director of Freshman Writing, the core program that all Plebes had to take for two semesters their first year. A very bright and more senior ranking PAP named Tony, was placed in charge of the Philosophy group. Since we on the permanent faculty often exchanged the leadership of the various core programs the change was certainly no demotion, but it was a clear sign that my efforts to chew the wafer had become a little too public. I would cease teaching Philosophy and Ethics, and instead concentrate on argumentative writing and teaching cadets how to write coherent sentences and essays.

When I had agreed to spend just two years in grad school to finish my doctoral studies, part of the unspoken agreement was that when I returned to the Academy to teach, I would be assigned a very limited teaching schedule in order to research and write my doctoral dissertation on The Entropic Narrative Style and World View of Thomas Pynchon's Fiction. All that changed after the *How Should We Then Live* lecture series, and I was assigned several classes to teach, an ethics journal to write, committees to chair, and numerous other time-consuming departmental duties, making it impossible, in my mind, to finish it while on the faculty. Seeing the writing on the wall, nothing as graphic as *mene mene tekel upharsin* (Daniel 5:25), but just as prescient, I told our department Not-head—a brilliant and respected leader who himself eventually became the Department Head—that I thought it best for me to leave West Point and be reassigned elsewhere. His answer said it all. He told me that was probably a good idea and to let him know how he could assist me in making that reassignment happen.

During the previous year when attending the Armed Forces Staff College (AFSC), part of National Defense University, I had gotten to know General Ken Jolemore, the Commandant of the school and President of that college. Ken was a former Special Forces sergeant during the Korean War who, after that conflict, had gone to OCS, been commissioned, and had risen through the ranks and had been eventually promoted to Major General (a two-star rank). In the mid 1970's he had been diagnosed with stomach cancer, had part of his stomach and two thirds of his intestines removed, and had received a virtual death sentence by the oncologists at Walter Reed Medical Center, and given only a few months to live. Ken had been apparently given the assignment as President of the College as a way of easing out of his career in a less stressful academic assignment. In the previous year, he had committed his life to Christ and became passionate about his faith. I had gotten to know him because he faithfully attended the student and faculty *Bible* study that I led each week at the college, while assigned there as one of his students.

Once I knew I would be departing West Point, I decided to try to preempt the normal Department of Army reassignment process and called General Jolemore. Without offering any reasons, I told him it was time for me to leave the faculty at West Point and that I would like to join the faculty of the AFSC where he was still the President, if he thought I would be an asset. When he agreed, I told him I would come only if he would give me a free hand to run the entire ethics program at the college. I could almost hear him smile over the phone as he said, "How soon can you get here, Colonel?" Because my permanent appointment on the faculty at West Point had required Congressional approval, I was told that it would also require an act of Congress to "un-appoint" me. I am not sure how all that happened. I just made the request and let the process play out. General Jolemore said he would take care of it, and he did. That process took about three months, and I was on my way to Norfolk, Virginia after having been recommended for the Legion of Merit and receiving another Meritorious Service Medal for my work at West Point. As far as I know, the reason I was suddenly leaving such a plumb assignment was never announced within the department and came as a surprise to most of the permanent faculty. Once appointed as a PAP, no one ever left.

True to his word, General Jolemore appointed me the Course Director for all the programs in Executive Development and Ethics at the College, and for the next four years, in addition to serving as the Seminar Chairman for several classes of students, I taught all the courses in ethics, personal development, and executive fitness until I retired from active duty. Had I not left West Point when I did and gotten my subsequent faculty appointment at the Staff College, I would not have been able to launch the international coaching and consulting business I currently lead. God always answers prayers—often in unexpected ways—if we are faithful to chew the wafer. West Point once again served as the training ground for living a practical apologetics and putting the finishing touches on a Christian world view.

> Duty, Honor, Country — **those three hallowed words reverently dictate what you ought to be, what you can be, what you will be**. They are your rallying point to build courage when courage seems to fail, **to regain faith when there seems to be little cause for faith, to create hope when hope becomes forlorn**.

As icing on the cake, after having been diagnosed with terminal cancer and given only a few months to live, General Jolemore lived for 42 years and became a great spiritual warrior within the war college system and later in his retired life. His support was critical for the ministries we launched there for the mid-career and senior officers who would be assigned to the college with their families for the nine month course of studies.

Even though AFSC was an intermediate "Joint" War College (ie. Involved mid- career officers from all 5 military services), the Navy had proponency over the staffing. The navy chaplains who would be assigned to the college for posh two-year shore assignments were very professional and performed their chaplain duties with great integrity but, let me say, were often less than rigorous about their knowledge of scripture and represented several liberal denominations; rarely in those days, in my experience, could one find an evangelical chaplain in uniform. Because believer baptisms and celebrations of the Lord's Supper were not their long suits, we who worked with the campus chaplains had to take on those duties ourselves. I remember personally coaching a Presbyterian chaplain on performing believer's baptisms and had the joy of assisting him in baptizing one of my daughters in the Chesapeake Bay by the lighthouse off First Landing

Beach on Fort Story. It was an event that forever changed his ministry. What a joy to assist in the baptism of your child!

Communion was another issue. We had a mostly perfunctory one (usually led by Methodist, Lutheran, Episcopal, or Roman Catholic chaplains, who seemed to be in the greatest number in the Tidewater, VA area) every couple of months, after the regular services in the campus chapel, a small room on the second floor of the base recreation hall. Most of our small evangelical community chose to attend these sessions in lieu of or in addition to local churches in the Tidewater area, to support the ministry, and to demonstrate publicly our faith, but also to try to grow our Christian community on base. General Jolemore and his wife also allowed us to use their large government quarters at the NOB (Norfolk Naval Operating Base) once a month for a celebration of the Lord's Supper, which I would lead after our *Bible* studies. While there are many different approaches for celebrating this sacrament, our approach was usually to use a small loaf of bread and a common cup of wine that we would pass around our group to reinforce our Christian unity. Now, bread, unlike a thin wafer, you can really chew! It was always the highlight of our small team's (about 30 officers from four different military services) time together.

As an evangelical, I readily admit that formal written prayers tend to leave me cold, but the one we recited every Sunday in chapel while a cadet, hung in our youngest son's room for many years and since he has moved out after college hangs on my office wall. It is called simply the "Cadet Prayer." Every event of my life and humble attempts to live out a Christian world view seems captured in it, as it simply affirms:

God our father, thou searcher of men's hearts, help us draw near to thee in sincerity and truth. **May our religion be filled with gladness** and may our worship of thee be natural.

Strengthen and increase our admiration for honest dealing and clean thinking, and **suffer not our hatred of hypocrisy and pretense ever to diminish**. Encourage us in our endeavor to live above the common level of life. **Make us to choose the harder right over the easier wrong, and never to be content with a half truth when the whole can be won.**

Endow us with courage that is born of all that is noble and worthy, **that scorns to compromise with vice and injustice and knows no fear when truth and right are in jeopardy.**

Guard us against flippancy and irreverence in the sacred things of life. **Grant us new ties of friendship and new opportunities of service.** Kindle our hearts in fellowship with those of a cheerful countenance, and soften our hearts with sympathy for those who sorrow and suffer.

Help us to maintain the honor of the Corps (the West Point Corps of Cadets) untarnished and unsullied and **to show forth in our lives the ideals of West Point** in doing our duty to thee and to our country.

All of this we ask in the name of the great friend and master of men, Jesus Christ our Lord. Amen.

Some phrases have had more relevance than others during my life but the whole prayer, for both cadets and non-cadets, is worth considering.

CHAPTER XIX

Art in a Different Form

In the summer of 2018 my wife and I saw a commercial movie entitled *An Interview with God*. Cloaked in fiction, it is nonetheless a brilliant, non-sectarian, biblically faithful presentation of some of the thorniest theological canards that have plagued mankind over the ages. While the thesis of the film is admittedly corny—someone claiming to be God contacts an agnostic young reporter named Paul Asher, who has recently returned from an assignment reporting on the combat in Afghanistan, and asks to be interviewed—the acting is surprisingly good, and the staged discussion at the end of the film—an innovative way to engage a public movie-going audience regarding the theological topics presented without scaring them off by delving into seminary jargon—brings many of the themes discussed in the plot to life. In the commercial theater in Indianapolis where we viewed the film, no one left during the twenty-five-minute free-wheeling conversation led by author Eric Metaxis and two other syndicated columnists as they debated the influence of a Christian world view on our culture.

Once again, I had been feloniously anticipated. What does that mean? It means that someone, far more brilliant than I and less afflicted by creative and mental entropy, pounced on a subject and produced a creative product before mine hit the shelves. This is a script I could have written—indeed, that I should have written—as it dealt with the very same questions I have mulled over posing to God, myself, for years as I exercised on a treadmill, swam endless laps in our backyard pool, pedaled for miles on my Life Cycle, skied imaginary black diamonds on my Nordic Track, crisscrossed oceans in business class flights, or ran marathons in Boston, New York, Berlin, Virginia Beach, Texas, and Washington, DC. My body just goes into auto pilot, and mostly to prepare myself to answer the honest questions of others regarding my world view, I frame questions of eternal consequence to myself and hubristically try to answer them, as I believe God would want them answered. The movie raised a few of the larger questions, but there are many more than just those the movie posed; it will probably take me most of eternity to get them all answered to my satisfaction. I hope that the Lord and his team of angelic apologetics experts are patient with my persistent questioning. We'll start with God's telling Abraham to go sacrifice his son—a divine order I admittedly could not have obeyed—and move on from there.

A similar thing happened several years ago as I was considering writing a book about the power of statistical outliers to revolutionize a business, an industry, a sport, or an institution. Out of nowhere popped up Malcolm Gladwell's provocative book, *Outliers: The Story of Success*, a book that if anyone still reads in today's blog, Twitter, Instagram, Ted Talk, and U-Tube infected culture, should be mandatory reading for every leader, student, teacher, politician, coach, manager, engineer, and…yes…you. My wife, who is a brilliant chemical engineer, innovator, and business leader, and I had been mulling over these very issues for a few years before Gladwell's book hit Amazon's best seller listing. Since Gladwell feloniously anticipated me—knew what I was going to say and once again, with far better stories than mine, beat me to the punch—I was relegated to writing a companion piece a few years later in 2017, entitled *Inliers: The Curse of Polarity Thinking*, a populist organizational study now used in several Fortune 500 companies and a few B-schools, that highlights what must change inside most organizations before any effort at embracing *Outliers* can be successful. Perhaps I should thank Malcolm, instead of being put out by his creativity and wisdom.

In the same year, I published my fourth novel entitled, *Framing the Sacred: The Shadow of Death*. The plot, which is somewhat fictional, proposes how any of us, regardless of our presuppositional world view, theology, politics, or personal morality can be turned into an unintentional domestic terrorist through the intentional creative and subversive use of social media, sometimes using subconscious sacred framing, advanced quantum stenography, or even more complex AIT Stegs implanted in anything from cat videos or enticing ocean views, to graphic videos of beheadings in Iraq. When our world views are not premised on clear biblical absolutes, we are even more vulnerable. Another rationale for truly embracing 2 Timothy 2:15.

I sent the final manuscript to the publisher on September 15, 2017 and, while the ink was still drying on the first edition being shipped out to bookstores, less than two weeks later on Oct 1, 2017 an innocuous nobody named Stephen Paddock, for no discernible reason, fired over 1,100 rounds from the window of his 32d floor room in the Mandalay Bay Hotel and Resort in Las Vegas, Nevada killing 58 people and injuring 851 innocent attendees of the Route 91 Harvest Music Festival, as they frantically scrambled for safety in a hail of bullets. *Framing the Sacred* suggested in advance of the incident why and how Paddock could have become transformed into one of the worst domestic terrorists in US history, controlled by, well, you really should read the book (The Book Store at www.execustrat.com). For his world view, he chose poorly, and his story reflected it.

To date, no motive for the massacre has been uncovered by the Las Vegas police, the FBI, and the other federal agencies that swarmed over the crime scene for weeks. After issuing a 187-page report quashing all rumors of conspiracy in 2018, the Las Vegas sheriff ended the investigation. The case is now officially closed, and all that has happened in the wake of this horrific terrorist attack is resurrected interest in FEMA conspiracies, a renewed debate over bump stocks and extended magazines, and totally predictable, uninformed, media babblings regarding mental illness and what constitutes an assault rifle. Forget mental illness—that is the politically correct implied causation for every shooting arising from a purely Naturalistic world view masquerading as an excuse—the real reason is called sin. The only world view that acknowledges such a truth is the Christian one. Oh, and Paddock's fourteen bank accounts containing just over $ 2 million have been frozen, and his brain has been sent to Stanford University for further study—good luck—just more, all too predictable, polarity thinking. **Sin is not identifiable in a CAT scan, and researchers will find no world view hiding in his cerebral cortex or bank accounts**.

Forgotten in the stacks of paperwork surrounding the case are the inevitable and predictable differences in world views and the theological conflicts between Judaism, Islam, and Christianity. These differences, primarily eschatological ones, formed the basis for the conflict in my 2009 apocalyptic novel, *Spirit of the Oryx,* and reach their possible denouement in *Framing the Sacred.* The adventure novel, *Framing the Sacred,* is just fiction, after all, notwithstanding the number of federal agencies that have rung me up or dropped by for informal chats since the novel's publication. This time it wasn't another writer who did me in but a real life, aging gambler who feloniously anticipated me. He acted before I could predict why and how it could be done—and, it will be done again. Each time, that unpopular word "sin" will be studiously avoided by the psychologists, journalists, politicians, local police, and academicians who will be called in to discuss the causes and "cures" for what they will call a "pattern of mental illness," a lapse in security, or the failure of government to control the use of, purchase, or transfer of weapons. Psychologists believe they can assist someone if the cause is mental illness—just drug them and provide ongoing expensive therapy; Satan applauds their naivete, regardless of their political motivations. **Psychologists can't do a thing about sin.** Reality, these days, so often seems to trump (no pun intended) fiction.

Alright, I am done whining. Since I can't interview the Almighty, as the young reporter did in *Interview with God,* I'll be forced to use secondary sources to see what the Almighty would tell me. Full disclosure, if not clear yet, let me reiterate. I am a believer; why else would I care what the King of Kings, the Lord of Lords, the Creator of the Universe, had to say about leadership, team building, coaching, and building exceptional organizations? What that means is that as an evangelical Christian I believe in the reality and eternal existence of the God of the Hebrew *Tanakh*, what is often abbreviated as the *Torah* or part of what is more commonly known as the *Old Testament*, and in the personal revelation of Jesus the Christ who came to fulfill the Law and provide us with a pathway for salvation. I am one of his blood-blessed redeemed. That is my admitted bias, so this is an inside story.

I believe further that the God of the Universe has spoken dramatically in history and his message has provided mankind with guidance about how to live. That premise is the foundation of a Christian world view. As the Christian apologist Francis Schaefer stated so well in several of his books, ***He is There, and He is not Silent.*** Given that premise, and for me that premise is an historical, cognitive, and epistemological fact, the natural follow-on question always must be *How Should We Then Live?* **Since we are talking about being clear to live out a practical apologetic, that consideration is at the forefront of our thinking in every aspect of our business life.** No company hires us because they think of us as a "Christian" company, whatever that means, because we are not. There are no crosses on our vehicles, "AGAPE" on our license plates, or fish on our business cards—if there were, I am sure mine would be routinely swimming in the wrong direction, but **every tool, assessment, approach, and technology we use has its background story rooted in a Christian world view. That is how we can impact the world with a practical apologetic, even in our business.**

In that regard, I admittedly have taken a lot of space here to relate events in my personal story in order to underscore how my Christian world view was forged in order to show how and why it has become the backstory for all of our current work in the business world. **All the small stories I have related are but subplots in God's much larger narrative. It is His story that ultimately counts** the most.

If I am right, then surely that God has some things to say about the principles of leadership and how effective people should work together to achieve the best outcomes in the world he created by living a practical apologetic. Anything else would be an irresponsible and anti-intellectual *Escape From Reason* and an unwarranted "leap of faith."

> One who is faithful in a very little is also faithful in much,
> and one who is dishonest in a very little is also dishonest
> in much (ESV, Luke 16:10).

Not only is this a biblical principle, but it is also a guiding tenet of any organization that wants to be know as exceptional.

CHAPTER XX

Paul—My Man

The Apostle Paul, now there's my man! It may sound almost trite to say, but if there were ever a fleshed out portrait of what it looks like to embody a transition from a generically Theistic world view, even one nurtured in the best Jewish schools of his day, to a practical Christian world view, it is Paul. Every time I think about the fledgling first century church, Paul's brilliance and fearlessness astound me.

First, this unknown rabbi emerging from Galilee, the earthly son of a carpenter, actually does what numerous prophecies in the *Old Testament*, most prominently those in Isaiah, predicted he would do when he arises from the dead and appears to hundreds of skeptical witnesses throughout Judea. Small groups of *sub rosa* followers spring up in fellowships all over the then known world, and as far away as Turkey, Iran, and Greece (Some sects would claim as far away as North and South America), to worship this formally unschooled rabbi and spread his gospel of eternal salvation, cultural harmony (1 Peter), and personal resurrection. The missing years of Jesus' life (age 12-30) have always spawned a lot of fictional speculation and post canonical writings, but I'll stick with the more geographically limited biblical record.

All with the best intentions, these small assemblies of believers attempted to start churches, oh they were not called that at first, but small assemblies of fledgling believers who would proclaim the gospel of Jesus the Christ despite the persistent attacks from the Jewish hierarchy and Gentile intellectuals. The closer they were to the events, the more accurate their observations and faithfulness to the teachings Jesus proclaimed while he walked the earth. The further away they were from the events, the more errors of doctrine tended to creep in from those teachers whom the Apostle Paul talked about in his second epistle delivered to the Thessalonians. Jesus had come to engage the world and spent his time speaking with and dining with real people—sinners, fishermen, tax collectors, and other scalawags with whom the pharisees and traditional church fathers would have nothing to do.

I can't begin to understand the excitement as well as the fear and theological misunderstandings that must have permeated every one of these hundreds of small groups as they initially worshipped in caves, homes, and upper rooms fearful of Roman soldiers and Jewish scholars who threatened them with violence for trying to destabilize their world or simply disrupt their economy (Acts 16:16-40), with their primitive beliefs. In our country, we know nothing of real persecution for our beliefs and occasionally have to be startled awake by such realities as the death and persecution leveled on believers in other cultures. Even a quick visit to the Church of Martyrs in Medina, Italy, where 800 men were beheaded for refusing to renounce their faith, is a wake-up call worth the trip. To this day, you can still see their skulls embedded behind glass panels in the chapel's walls. Their Christian world view cost them everything valued in this world.

According to the current World Watch List website, on the average, 345 Christians are killed worldwide every month, 105 churches are burned or attacked, and 219 more Christians are arrested and charged for expressing their faith. In 2019 alone, in the top 50 countries allowing if not actively encouraging the persecution of Christians, 4,136 believers were killed for faith-related reasons (in case you are STEM challenged, that's about eleven/day), 1,266 Christian churches were burned to the ground, and 2,625 Christians were sentenced and incarcerated for little more than being Christians (World Watch List 2019). Even in the USA, a country alleging to have been founded on Christian principles and institutionalizing freedom of speech and assembly in its founding documents, Christians are hauled into court every year for daring to have their Christian world view influence how they choose to do business, protect human life in the womb, or make decisions regarding marriage, usually regarding LGBTQ issues.

Notwithstanding the outright slaughter of Christians in some predominantly Muslim countries in the Middle East and Southwest Asia, perhaps the most virulent of these attacks on Christians in 2019 occurred in China where the Communist Party began rounding up and jailing Christian ministers and closing hundreds of house churches across the country. In the same year, Chinese Christian churches were ordered to take the Ten Commandments and *Bible* verses off their walls and replace them with sayings of President Xi Jinping. In several more prominent Christian churches the Chinese government uses facial recognition surveillance systems to identify Christians coming and going. Reports from furloughed missionaries and more formal events like Secret Church held quarterly at the McClean Bible Church, outside Washington, D. C., are crucial for helping us understand the plight of our brothers and sisters in other lands. We suffer very little for living out a Christian world view in the United States—maybe just the loss of a friend, a job, or a faculty position from time to time. Our prayers need to be with Christians elsewhere who often lose far more than that. As the Apostle Paul reminds us, in regard to the local church—the Body of Christ, "If one part suffers, every part suffers with it; if one part is honored, every part rejoices with it" (NIV, 1st Corinthians 12:26). Christians in China, Syria, Somalia, Thailand, Myanmar, Iran, Toga, and Chad are as much a part of the Body of Christ as the person sitting next to us in the pew on Sunday morning.

In the first century, chief of those scholars trying to eliminate the "Jesus" threat was Paul, himself, at the time still known as Saul of Tarsus, who even participated in, if not himself inciting, the beheading of the Apostle Stephen. His career was as surprising as some of ours. After having his sight restored, his very life screamed the world view of his Messiah, the Christ. Some of the chapters in his story are hard to document; others are easier to track down as we watch God change Saul's name, as well as his motives and directions, several times during his life. At times he just had to say that the Lord forbade him to go certain places. He was never in charge; God was. His life was a practical apologetic the rest of us can only hope to emulate. Not surprisingly, his world view likewise took some time to develop.

We know that he was born a Roman citizen in Tarsus to Jewish parents in 5 or 6 AD. Tarsus would have been in what today is eastern Turkey, a thoroughly Muslim area—a warning to all of us regarding what can happen to our culture as well when we are not clear enough about our world view. As recently as 2014, the Turkish Christian population was still listed at 20% but as of 2019, a mere five years later, was down to less than .2%--a 99% reduction in five years. Paul was probably the best educated of Jesus's followers, having studied under the tutelage of Gamaliel, the most prominent Doctor of Law in his time and President of the Jerusalem Sanhedrin for several years.

Saul became a respected Pharisee and spent at least three years persecuting Christians until on that dusty road to Emmaus, Saul of Tarsus, the chief persecutor of these new fledgling believers, meets the Lord and all of history as well as his name changes. Saul became Paul and was transformed into perhaps the most important figure in Christianity since Jesus.

In AD 46-7 Paul took his first missionary journey to engage Gentiles in Cyprus and Galatia accompanied by his trusted companion Barnabas. To convert these intellectuals, Paul had to begin with an apologetic approach to his ministry so others could recognize his own intellectual bona fides. At the Council of Jerusalem in AD 49 he debated with Jewish scholars the controversial position that Gentile Christians were not bound by Jewish law. If you know your MBTI technology, the consensus in the field is that Paul was an INTJ, always challenging the status quo and demanding that those in charge back up their traditional beliefs with truth.

In AD 49-51 he went on his second missionary journey, apparently settling in Corinth and writing his letters to the Thessalonians, whom he had visited and established earlier, and who were now having questions regarding Jesus' promised return. In the beginning of AD 52, he went on his third missionary journey.

From AD 55-57 God directed him to travel to the section of Greece known as Illyricum (What later became known as Yugoslavia and since 2005 is most likely the section of that country presently known as Serbia). We forget sometimes with all the bad news coming from that part of the world exactly how Christianity has thrived since Paul established it there. Sometimes just living a practical apologetic, plants fertile seeds the outgrowth of which we may not be aware of in our generation. Today, amidst all the Muslim uproar and violence surrounding that part of the world, Serbia has 79 % of the population who are professing Christians—many of whom are evangelicals. They face life-threatening persecution every day from the ruling Muslim minority who would willingly institute an oppressive caliphate if they could.

From AD 57-59 Paul was imprisoned and then in late AD 59 famously appeared before Festus and made his well-reasoned appeal, as a Roman Citizen, to Caesar. Unafraid of expressing his world view, he was willing to confront the head of the Roman hierarchy.

For the next year he was under house arrest in Jerusalem, living out a practical apologetic even to his jailers.

After a hazardous trip, he once again wound up under house arrest in Rome.

While in prison, he wrote the Epistles to the Philippians, Ephesians, Colossians, and Philemon. Just think about the doctrine we would have missed out on had Paul not been imprisoned. **Isn't it rather ironic but extremely sad that in the USA, *Bibles* are routinely allowed and even distributed to those convicted criminals in prisons, but banned in most public schools?** Freed once again, Paul traveled to parts of current day Spain and wrote his letters to Timothy and Titus.

Step by step Paul is directed where to go and with whom to speak. Always God's plan, not necessarily Paul's. History seems to lose track of him here, and all we know is that around AD 64, at a very young age, Paul returned to Rome and was martyred for his faith and ministry. **Chewing the wafer in public is frequently hazardous to one's career and sometimes to one's health**.

As scripture tells us, Paul's purpose throughout his life, became to engage the world and, in particular, to open the Gospel to Gentiles—all those of us who are not Jewish. That's probably why I love to read Paul's various letters. He examines the strengths and infelicities in doctrine in each of these scattered churches whether it be Ephesus, Philadelphia, Thessalonica, Philippi, or others and goes to the heart of their doctrinal errors and gently nudges them back toward the truth. Where these fellowships can be praised, Paul does so; where they need to be coaxed back to the truth, Paul does that as well. We could use him today to help several of our local churches correct their flawed doctrines and return to their first love. Inspired by God's wisdom, Paul writings gives us our most complete picture of what the *New Testament* church should look like, particularly in his letter to the church at Ephesus. Hard to find one these days, to be sure, but well worth the search.

The local church is the way God intends to accomplish his mission in the world. It is primarily though the local church that God wants to be made known. Of all the evangelism strategies in the world, of all the ministries in the world, none is more central than the local church. It's interesting to note that Paul considered his ministry in a geographical area fulfilled not when every person was reached, but when churches had been planted (Romans 15:19-20). Paul knew that the churches there were how the gospel would spread into all of the individual neighborhoods. Politicians are wont to opine that all politics are local. The same is true of the spread of Christianity. "Local churches do local evangelism." The church is God's plan; it is God's mission. The local church should matter to us because it matters to God. The church is Jesus' body on earth (see Ephesians 1:22-23) and it is made up of all kinds of people from all walks of life. Together we represent Christ here on earth through our diverse body of believers. The church exists for God's glory and showcases it in a unique way. Since we represent Christ to the world it follows that our doctrine should be sound. Few things are worse when reading a story than to find that several plot points just do not fit. How about your story? Does it fit with God's narrative? "The church is built for Jesus, by Jesus, and on Jesus….If it matters so much to God, it needs to matter to us just as much" (Tim Challies, Blog: "Why the Local Church Matters").

CHAPTER XXI

Where two or three are Gathered together...."

As you have no doubt already surmised, my background is different from many of you. Forget about the specifics in each of our lives but focus instead on all the vectors from different inputs that help a world view develop. The point is not where we come from but where we arrive. Our world view seldomly sprouts full grown all at once but accretes as life's events shape us. That's why telling our individual stories is so important to germinating our world views and building up the body of Christ. Since the holy scriptures are God's narrative of salvation related to us, it follows that our individual God-driven narratives can be critical to living out our practical apologetic.

Throughout high school my family attended a fundamentalist Baptist Church in Ocean City, New Jersey (OCBC). It was very well known up and down the east coast for its Summer Bible Conference. For two months every summer, the church would bring in the best preachers, evangelists, and *Bible* scholars from around the country for a week at a time. Every night there would be evangelistic services which thousands of summer visitors to the South Jersey shore would attend before hitting the famous boardwalk later in the evenings. That was the church in which I was baptized as a high school junior and subsequently joined.

Until four years ago, it was the only church I had ever joined. Yes there are a couple stories there. Don't misinterpret my intent. I believe that joining in fellowship with a local church is very important and is the preferred *New Testament* model for believers. It is not membership per se that is important, but the implied fellowship that follows from such an association. Spending a first career in the military, however, offers a different challenge. Once I left for West Point, my association with the OCBC, essentially came to an end. Oh, to be sure, I got their monthly contribution envelopes in the mail, but I probably only attended it fewer than a half dozen occasions again when I was in town for a brief time, visiting my parents in neighboring Somers Point, New Jersey.

The times were somewhat confusing back then and the Vietnam War was very controversial. Many *Bible* believing congregations were themselves divided by their beliefs regarding the morality of the war. When I did return to OCBC, proud of my service to the country, I wore my uniform to church, much to the dismay of the pastor and, I assume, some of the elders. I eventually found out that my membership had been revoked because I was in the military and because I had actually volunteered a couple times to go fight in Vietnam—go figure. Such was the narrow mindedness of some local congregations. As my dad so often reminded me, there is no such thing as a perfect church. So much for affirming diversity within the body of Christ. Think Jesus would have booted the Roman Centurion from the local assembly for going to war (Matthew 8:5-13)?

Once I was on active duty, the church model changed. There is no such thing as church membership on military bases. Every large military base has at least one post chapel where services are held by any and all Protestant, Roman Catholic, Jewish, Holiness, Mormon, and Muslim chaplains that might be assigned to the base. No one joins anything because soldiers come and go as their units are moved in and out. Some posts can be complete spiritual deserts. For that reason, most soldiers never darken the doorway of a church. If they were ever active in their faith before enlisting, they just retain token memberships with churches where they were raised and attend whatever base chapel services are most convenient, when duty allows. Membership is not an issue and is never spoken about from post chapel pulpits. Over time one begins to lose the importance of consistent fellowship—something much more important than actual membership, per se. Talk about a mission field ripe for the harvest! If you are a Christian in the military, support your local chaplains, whatever their affiliations; they need your help.

Since you can never be sure what the denominational affiliation of the chaplain who shows up in the pulpit might be—by regulation, every military chaplain, regardless of denominational or sectarian affiliation (yes, even Jewish, Holiness, Muslim, and the one Wiccan recently commissioned) is obligated to be willing to and capable of ministering to soldiers of any faith—those more committed to their faith often seek out civilian churches in the local area off base, where they can be more certain of the theology behind the pulpit and comfortable with a specific denominational approach. Some also get involved with the OCF, the inter-service lay led evangelical ministry on many major military installations of which I have previously spoken, or other church related organizations.

Sadly, what that often means is that those more committed to their Christian faith are not part of the mix on base in Sunday services, because they have sought fellowship elsewhere. To their credit, military chaplains on large military bases in the USA have tried in recent years to mitigate this dilemma by offering a variety of services each week from Protestant to Roman Catholic, to Gospel, to traditional, to Mormon, to those with less formal liturgies in order to try to meet the needs of soldiers from different denominational and theological backgrounds. These chaplains need the active support of uniformed Christians within their areas of responsibility. Out of necessity, while various denominational meetings are sponsored by the Chaplaincy, many of these services must be lay led or assisted.

This problem is exacerbated when soldiers are serving overseas where those civilians in the local communities may be from dominant religious groups very foreign to Christianity, such as in Southwest Asia or the Middle East. Those who wish to be involved with their denominational Christian groups are then relegated to the base chapel only, where the spiritual leadership or an emphasis on biblical understanding is often questionable. I'm sorry, but an Iman chaplain is not going to be capable of ministering to my spiritual needs, even though he may be charged to do so by his well-intentioned commitment to the chaplain corps mission statement. Even in geographical areas more or less friendly to mainline Christianity, such as in Europe, South or Central America, or some places in Asia, such as South Korea that has a large Christian population (about 13.9 million, Wikipedia), should soldiers wish to attend religious services off base they are most likely held in a different language, even if soldiers can find necessary transportation. The fallback position then is just to sleep in—always an attractive alternative after a twenty-four-hour duty shift—or attend the base chapel where membership is irrelevant. Often it is up to the local commander to exercise some creativity. Because living a practical apologetic is as important in the military as in our civilian callings, let me tell two stories about such possibilities. Wherever we find ourselves, we can be challenged to live out our Christian world view and may have to find creative alternatives to the circumstances in which we find ourselves.

In one leadership assignment I had as the commander of a nuclear missile site in Balesfeld, Germany, a very isolated part of the Schnee Eifel near the Belgian border, there were no English-speaking churches anywhere for our soldiers to attend. I was the first commanding officer ever based there who spoke German, so ties with the local community were also almost non-existent when I arrived. Even if there had been English-speaking churches available, my 150 plus soldiers were mostly young enlisted soldiers with no personal transportation and were, because of our 24/7 tactical mission, confined to the base unless they could earn an occasional pass to walk the eight kilometers to the local village—usually to spend a few hours sampling too much of the local *Bitburger Pils* brew or cavorting with locals at Alphie's *gasthaus*. All of them were required to live in barracks on site and be available around the clock for possible engagements thwarting air attacks from Warsaw Pact countries.

Our air defense battery rested on three separate geographical sites (missile launch area, fire control area, and administrative housing area). Each of the sites was surrounded by two barriers of ten-foot high cyclone fences topped with razor wire with guard towers every 25 meters staffed with heavily armed soldiers twenty-four hours a day and guard dogs with handlers constantly patrolling between the fences. During the late 1960's we were frequently probed at night by communist agents, and on one occasion our security sergeant was kidnapped for several days by East German agents for interrogation. The threat was real in those days even in "West" Germany. Of necessity, we were almost entirely self-sufficient; one needed a high security clearance just to enter our heavily guarded compound.

As the battery commander, I was not only the tactical commander for our air defense mission but also the base commander and by default basically the mayor of a small city with police force, guard dogs, restaurant (mess hall), hotel (several barracks), bars (enlisted men's and officers clubs), a casino (a room full of slot machines for soldiers who were off duty), as well as all the weapons, high explosive and nuclear missiles, radars, and associated classified hardware that came with our mission of defending West German and Belgian air space against possible air or ground attacks. All these amenities were required to be on site because of the prevailing Status of Forces Agreement with the German government. Because our soldiers were confined to the site for their entire eighteen-twenty-four-month tours of duty, the army tried to make sure the soldiers had all their physical needs met, without leaving the site.

What was not provided for was their spiritual needs. There was no chapel on our small base or chaplain assigned for just 150 soldiers. Because we were an isolated site with the nearest other American facility over 60 kilometers away, every month of so one of the base chaplains from Spangdahlem Air Force Base, where our army battalion headquarters was located, might try to drive out to provide religious services, usually with little advanced warning; so rarely did anyone show up for the meetings, even if they had the inclination, and the visiting chaplain just drank stale coffee and ate sweet rolls for an hour in the mess hall. Aside from that there was no hint of spirituality in the vicinity.

As the senior officer assigned as the base commander, I was able to live in government housing off base in a small community called Prum, Germany, about twenty klicks (kilometers) from my missile site. If I were not personally on duty on site every other Sunday, if I so desired, I could drive to a post chapel located on Spangdalem Air Force Base (AFB), Bitburg AFB, or Baumholder Army Post (all located within about 40 klicks from Prum), or, since I spoke German, could opt to attend a local German church—always Lutheran in the Schnee-Eifel area, where women and men still sat on opposite sides of the congregation—not my cup of tea. My soldiers, however, could not attend such services even if they so desired. They were confined to the site. I decided to try to change things, so I met individually with the various chaplains on Spangdalem Air Force Base and Bitburg Air Force Base until I found one whose theology, in my opinion, was consistent with sound biblical beliefs. After interviewing a few of them, I found Jerry.

Jerry was an army major, and a *Bible*-believing chaplain from Alabama who had a genuine passion for Christ. I invited him to come to our site every weekend to hold chapel services in the casino. As he explained it, he had not had such a request before, but he would try to work out the details. The other four artillery units in our battalion (about 800 soldiers) spread out over south western Germany, had no such services either. The times would have to vary because Jerry had other duties in other geographical locations as well, but we pledged with one another to make sure he made it to our Balesfeld site some time every Saturday evening or Sunday morning. As a rule, after our base casino and beer hall would close down at 4 am (staying open late in order to accommodate entertainment for the off-hour tactical and guard shifts) each Saturday evening or very early Sunday morning, my on-site duty officer or our First Sergeant would cover the liquor supply on the bar and all the slot machines with clean sheets and make sure there were several folding chairs brought in. Jerry would arrive a few hours later with *Bible* in hand and hold services. What began as a half dozen or so soldiers coming out of curiosity morphed into over fifty faithful attendees in a few weeks in our makeshift chapel. How I wish I had photos today of my soldiers standing with locked arms singing hymns surrounded by dozens of white sheet-covered one-armed bandits as Jerry preached his fire and brimstone sermons.

That was our local church in Balesfeld, Germany. No small groups, no stained-glass windows, no candles burning, no board of elders or deacons, no incense being lit, and no crosses hanging anywhere. Indeed, there were no hymnals or *Bibles* anywhere, just the perpetually lingering smell of the previous night's spilled beer. Most significantly there was no offering plate passed and no church membership. God may have kept roll; we certainly did not. That is too often the model within the military, regardless of geographical location, so Christians in the military tend to lose focus of the power and the support of the local church, which is admittedly the *New Testament* model, just not always feasible. Our world view has to be expressed in other less obvious ways.

Like the Apostle Paul, Jerry would go wherever he was called and preach to anyone who showed up. After a year of commanding that unit, I was reassigned about 60 kilometers away to a unit in Butzweiler, Germany overlooking the Mosel River, to "fix" another large isolated missile site whose commander had just been relieved of his duties owing to the Group Commander's lack of confidence in his leadership abilities for all kinds of legal offenses and violations of moral turpitude. Within a month, I invited Jerry to come with me and he was soon holding weekly services there as well. The local church is where you make it—membership not required. **Our work and position should reflect our confidence in our world view. That is living a practical apologetic without having to preach**, which in this instance, my command position of authority would have prevented.

Let me relate one more admittedly parochial story about church in the military, because it too was spurred on by my enlarging Christian world view. After a year commanding the Butzweiler missile site overlooking the Mosel River, I was transferred to my third command assignment in Kaiserslautern, Germany to take command of a Headquarters Company of about 500 soldiers in the 94th Artillery Group's Kleber Kaserne. Many of the young soldiers assigned to that unit were "short," meaning they would be leaving Germany in just a couple months and most, along with me, would be reassigned to combat units in Vietnam or other unfriendly hot spots. I also had sixteen young lieutenants and captains who were under my authority, in my chain of command, who would also, within less than six months be transferred from NATO to combat assignments in Vietnam or other hot spots in Southeast Asia and would most likely be leading their own soldiers into combat for the first time. I did something that I could most likely not get away with these days, in our hyper vigilant, overly litigious ACLU tainted culture, but I felt was ethically imperative then. Fortunately Facebook, U-Tube, I-phones with cameras, and Twitter were not available, at the time.

I told my officers that regardless of their personal religious beliefs or lack thereof, I didn't want them attending local churches off base—not a problem at the time because none of them did—or taking any more Sunday mornings off. I informed them that Sunday just became a duty day dedicated to leadership development while they were assigned to my command, and I had their assignments. I informed them that I would be on the front row of the post chapel each Sunday at 10 am and I expected my junior officers to join me there for their weekly leadership training class.

I explained to them that whether they themselves realized it or not that their very physical presence in chapel would be crucial someday for the example it set for their soldiers to have seen them there and to know that when they were sent into combat within just a few months, that they were not going alone. They would be led by officers who, apparently by their physical attendance in Chapel, believed in and relied on something and someone far greater than themselves for victory. My First Sergeant (the senior NCO in any unit), although a dedicated Mason was not a believer, but a good leader and a loyal partner in supporting my policies. He apparently let it be known to all of his sergeants that the "Old Man" (the title given to the senior officer in every command, ie, me at the age of 24) and his officers would be in chapel each week for "leadership development" and they should probably consider joining us; subtle pressure to be sure, but very effective. Within two weeks, much to the bewilderment of the post chaplain, half the chapel attendees each Sunday morning were from Headquarters and Headquarters Company, 94th Artillery Group. In addition to being a witness to a Christian world view, it was a confidence builder for our soldiers. That, in my mind, was living a practical apologetic by demonstrating leadership.

By now you should recognize this kind of model as a non-Naturalistic one. A few of my officers disagreed with my methods, as no doubt some of you probably do as well—I know the ACLU would—but they all committed to being there. After all, when you soar like an eagle you should expect to attract a hunter or two (1 Peter 5:8).

I had given them my Vision of leader responsibilities and had begun to build our leadership team around certain demonstrated Core Values. As I admitted, I most likely couldn't get away with such a behavior today, nor would I try to, as I'd probably be lit up on Facebook or find some MSNBC or CNN reporter taking notes in the second row. But desperate times call for exceptional measures. Whether they personally believed what they heard or not, I wanted my officers to set the example for their soldiers. Our world view should be demonstrated in our work. **Chewing the wafer is sometimes very risky**. I am happy to say that a few of them who made it back from Southeast Asia alive, as well as my First Sergeant, still stay in touch with me a few decades later.

Where I got this idea, I am sure, is from my time as a cadet at West Point, where we were always watching respected senior officers to see what various leadership models we could identify in order to know which behaviors to ignore and which ones might be admirable to attempt to emulate some day. In the Cadet Chapel, the front pew on the right was traditionally reserved in each Sunday morning service for the Superintendent of the Academy (a lieutenant general—three stars on each shoulder) and the Commandant of Cadets and the Dean of Students (each a brigadier general—one star). Every Sunday morning, as we were marched into the chapel, I could look to the front of the chapel and see two, three, four, or six shiny stars sitting there as well. I have no idea about the personal beliefs of most of these generals, except for a couple with whom I have personally served over the years, but I can affirm that week in and week out, they provided a model of behavior that shouted to all of us cadets—"leaders in training"—that those leading the Academy were willing to model behaviors that affirmed publicly that they acknowledged a power far greater than themselves. Such a model of leadership, regardless of the personal motivation involved, instills confidence in those watching. As General Colin Powell, has stated so well in his *Biography*,

> The most important thing I have learned is that soldiers watch what their leaders do. You can give them classes and lecture them forever, but it is your personal example they will follow.

From a Christian perspective, that is living a Christian apologetic. As the Apostle Paul advises, "Join together in following my example, brothers and sisters, and just as you have us as a model, keep your eyes on those who live as we do" (KJV, Philippians 3:17). Twenty-six years after graduation from West Point, when Cheryl and I were married in that same Cadet Chapel, I stood by the altar rail waiting for her to walk down the long aisle surrounded by beautiful stained glass windows all expressing examples of the grandeur of God and scriptures chosen by classes before mine as well as battle flags from every war hanging from the rafters. As I waited for Pachelbel's *Canon in D* to begin, I could glance at the wooden bar in front of the first pew where I stood and see the brass name plates for General Douglass MacArthur, General William Westmoreland, General Maxwell Taylor, General Sid Berry, General Andrew Goodpaster, and many other famous generals who had sat there every Sunday morning as Commandants, Deans, and Superintendents, leading the Academy in both peace and war, and leading the Corps of Cadets, proudly modeling symbolically for us their fundamental association with a Christian world view.

We can sometimes have doubts about God's presence during difficult times; I know I have, but our Christian world view can always affirm to us and to those with whom we work, that God is there, and he will not be silenced. One of my favorite *Old Testament* passages through the years has always been II Kings 6:15-17 (KJV).

Now when the attendant of the man of God had risen early and gone out, behold, an army with horses and chariots was circling the city. And his servant said to him, "Alas, my master! What shall we do?" So he answered, "Do not fear, for **those who are with us are more than those who are with them**." Then Elisha prayed and said, "O LORD, I pray, open his eyes that he may see." And the LORD opened the servant's eyes and he saw; and behold, the mountain was full of horses and chariots of fire all around Elisha.

Those chariots have accompanied me to 39 countries. **As we live our lives, we can count on the fact that He who is with us is always far greater than anyone who is with them.** Resting on that confidence, our obligation is simply to live in accordance with scripture and do the right thing (*Fac recte et nil time*—Do Right, Fear Nothing)—that's the Christian world view. The rest is in God's hands (1 John 2:29 KJV). Nowhere is this obligation more important than in our day jobs.

Faith is daring the soul to go beyond what the eyes can see. "Now faith is the substance of things hoped for, the evidence of things not seen" (NKJV, Heb 11:1).

Will there be criticism and possible consequences for such a position? As a rather infamous former Governor of Alaska and VP candidate once said, "You betcha!"

As a former member of the 1st SOG in Southeast Asia puts it in his on-line webcasts, "If you are going to lead, you should expect to be hit." For him, as a Green Beret, that meant wearing a Purple Heart. For others, it means verbal and written attacks, maybe personal criticism, and occasionally getting fired for their beliefs.

CHAPTER XXII

Thessalonican Concerns

Let's get a little more controversial. This chapter alone will prevent some "Christian" book publishers from adopting this manuscript. I warned you that we would have our differences. Having the same Christian world view does not guarantee that we will always have interpreted scripture the same way, just that we wind up at the same place on the basis of the same faith for all eternity.

Chief of the concerns that the Apostle Paul tried to assuage when writing to his dear friends in this new local church was their question regarding the status of the dead—those who had died acknowledging Jesus as the Messiah and their Redeemer. Paul, who had launched many of their small assemblies of believers and initially grounded them in their faith, wanted to ensure that they understood that those believers who had already died would not be left behind when the Lord returned, but would be included in the numbers who would meet the Lord "in the air" with other believers during what even Paul assumed would be Jesus's immanent return. That occurrence has become known in fundamentalist circles as the Rapture of the church (admittedly, a term never used in scripture). Indeed, Paul confirmed for his friends that the dead would not only join those believers who were still alive at his coming but would precede them. While the Thessalonians had only the *Torah, Old Testament* prophets, a few months of Paul's personal ministry, and a few circulating epistles to use to try to understand what would happen in the future, we are blessed with having the entire *Bible*. Yet, despite those additional insights, and almost 2,000 years of "scholarly" exegesis, confusion regarding the events of the end times persists in the local church. For that reason, except in fundamentalist circles, the topic is usually just ignored from the pulpit.

I never expect to hear sermons on eschatological topics when attending Lutheran, Episcopal, Methodist, or most Presbyterian churches or during homilies in Catholic masses, so I am never disappointed. Sadly though, there seems to be increasing reticence in Baptist, and *Bible* churches, and too many non-denominational evangelical fellowships, particularly mega churches from a more Reformed background, to address the same topic. Sure, there may be a general unspoken belief that Jesus will return some day, but to get all worked up about the time and the manner doesn't make sense to church leadership, too often concerned with simply growing the church or launching new ones in their communities. Personal salvation of course, giving our lives to Christ and growing in our faith, sure, impacting our world, of course, sacrificial giving, oh most definitely! But teaching when and how Jesus will return for his bride, that's a hot potato, easily dropped. The split between Reformed and non-Reformed biblical perspectives on the Lord's second advent has ruptured many local assemblies and denominations.

Too many local assemblies are fearful of even mentioning the coming events of the end times and their possible sequence laid out in Daniel, Thessalonians, Jeremiah, Micah, and Revelation lest they insult or disenfranchise some members who may disagree with their biblical order of events. Such topics are deemed potentially too divisive, so they are just not mentioned from the pulpit. That is a problem. **We can opine about diversity in the local church till we are blue in the face, but all that usually boils down to is racial preferences in music, prayer, and preaching styles and a few different color faces in the pews.** Meanwhile the church leadership sidelines a topic that may well demand a true appreciation of believer diversity. What happens if, when, and how Jesus returns is far more important than race, gender, or diversity of worship styles. His second advent will impact all of us regardless of our skin color, accent, gender, or preferred pronoun.

Particularly if we want to be able to engage colleagues and students with an apologetic approach, we need to be very clear about what we believe regarding the events of the end times. If Christ may return unannounced tomorrow before lunch (the position of those who believe in the sudden Rapture of the Church), believers should have a greater sense of urgency when it comes to reaching the unsaved. If the church is going to be present and purged and undergo suffering and turmoil for at least seven more years (Daniel's seventieth week for those who study prophecy), then believers have some time to try to reach the three billion unsaved that are growing in numbers daily (60,000 / day according to Operation Mobilization). Just purchase a good generator, get your Concealed Carry permit, load up on ammo, avoid computer chip implants and forehead tattoos, and stock survivor food, and we'll get through this together. I know, that is a bit glib, and no one writes like this, but let's get real; these are just some of the practical consequences of such a viewpoint. Such differences can divide a congregation.

Sadly, to avoid such difficult conversations, many pastors simply avoid the topic altogether as they believe that such differences will become divisive for the membership. Consequently the membership remains unschooled in this very important topic. Often such reluctance to engage the topic is because local church leaders themselves span both pre- and post-trib believers, and hold both Reformed and un-Reformed doctrinal positions regarding the second coming and the millennial reign of Christ, usually depending on the seminary they attended. I have sat in on pastor, elder, and deacon selection conversations in churches and the topic is rarely broached. As too many seminaries and *Bible* schools teach these days, concentrate on just the "main" theological doctrines and do not be side-tracked by extraneous issues that can divide a fellowship. Sound advice to be sure. It is what is "main" or "extraneous" in the minds of those teaching in seminaries and in the minds of elders that concerns me.

When we believers align ourselves in fellowship with a local church, we are expected to abide under the leadership of the elders and be subject to the discipline of the church. That is a biblical principle (Hebrews 13:17). But there is a not so fine line between assenting to the leadership of the elders or board of a church and standing for a biblical truth we believe they are shirking. Since we are of one body, members of the body of Christ have an obligation to alert the head when it is not doing its job. When the differences are too extreme, it is time to leave and seek out a fellowship more in line with biblical principles as we perceive them.

Without getting down into the weeds, right away, my experience is that one of the many questions that believers hear from the lost, particularly when they are actively searching is, **"So when is this Jesus of yours coming back?"** This has been the question that has opened the door for "my story" any number of times. What is your answer to that question? What is your church's answer? Can you give me a tentative agenda? Maybe tomorrow? Maybe tomorrow plus seven years? Maybe tomorrow plus 1,000 years? Nobody knows. **Just saying, "someday," won't cut it. It sounds like a cop out—because it is.** And such apathy regarding the topic probably frustrates the Holy Spirit who spent so much time infusing scripture with evidence of the Lord's return that you are ignoring. If you are personally not getting that question, that can also be a problem with your walk and practical apologetic as you live your Christian world view. You haven't caused anyone to care enough to ask.

Last year, in one of the two weekly *Bible* studies I was in, we focused on the Apostle Paul's letters to his friends in Thessalonica. As you will know from your study of those letters, the local assemblies, as did Paul himself, believed that Jesus was going to return at any minute. Since some of the local assembly had died since hearing his message in person, Paul's friends were worried about the status of the dead. Would these recent converts be left behind when Jesus returned? Who would rise and when? What happens to those already in the grave? In one meeting, raising a question posed in the study guide we were using, the leader asked our group, "So, in regard to Jesus' return, how many of you would say that you,

1. Are nervous and antsy
2. Are irritated by some people's obsession with the topic
3. Are excited and motivated to live for Christ
4. Come away with more questions than answers when thinking about the topic
5. Are motivated to study the *Bible* more diligently,
6. Are generally bored by the topic
7. Or 'other'—I guess this category is like the 'no opinion' response for most political surveys these days."

Of the nine persons present, all of whom are professing Christians who in some cases have studied the scriptures for years, one said he never really thought about it, three said they were irritated by the way in which some people get all worked up about the topic and see it as a distraction, one said he would find out the answer when he got to heaven, and two admitted to being totally disinterested: "I'm saved, so what will happen will happen. *Que sera, sera.* I can't see the need to get all worked up by how events turn out," was the expressed sentiment. There was even general dismissal of the whole "Left Behind" series of novels by LaHaye and Jenkins—clearly popular fiction—several years ago, as just being silly and fear mongering. Only one other person present—the *Bible* study leader—agreed with me when I said that I am personally excited by what will take place and how the events of the end times will unfold, and personally pray every day that today will be the day that I will hear Jesus's shout, calling us to meet him "in the air": "Even so, come quickly Lord Jesus." When I asked the group, how would you live differently today or whom would you go to speak immediately to share your belief in the Gospel, if you KNEW Jesus could return by close of business or sunset, there was general silence around the table. That is also a problem, because my *Bible* says he just might.

Many "Christian" publishing houses, probably to ensure they do not drive away potential book purchasers, even make it clear that they will not publish books about end times events. The topic is just too divisive. That's their choice to be sure, but it is also a problem. Terms like tribulation, rapture, Great White Throne, Millennial Age, Judgment Seat of Christ, and other theological "jargon" like justification, sanctification, predestination, and regeneration can seem too much like "seminary cant" and unrelated to contemporary spiritual reality. Too many evangelical pastors totally ignore such terms so as not to disaffect Millennials and others the church depends upon for support. Often by sheer neglect, local church members are subtly encouraged to relegate such topics to smaller *Bible* studies or perhaps to explore them in small groups outside of Sunday morning services, if at all. Even in such smaller groups, it is rare that such studies tackle the books of Revelation, Thessalonians, Micah, or Daniel for fear of causing disunity. **Church unity and harmony within the local church, too often takes precedence over a passion for truth**. Having worked with some professional church consultants in the USA, I know that such is the model taught by several of them hired to assist in church growth and church planting. For those of you wishing to live a practical apologetic, clarity in knowledge about such topics is imperative. We can certainly disagree about this topic, but you should at least know why and be able to justify your view based on a sound interpretation of scripture.

Even very sound *Bible* scholars like John MacArthur, whose study of Thessalonians we used as a guide in another of our groups, warns in his study of Daniel, that "tragically, some people get so caught up in the study of eschatology that they neglect the basic principles of spiritual growth and evangelism that the second coming is designed to motivate." That observation is no doubt true, but it is a sorry excuse for ignoring the topic. This should not be an either-or conversation. Many pastors and *Bible* teachers are so worried about a handful of reckless TV evangelists who thump this topic every week on their shows and hawk copies of their most recent books and CD's helping viewers to understand world events in the context of scripture (for a tax deductible "contribution" of just $ 89.50, of course) that they shy away from any such discussion. That is a problem.

Worse yet, some evangelists and whole sects have routinely misinterpreted events even to the point of foolishly setting or implying dates for end times events, something the scriptures clearly warns us not to do. Others unabashedly name contemporary political and religious leaders and imply their relationships with figures in Revelation. They have been wrong multiple times in the past and will be wrong again. The consequence is that many Christians have just given up trying to understand the sequence of events surrounding our Lord's return. Such study often smacks of religious fanaticism and the kind of old-style fundamentalism that embarrasses too many Gen-Next, Millennials, Gen-X's, and Gen-Y's who make up the base (both financial and attendance) for many mega churches.

We do not have to be *Bible* scholars or even passing fans of older popular writers like Hal Linsey, John Hagee, Jack van Impe, John Piper, John MacArthur (5 very different eschatological viewpoints, by the way, but all ridiculed by some *Bible* schools as "fundagelicals"), and others who write and preach about end times—many of whom can be routinely wrong about such events—to try to understand the "times and seasons," of the end times (KJV, Daniel 2:21; Acts 1:7). Unfortunately, trying to understand the events surrounding the end times, demands a careful study of some of the most cryptic scriptures: the books of Daniel, Ezekiel, Joel, Thessalonians, Jeremiah, Revelation, Micah, and others—study that frustrates too many casual Sunday morning believers and makes it difficult to cover in a thirty-five-minute sermon or fifteen minute homily. Terms like Rapture, Day of Christ, Believers Judgment—essentially a rewards ceremony—Day of the Lord, Millennium, Great White Throne Judgment, and many others scare off the casual Sunday morning Christian.

I for one, however, as I have tried to chew the wafer—exemplify a Christian ethic—in the military, at work, in the private sector, while consulting and coaching, and just trying to make sense of the daily news, can't think of a more important topic about which a Christian should become more passionate. The play clock is running, and as I view world events, we may be close to sudden death overtime. In my experience, it is one topic that is always in play when one engages others with an apologetic approach to faith.

Maybe God will direct Jesus to return for his Bride after Superbowl CLIV in 2173, or maybe sooner on the drive home from work this afternoon before you finish reading this chapter in Starbucks. No one knows, apparently not even the Lord, Himself: "But concerning that day and hour no one knows, not even the angels of heaven, nor the Son, but the Father only (NIV, Matthew 24:36). See also, Acts 1: 7. He waits for the Father to tell him that the time has come. Whenever it occurs, I, for one, can't wait. So, without setting any dates, let's explore what the scriptures tell us about the "times and seasons." I know that hundreds of volumes have been written on this subject by "scholars" from every persuasion; although, regrettably, not a one is in the bookstore at our church, so think of this brief summary as a poor man's *Cliff Notes* to eschatology. Even worse, just Bing or Google "eschatology" or some related term and get ready for a dizzying display of biblical ignorance and speculation. Feel free to check me out and use scriptures to show me where I am wrong. **If we are going to "chew the wafer" and be ready at all times to give a reason for the hope that is within us (KJV, 1 Peter 3:15), this topic is more than just relevant; it is seminal**.

The events surrounding the end times are too often collectively referred to as the Second Coming. That is a far too generic term encapsulating several events. The first coming, of course, was Jesus' coming to earth and living for about thirty-three years until he died on the cross and ascended into heaven (KJV, Acts1: 8-11). But the Second Coming or the Second Advent (terms often used interchangeably) have become catch all phrases with little specificity attached to them, even within the evangelical community—they are just thrown about glibly and, therefore, invoke no sense of immediacy or at worst, ridicule. While a nice generic description, this concept is far too general and subsumes many other events with a specific intended flow. The Second Advent is too often considered metaphorical and not actual. While the specific flow of events rightly ought not to divide our fellowships, it behooves each of us to be clear about our understanding as part of our practical apologetic, while trying to live out a Christian world view.

Sadly, many Muslims I work with are far clearer about their view of eschatology found in the *Qur'an* as well as the multiple hadith written over the centuries, than are Christians. It is a genuine point of attraction for many new converts to Islam. Even though the *Shia* and *Sunni* sects differ somewhat on their individual eschatological frameworks, the bulk of educated Muslims know what they believe. That is a problem. It is a problem for lazy individual Christians, and it is a problem for local church leadership—too many pastors, priests, ministers, and elders—who have failed to teach the truth from the pulpit. In that regard, the prophet Ezekiel provides a warning for all of us, but in particular to those charged with shepherding their flocks:

> But if the watchman sees the sword coming, and does not
> blow the trumpet, so that the people are not warned, and
> the sword comes, and takes any one of them, that person
> is taken away in his iniquity, but his blood I will require
> at the watchman's hand. (ESV, Ezekiel 33:6)

At the risk of alienating some more of you—but if you really value diversity in the body of Christ, you will hang in with me for a bit longer—the following is how my study of scripture leads me personally to describe that flow of events. While we are warned about setting dates, we are encouraged to know the times and the seasons. So, let's talk large concepts first. I come from an unashamedly un-Reformed background, believing in the immanency of the return of Christ and its importance to the believer's life, world view, and service. While I have attended churches with various eschatological approaches over the years, I have never found a biblically based rational argument to make me waver in that approach. If you disagree, feel free to skip over the rest of this chapter where I get more specific and move on. We can stay friends.

Within that framework, the Second Coming often includes what is referred to by some as the Rapture of the Church—an eschatological concept primarily within North American evangelicalism first appearing during the eighteenth century and later systematized by the Anglo-Irish *Bible* scholar John Darby in the nineteenth century—during which those who have died in Christ (in the grave and those still living believers) will all suddenly—without warning—be raised with Christ and taken to Heaven. This event, as I read scripture, is the import of 1 Thessalonians 4:16-18 and Luke 17: 34-37. According to scripture, those believers who have died have had their souls already in Paradise in fellowship with the Lord (KJV, Luke 24:43), but at the Rapture—a sudden snatching away—when everything seems well on the earth (KJV, 1 Thessalonians 5:3), these souls will be joined with their changed bodies and be reunited with the Lord "in the air." That is the point I believe the Apostle Paul reaffirms for his friends in Thessalonica. Note that, according to scripture, Jesus does not touch earth at this point; that event, by my reading of scripture, is reserved for another seven years. Such seemingly small details are critical to our understanding the flow of events. **If such details were not important, God would not have included them.** Our Redeemer meets believers from all of time, dead and alive, "in the air" (KJV, 1 Thessalonians 4:16-17).

The next event on God's day planner is variously described as a time of great troubles, normally referred to as the seven-year Tribulation period (the Book of Daniel's 70th week), usually broken in to two, 3 ½ year segments of escalating troubles and persecution of new Christians and all Jews (KJV, Daniel 12:1-2). This seven-year period is reserved for the refinement of the nation of Israel and the salvation of additional Gentile believers. The witnesses to the faith during this time are primarily the 144,000 evangelists (Revelation chapter 14) culled out from the 12 tribes of Israel who refuse the Mark of the Beast and risk martyrdom for their newfound belief.

"Reformed" theologians generally see the promises made to Israel transferred to the Church. I do not, nor, by recent polls, do 67% of evangelical theologians. When the Book of Revelation speaks of the seven Trumpets (chapter 16) and the seven Vials (chapter 8) being poured out, these will all occur during this period. This horrible tribulation and persecution will be permitted because, by my un-reformed reading of scripture, the Body of Christ—the Church—will have been removed at the Rapture, so there is no further need for the restraining ministry of the Holy Spirit to hold it in check. Only with the removal of this restraining force, can evil run rampant.

The removal of that aspect of the Holy Spirit's ministry is reminiscent of the account in the Book of Ezekiel (chapter 10) where we learn of the temple's being protected, as long as Yahweh dwelt inside it. Once Yahweh removes himself to the hill outside Jerusalem, the temple is destroyed. This historical event foreshadows the end times when the restraining ministry of the the Holy Spirit will also have been removed for the entire seven years of tribulation. Note that the Holy Spirit, Himself, has not been removed (after all, God is still present and the Holy Spirt is part of the triune Godhead), because His presence is necessary for the salvation of the nation of Israel during this time of momentous Jewish revival. Those from a reformed tradition believe this is mostly metaphorical. I won't be here to tell them they were incorrect, but praying they can avoid receiving the mark of the Beast.

There are three variations of the sequence of these events. Scholars who believe that Jesus will return unannounced (The commonly called Rapture of the church) before the time of Tribulation are referred to as Pre-Trib (overwhelmingly, the vast majority of evangelicals and other fundamentalists). Those who see Jesus returning after 3 ½ years of troubles are called Mid-Trib (by far the fewest number of scholars, about 3-5 %). Those who believe that the Lord will return only after the Church has been thoroughly purged and refined by fire, violence, and death for not receiving the Mark of the Beast during the seven years, are referred to as Post-Trib (about 5-8% of *Bible* scholars—often the most vocal, particularly on late Sunday night cable TV, and the majority of "Reformed" pastors and theologians like John Piper). Pay heed to which contemporary authors your pastors cite in their sermons and you will get a glimpse into their unspoken eschatology. Whatever one believes regarding these events, one must be prepared as part of living their world view to speak with clarity regarding the sequence of events when pressed by non-believers.

While this period of "troubles" (The Tribulation period) caused by the Beast (The Anti-Christ) and the False Prophet takes place on earth (having a free rein because the restraining power of the Holy Spirit will have been removed), in Heaven there are exciting events taking place as well. There will be a war in Heaven, and Satan (The Dragon) will be thrown out once and for all (Rev. 12: 7-12). He has of course had access to the Throne of God through the ages in order to accuse believers (Rev 12:10). This detail alone often surprises the casual Sunday morning Christian. During this period, there will also be the Judgment of Believers at the Judgment Seat of Christ, where all believers will be "judged" for their works. Don't be confused by the language. This is when we believers get "rewarded" for trusting in Jesus' sacrifice and the quality of stories we have lived. **Think of it as a believer's Tabard Inn at the end of our pilgrimage. During this time, at least five kinds of crowns will be awarded (Life, Incorruptible, Righteousness, Glory, and Exaltation)** for the various works described in the Book of Revelation. Believers, realizing they have personally earned nothing by their own merit, will humbly cast these crowns at the feet of Christ who has secured their salvation (KJV, Revelation 4:10-11). This period will culminate in the Battle of Armageddon resulting in the Second Coming—The Day of the Lord—where Jesus returns to earth with his Bride, the raptured Church.

Put those thoughts on hold. The next mysterious term that enters into the conversation is the Millennial reign of Christ, described in the book of Revelation as a thousand-year reign of Christ and believers on a renewed earth, where Israel is the Head of the Nations (KJV, Deuteronomy 28:13) and Jesus sits on the Throne of David in Jerusalem (see also the Book of Micah). There are some *Bible* scholars who are Pre-Millennial, meaning that any of the three above views of the Second Coming take place before the beginning of the literal 1000-year period (by far the overwhelming number of evangelical believers), those who are A-Millennialists—those who do not believe the event will take place at all and that such a period of God's earthly rule is more figurative than literal, and Post-Millennialists who believe that Christ's second coming will occur only after a "Golden Age" during which Christian values and ethics will flourish on earth.

For some Post and A-Millennialists, the Church is in that "Golden Age" now. These beliefs increasingly in the evangelical church—particularly non-denominational mega churches—are presented as the Reformed positions, where at the end of this age—whenever that occurs—there will be a one-time coming of Christ who will then pronounce judgment on the non-believers. Because we can't prepare for this event, many naïve local churches simply ignore it. It will happen when it happens. Nothing to see here…just move along. I guess the Holy Spirit was wrong to bring it up.

All those events surrounding what other evangelicals see as the Rapture, a Day of Christ, or a Day of the Lord are seen as "spiritual" in nature, not chronological and literal, and will be fulfilled in various metaphorical ways during the current Church Age. Please pardon my sardonic skepticism, but if we are currently living within a Golden Age of Christian ethics and values, I am very disappointed in God. I expect much more out of holy and sovereign God than what I see around me today. Just check out the weekend murder rate in Chicago, Baltimore, or Indianapolis, the homeless and rat-infested streets of San Francisco, Austin, and Los Angeles, the slaughter of millions of innocents in the womb every year, the spread of COVID-19, our North American opiate epidemic, and the worldwide assault on Christians and the Christian world view everywhere—no Golden Age in Yemen, Syria, Somalia, Pakistan, China, or thirty other countries I could list, had I space to do so. Such a position, by my understanding, is as illogical and unscriptural as the Neo-Orthodox position that says that Jesus probably rose from the dead spiritually but not physically. In other words, he probably did, but if you had been there at Golgotha you would not have seen a thing.

As an unabashed Pre-millennial, Pre-Trib believer, the following is how I interpret the times and the seasons, the order of events, whenever they begin. These are the events I hope to honor in living a Christian world view.

1. From the past up through the current age: All those believers who have died over the ages have had their conscious souls go directly to Paradise (Heaven) or Hades (Hell) depending on their status as believers or non-believers, while their bodies remained behind on earth, in the grave, lost at sea, or, for some, in a decorative urn on Aunt Ethyl's fireplace mantle (KJV, Luke 23: 43; Luke 16:19-31).
2. Jesus is presently acting as our advocate at the right hand of the Father (KJV, Ephesians 1: 20-23) and preparing Heaven for believers (KJV, John 14:1-3).

3. The Rapture of the church (The Day of Christ). The Lord returns with a shout, the voice of the Archangel sounds (KJV, 1 Thes. 4:16). The Trumpet of God sounds, and the dead in Christ will rise first, followed by all those believers who are currently alive (KJV, 1 Thes. 4:13-14, Mark 13:37, Matthew 24: 30-31).

4. Those Christians still alive will rise next to join the deceased (those in the grave) all with renewed bodies, in the air. Beam me up, Scotty!

5. The Believers' Judgment in Heaven (KJV, 2 Corinthians 5:10). This is the rewards ceremony mentioned earlier. **Think of this event as analogous to the Tabard Inn celebration at the end of Chaucer's pilgrimage.** Be prepared to have your story judged. By the way, God is a tough critic, but his criteria are clear.

6. Beginning of the seven-year Tribulation period (Rev 8:6 ff and Rev 13). The Church has been removed (Raptured) and the restraining ministry of the Holy Spirit has been curtailed: Elvis has left the building (Ezekiel 10).

7. The nation of Israel (not the Church, because she is gone) will be refined over the seven years of torment, ending in the Battle of Armageddon (Rev 16-17). While the entire nation of Israel will be purged, refined, and saved during this period, some non-Jews will also be saved, and many will be martyred for their beliefs, refusing to accept the mark of the Beast. This is the period when the numbers 666 and 144,000 become so important.

8. The Day of the Lord (The Second Coming) when Christ's feet hit the earth for the first time since he was translated following his appearance to hundreds after the resurrection (Mark 13:24-27).

9. Satan will be bound and cast into the Bottomless Pit for 1,000 years.

10. The Lord returns to earth with all believers to set up a 1,000-year theocracy with Jesus on the Throne of David and prominent believers from all ages as rulers. During this time, Satan will be bound (Rev. 20: 1-3). At the end of this age, he will be loosed for a short time (Rev. 20: 7).

11. When Satan is loosed for a brief time, he will be utterly defeated by the Lord and thrown into the Lake of Fire (Rev 20:10).

12. Great White Throne Judgment (Rev 20:11) of all non-believers who will be judged by their works and found guilty and inadequate (Ephesians 2:8), because they have relied on their own efforts not on the vicarious sacrifice of Jesus on the cross. Imperfect human effort—works—just don't hack it for a holy God who demands a perfect sacrifice (his own perfect son) in order to be pardoned. Just FYI, if you see a Great White Throne in the future, you are in deep *kimchi*. In other words, Christians will not be there for this judgment.

13. A new heaven and new earth will be created to last for all eternity (Rev 21:1).

I'm sure some of you will find places to quibble with this flow of events; some may even feel insulted. Feel free to give me a call, but bring your *Bible,* and we will discuss why you are mistaken. Again, all of us who claim the name Christian can have different interpretations of what will occur when, but I charge the local church leadership to teach what they believe about these events and to be clear regarding what they believe the biblical position is regarding them. Not to do so is to shirk their responsibilities in Ezekiel 33. Don't be a biblical ostrich. Ignoring these events does not mean they will not take place.

Before you come ready to debate, however, since some of you from a Reformed theological position see the Rapture (described by John 14: 1-4, I Corinthians 15: 51-58, 1 Thess. 4 13-18), and the Second Coming of Christ (described in Zech. 14: 1-21, Matt. 24:29-31, Mk 13: 24-27, and Rev. 19) as essentially the same event, you will need to resolve some contextual linguistic differences in Scripture between how the Rapture (The Day of Christ) is described and how the Second Coming of Christ (The Day of the Lord) is described—again, from my perspective two very different events separated by seven years. As you will see in the following examples, mere word choice by the Holy Spirit dictates that they be different events. One of my previous careers as a professor of English demands that I pay attention to the language the Holy Spirit uses to describe each event.

1. **Rapture:** Believers from the grave and on earth meet Jesus in the air.
   2d Coming: Jesus returns to the earth—The Mount of Olives—and meets believers there. Clearly these are two different events.

2. **Rapture:** The Mount of Olives remains unchanged.
   2d Coming: The Mount of Olives is divided and forms a valley to the east of Jerusalem. Either the Holy spirit is confused, or these are two different times.

3. **Rapture:** Living Christians receive new "glorified" bodies.
   2d Coming: living believers keep their same bodies. I want the glorified one.

4. **Rapture:** Believers, those who are taken from the grave and those alive at the time go to Heaven.
   2d Coming: Glorified believers come down to earth from Heaven and meet those alive at the time on earth.

5. **Rapture:** The earth is left unjudged and those alive living in sin.
   2d Coming: the world is judged, and righteousness is established on earth.

6. **Rapture:** The Church is delivered from wrath.
   2d Coming: Believers who endure God's wrath are delivered.

7. **Rapture:** No signs precede it—the event is sudden and unexpected.
   2d Coming: Many specific signs outlined in the *New Testament* predict it.

8. **Rapture:** The event is revealed only in the *New Testament*.
   2d Coming: The event is discussed in both the *Old* and *New Testament*.

9. **Rapture:** Deals with only the saved—those who have been born again.
   2d Coming: Deals with both the saved and the unsaved.

10. **Rapture:** Satan remains free.
    2d Coming: Satan is bound and thrown into the abyss (Nathaniel Jones, Lion and Lamb Ministries).

The Church is a large tent, and true believers come from all three camps: pre-, mid-, and post-trib and can likewise have different views of the Millennium (both Reformed and un-Reformed). As I suggested earlier, **regardless of which view you hold in no way means believers cannot worship together, nor should we let it divide us.** You would not recognize the truth of that sentiment, however, if you listened to any of the vitriol expressed on social media by some of our brothers and sisters in Christ at conference speakers who dare to express one view or the other. Sadly the current day split between Reformed and un-Reformed theologians must excite Satan in his efforts to divide the church. Only one thing matters to my mind and it is nicely summed up by Russ Taff in his song, "We Will Stand."

But I, I don't care what label you may wear…
You're my brother, you're my sister
So take me by the hand
Together we will work until He comes
There's no foe that can defeat us
When we're walking side by side
As long as there is love
We will stand

That is what really matters. But if you want to be an effective practical apologist, you need to be clear about your personal understanding of the end times. It may well depend on how you live out your Christian world view. I have done my homework; I suggest you do the same. If they haven't done so yet (and, if that is the case, that could be a problem), someone will eventually press you on the "destiny of man," and how current events match your understanding of biblical predictions. Your ability to relate the two may well determine the extent to which unbelievers are willing to listen further to your story (see Chapter XXXI). Just saying your savior will return "someday," will not be enough for enquiring rational minds. It may sell from the pulpit on Sunday mornings, but fails miserably on campus, in the workplace, and on your battlefield.

If we were not meant to understand the sequence of events in the end times, the Holy Spirit has certainly wasted a lot of time crafting obscure references in both the *Old* and the *New Testament* to confuse us. But we know that "God is not the author of confusion" (NKJV, 1 Corinthians 14:13). So what is your conclusion? How does your story end? After all, we start with the end first. Airborne! That is why God promises a special blessing to those who study Revelation and then work backwards from that Vision to today. What a confidence builder it can be for the believer to know that the battle is already won! What is your Vision of eventual success and how will you get there?

Reconcile the textual differences above between how the Day of Christ is described and how the Day of the Lord is described, and we can begin to have an honest rational conversation. In the meantime, if you still believe in a post-trib view of the end times, where the Rapture does not exist and merely conflates with the Second Coming, while you are stocking up on water, food, prescription meds, and ammo—behaving like a genuine Naturalistic end times Prepper—I'll be preparing to meet my savior in the air at any time.

> And you shall know the truth, and the truth shall make
> you free (ESV, John 8:32).

CHAPTER XXIII

"Secular" Attacks on Credibility

Let's take this world view to work and see how our belief in a Christian world view can inform another aspect of our lives. My work as a consultant and executive coach is no doubt very different from much of what you do, but I hope that by showing how even the selection of some of the tools and methodologies we choose to use in our particular business should be reflective of our world view, can encourage you to consider the approaches you take in your life and work as well.

As one of the fundamental approaches to Christian apologetics, writers often talk about the various philosophical "proofs" of God's existence. Many of these arose from the work of well-known Catholic moral theologians such as St. Thomas Aquinas and St. Anselm. Traditionally such proofs are known as the Cosmological, Ontological, and Teleological proofs. Modern apologetics organizations such as the C. S. Lewis Institute and others will expand these proofs to include the Argument from Desire, the Argument from Morality, and the Argument from Prophecy. Any of these may be appropriate to reference from time to time, but none are immune to criticism; each attacks a nonbeliever's basic premises from a unique perspective. The Argument from Desire, which I prefer to call the Argument from Personality, demands a look inside each of us who have been "fearfully and wonderfully made" (KJV, Psalm 139). The very best of these I believe addresses why each of us has been created with a unique set of neurologically based preferences that help us perceive and judge in diverse ways that can support the kingdom and provide true diversity in the body of Christ and by extension in the local church.

As some of you will know, the basis for a lot of our consulting and training is the very popular personality survey known as the MBTI® (Myers-Briggs Type Indicator), the origin of those four letter combinations I have mentioned several times. It has been the core technology our company, Executive Strategies International, has used for over thirty years to help individuals, teams, and larger organizations understand human personality, personal preferences, genetic heritage, leadership styles, team building, mental fitness, and many other issues. We always begin with this assessment because we want to stress the individual cognitive differences that exist among the members of any organization but **primarily because the implications such differences have on one's world view are profound**. As I believe will become clear, such an approach also has a clear biblical foundation. As one of the primary users of this instrument, we at ESI are frequently called on to answer the challenges of critics regarding the instrument's credibility. I, myself, have written three books on that topic and included its technology in discussing leadership and culture in several others. Some psychologists short cut this technology with just two letters they refer to as Temperaments, but while such a shorthand can be helpful, I find their behavioralist approach far too limited and less congruent with a biblical understanding.

In particular, since I volunteer as the Interest Area Coordinator for Management and OD for the APTi, The Association of Psychological Type International, the professional association that serves as the organization monitoring and coordinating the ethical use of the instrument worldwide, I am frequently called on personally to respond to such attacks, usually from competitors, trainers, the academic community, and individual consultants who choose to use a different model to understand personality differences as well as skeptical and sometimes outright antagonistic university faculty with little actual professional experience using the assessment. We use it because of its psychometric credibility and the familiarity that most people have with the language; about two million people around the world take the assessment for the first time each year. Most importantly, we use it because **the fundamentals of psychological type are deeply rooted in a Christian world view.** That assertion alone may come as a surprise to many of you who have had to endure some Naturalistic approach in training on personality development over the years.

That credibility as well as its scientific or psychometric validity and reliability seem to find new detractors every year, as more and more assessments or websites alleging to provide insights into human motivation and personal preferences surface. Every trainer and HR professional seems to have a system they trust and become more invested in its credibility the more they associate with those of like minds—sound familiar? In most cases it is a simple matter of "follow the money." Rather than pay the copywrite holder of the MBTI, they would rather create their own assessment tool and encourage others to purchase it. Every major leadership development company seems driven to develop their own instruments and instead of advancing them on the basis of their scientific credibility find it far easier to try to trash what has been the standard in the field for 70 years—the MBTI®. In general, it is less an issue of validity but the more common concern of "follow the money." I have no need to disparage any of them; we are responsible in God's eyes only to do the right thing and use the right tools, and then leave it to Him.

If you are a Certified, or in the past what was known as a Qualified, user of this assessment, you have weathered such attacks for years; indeed, the mother-daughter team who were the authors of the instrument, Isabel Briggs Myers and her mother Katharine Cook Briggs, faced similar criticism from its development in the 1950's and 1960's. Such uninformed criticism frequently pops up on LinkedIn and other "professional" linkage sites. Often the criticism leveled is because of the lack of advanced academic degrees and scientific credentials of both mother and daughter who were at various times, novelists, teachers, or librarians, but never psychologists or scientists. Worst of all they were women breaking into a male-dominated profession. They also dared to add to the extant Jungian theory and add their personal touch with the Judging-Perceiving dimension when discussing psychological type. Anyone from outside a traditional bureaucracy who dares to challenge the status quo becomes an easy target. If you are not familiar with this technology, you can read up on it in my book, *Still True to Type* or Otto Kroeger's (a Lutheran minister and psychologist) book *Type Talk*. I am more concerned here with the worldview undergirding it than the specifics of the technology itself.

When the reputation and credentials of the authors are not being sullied, the attacks, often from university faculty, historians, and theologians, turn instead to attacking the theorist beneath the technology lurking behind the mother-daughter team that actually developed the instrument. His name is Jung: Carl Gustav Jung, the Swiss-German psychiatrist and psychoanalyst who founded Analytical Psychology in the 1930's. His name itself is enough to scare off most unschooled Freudians, Adlerians, and Skinnerians, not to mention dozens of lesser Behaviorist lights who stroll ivy-covered buildings in tweed jackets puffing on pipes, vaping in their offices, or smoking crooked cigarettes behind the campus lecture hall.

What does all this have to do with faith and chewing the wafer? Even more aggressive sometimes in their skepticism or outright attacks on this application of psychological type are both Christian and Jewish clergy who are woefully uninformed and simply have not done their homework. Just go to your favorite search engine and look up Jung or Jung and Nietzsche and then hang on for a bumpy ride. You will find articles claiming that Jung was anything from an atheist to a Jew to an anti-Semite, or worse yet a Nazi sympathizer. Freudians hate him, because he debunked much of their mythology regarding personality and psychological illness. As some of you know all too well, when someone dares to attack orthodoxy, he or she is likely to attract detractors. For all those wanting something else to be insulted by these days, you will find plenty to attack Jung on and tear down any statues dedicated to him or deface murals containing his image. Thank the Taliban for that model.

For a good dose of professional irony think back to "The Pardoner's Tale" in *The Canterbury Tales* where we began. In the "Prologue" to his tale and in the first 200 lines of the story, the Pardoner preaches against vices while at the same time admitting and revealing that he has indulged in those very vices, himself. The point Chaucer makes is that even a person flawed in his or her own life can tell a moral story. That would include, at a different level, **each of us, because despite our flaws and sins we are called to live a Christian world view.** How concerned was Jung with the right view of God's human creations and one's fundamenal world view? As Jung himself stated the problem,

> I have treated many hundreds of patients…in the second half of my life…There has not been one yet, whose problem was not that of finding a [coherent] religious outlook on life. It is safe to say that every one of them fell ill because he had lost that which the living religions of every age have given their followers, and none of them has really been healed who did not regain his religious outlook.
> (*Modern Man in Search of a Soul*).

While Jung's comment is certainly no glowing affirmation of Christianity, I'd argue with Murray, Schaeffer, Lewis, and Zacharias, not to mention Indiana Jones, that the only choice that makes coherent sense is the Christian world view. If you do your homework and read more of Jung's works and academic studies than just his often cited controversial 1934 essay entitled "The State of Psychotherapy Today," you will find a staunchly Theistic world view expressed. What many critics fail to uncover in their Wikipedia approach to academic research is that for several years Jung worked for the OSS, the precursor to the United States' CIA, and that he was one of the planners for two plots to try to assassinate Hitler because of his inhumane treatment of God's chosen people. Let's put all that on hold for a different book. The authors of the MBTI refined Jung's latent Gnostic Theism into their Christian world view.

When Katharine Cook Briggs read Jung's 1923 landmark book, *Psychological Types*, she found a complete resonance with her personal faith and what she had discovered in her own teaching experience in the Washington, D. C. public school system, that there were eight very diverse learning styles valued by her students and that they correlated fittingly with Jung's eight dominant personality functions. Katharine wanted to make that theory of personality differences better known and understood throughout the general population. Jung provided the theory, but Isabel's and Katherine's personal faith and world view provided the incentive to go to work. As two Christians watching the events of WWII unfold, they were appalled at the devastation of property and loss of life that occurred and came to believe that—are you ready for this—if people actually understood one another and the source of their God-given identities and their purpose in life, we could end war. What a thought! (Sounds like Ephesians chapter one to me).

They knew their scripture and began with the Psalmist's wisdom that "I will praise thee; for I am fearfully and wonderfully made; marvelous are thy works and that my soul knoweth right well" (KJV, Psalm 139:14). In short, who we are and our ways of approaching the world, were shaped by God even before birth. He knows why He made us with the personality preferences he wanted us to express. That thought in and of itself is enough to boggle the minds of most Pantheistic and Naturalistic academics these days. Combine that verse with the assertion that "Before I formed thee in the bowels of thy mother, I knew thee," and the fact only recently being confirmed scientifically that our true personality preferences ("Types") are almost totally genetic, and one would have to wonder what Isabel's and Katharine's view would be of the 60,942,033 reported abortions of babies "fearfully and wonderfully made" since the Roe V. Wade Supreme Court decision in 1973.

We are not sure how much this mother-daughter team knew of controversies surrounding Jung when they crafted their practical application of psychological type on his theory. The best supposition is that they knew nothing at all—a supposition that Isabel herself confirmed to me when we met for an extended conversation in 1978 at the University of Florida, Gainesville—but we do know that they recognized that God created and used different people and diverse personalities for different reasons. The very title of Isabel's 1980 landmark book on psychological type, *Gifts Differing,* will have immediate resonances for anyone who knows their scripture. For those who might miss the subtly of the title, the dedication of the book, "To All Who Desire to Make Fuller Use of Their Gifts," will get them closer. As Isabel begins her book, she starts with a full quotation from the *New Testament* Book of Romans:

> For as we have many members in one body, and all members have not the same office; So we, being many, are one body...and every one members one of another. Having then "gifts differing"....
>
> (NIV, Romans 12:4-8)

The local church then, in Isabel's mind, almost becomes a biblical paradigm for the general population. That the percentages of the different individual preferences (Extraversion, Introversion, Sensing, iNtuition, Thinking judgment, Feeling judgment, Judging, and Perceiving) and those of the complete sixteen personality combinations referred to colloquially as Types have remained largely consistent around the world for the last seventy years should come as no surprise to the Christian. People are people, regardless of whether they were born in Nigeria, Kenya, Brazil, Saudi Arabia, Canada, Germany, Laos, Israel, Japan, Mexico, the UAE, or the USA. All of us, regardless of accent, gender, or skin color, are members of the same human tribe and have been "fearfully and wonderfully made," by an omniscient rational Creator.

Each of us with our unique preferences has a contribution to make to God's kingdom. This is an essential understanding in our team building process and why this theory of personality preferences, because of its clear linkages to the Christian world view, is the only one we will use. When working with faith-based organizations, we start with the individual who has a unique identity implanted by God and given a Purpose for existence and then through coaching help each member uncover her or his unique role in accomplishing God's Mission for us in this world. Our Core Values that we live are the cornerstones of the Christian world view. Even if we misunderstand that principle from time to time, God never does. ***Chewing the wafer* means recognizing our unique gifts and using them to further God's work of personal, cultural, and ethnic reconciliation, in our individual lives and in the local church**: that is the import of Ephesians 5:16.

For "secular" organizations our approach is identical to the above, because it matches the biological, ontological, epistemological, and axiological reality of this world. From our organizational perspective, it is the only theory that does; the rest are mere pop psychology. We don't lecture and we don't preach; we simply tell stories that express the key elements of exceptional organizations. This approach scratches the surface of a narrative approach to Christian apologetics. Again, the Myers-Briggs Type Indicator is the start of the process for any organization we work with because Kathy takes us right back to the Apostle Paul's understanding of the different roles that parts of the body play, as the analogy for the local church. **We each have *Gifts Differing*. Understanding our personality preferences allows each of us to live out our world view with greater clarity and understanding**.

That every Tom, Dick, and Dr. Harry these days, working out of a Naturalistic world view, tries to disparage the work of these two remarkable women, who premised their understanding of human nature on God's word and a Christian world view, and put some other Humanistic system in its place, should come as no surprise. Sincerity and truth are important, even in the business world. Diversity and Inclusion training is all the rage these days—often for the wrong reasons. Whenever we are asked to train and educate in diversity, we demand that we start here—genuine God designed "human" diversity. As one of the arguments for God's existence, this approach is fundamental to the internal Argument from Desire.

> Just as a body, though one, has many parts, but all its many parts form one body, so it is with Christ. For we were all baptized by one Spirit so as to form one body— whether Jews or Gentiles, slave or free—and we were all given the one Spirit to drink. Even so the body is not made up of one part but of many. (KJV, 1 Corinthians 12:12-14)

CHAPTER XXIV

Prophets in Their Hometowns

Most of our consulting, coaching, and training business is with just that— businesses, C-Suite executives, government agencies, middle managers, professional sports teams, and large NPO's. It is rare that we are hired to consult with churches or religious organizations. That group of clients tends to be a relatively closed society that is hard to penetrate. The all too prevailing sentiment is that if there is not a Reverend before the consultant's name or a DD after it, that he or she can have very little to contribute to the community of faith. This naive sentiment is particularly rife in the more fundamentalist Christian community. The worst of the offenders are evangelical groups who tend to be mostly in-bred in terms of denomination or theology and routinely express vocal skepticism about books written by secular writers or those proposing theories not based out of Dallas Theological Seminary, Westminster, Moody, Master's University, Gordon Conwell, Liberty University, or even the Vatican. For sure, you will not find any of their books in church bookstores. Indeed. Some "Christian" book publishers announce in their submission criteria that they will only accept manuscripts from those currently in the pastorate or teaching in *Bible* or divinity schools. What sad inbreeding! Servant leadership may be a biblical principle, but if someone from the wrong denomination, tradition, or sect writes about it, the work is pretty much dismissed. We need to be frequently reminded of Miguel Cervantes' admonition in his great novel,

Don Quixote: *Dondequiera que haya verdad, hay Dios,*" **wherever there is truth, there is God.**

Generally speaking, the higher the church—the more liturgical—(eg., Roman Catholic, Episcopal, and some Lutheran churches), the more they are open to hearing about leadership development, personality differences, Emotional Intelligence, or Team Building from someone outside the clergy. Indeed, the Lutheran Church, under the early entrepreneurship of Otto Kroeger, by his own admission, a very flawed "Pardoner," was one of the initial groups to popularize the MBTI. That openness presents a wonderful opportunity. The "lower" the church (non-liturgical), several nondenominational fellowships, Bible Churches, Baptist Churches, non-denominational evangelical, Holiness, and some Reformed Presbyterian churches, the more they fend off those not within their familiar arena of fellowship. Since the latter is my background, and as an evangelical most representative of my theological positions, I am saddened by their parochial nature. The real shame is that they miss out on incredibly important approaches to church leadership, personal development, strategy development, techniques for engaging the Millennial and Gen Next populations, marketing to the unchurched in the area, innovation in liturgy, the power of growing the skills of Emotional Intelligence, and a host of powerful speakers who could help them proclaim the gospel more effectively.

Naturally, there is a story here. An unusual opportunity presented itself to our company just last year. I was asked in to work with a Vestry committee for an Episcopal Church. A local entrepreneur whom I had trained in the science of psychological type and team building several years earlier was having a conversation with his priest regarding personality differences and conflicts within the congregation. The priest told him that she had been looking around the Midwest for someone skilled in the Myers-Briggs technology to work with her vestry committee and could not find anyone qualified enough. My friend assured her that I was one of the world's most preeminent "experts" in the technology, had written several books on the subject, and just happened to live in the area. I guess by default, she rang me up and asked if I would be willing to work with her parish. I assured her that I would be delighted to do so. Ideally this should be an opportunity to have our world view shine through.

As an aside, I was briefly describing this invitation to an elder in a local evangelical church, and his eyebrows raised, and he said "she? The priest is a she?" As I replied in the affirmative and assured him that such was frequently the case these days in the Episcopal church, he asked, "Why are you working with them?" My admittedly glib response was "why not?" What I did not say, was the even more culturally glib, WWJD? (What would Jesus do?). I may have just caught him by surprise, but please hear the implicit knee-jerk spiritual isolationism in his voice, an isolationism and perceived spiritual parochialism that impacts our daily walk. Where did Jesus go? With whom did he dine? To whom did he preach? Whom did he heal? With whom should we be discussing the gospel? Just those sitting in the front row of worship services swaying back and forth and rolling their eyes in agreement? Or all those with whom we come into contact. Would the same elder have questioned the managers of a local Chick-fil-A franchise or the local Jeep dealership as to why they were servicing non-believers or simply those with whom they may have some theological differences? Of course not!

Consider this even more egregious example of local church parochialism. On June 2, 2019, Franklin Graham encouraged hundreds of preachers across the USA to pray for President Trump, not because Franklin is necessarily a fan of everything the President says and does, but because it is a biblical mandate:

> First of all, then, I urge that supplications, prayers, intercessions, and thanksgivings be made for all people, for kings and all who are in high positions, that we may lead a peaceful and quiet life, godly and dignified in every way. This is good, and it is pleasing in the sight of God our Savior, who desires all people to be saved and to come to the knowledge of the truth (ESV, 1 Timothy 2:1-4).

Hundreds of churches across the country took the opportunity to do just that—unite despite denominational differences and pray for the President. In one large evangelical fellowship just outside Washington, DC, The McClean Bible Church, the lead Bible teacher, David Platt was in the middle of a service, preparing to celebrate the Lord's Supper with the congregation, when he received word that President Trump and his entourage had just arrived in the parking lot and was preparing to enter the church. No one had been previously notified of his coming and the church leadership was apparently taken by surprise by his arrival. When the President entered the sanctuary, David invited him onto the platform and greeted him warmly and then offered a sincere and powerful public prayer for the President and for all of our nation's elected leadership. The prayer was biblically based, and David acted in complete accordance with the scriptures (praying for those in authority over us). That is something that particular church routinely does, as should we all. The only difference was that the main object of the prayer this particular Sunday morning was present. What an opportunity! President Trump thanked him for his prayers and departed, not asking to say a word to the large and very surprised congregation. Well done David!

The outcry from some of the congregation after the fact implied that David should not have engaged in "supporting" a President with whom many in that very diverse congregation (attendees from about 100 countries) disagreed or concerning whom they had moral misgivings. The complaints were apparently so vocal, that Platt felt compelled to pen a long letter to the congregation and place it on Facebook, Twitter, and other media outlets explaining why he did what he did. Some thought he had been "used" and shouldn't have prayed for this President at all, and other members (or at least attendees) misunderstood his intent and accused him of apologizing in his letter for having prayed for the President. Shame on them. Leave you political biases in the parking lot. For some, it was not so much that he had prayed for the President, but that President Trump had been invited onto the platform for the prayer. Shame on them. Again, at the risk of sounding trite, WWJD?

First, the letter was anything but an apology; I have read it twice, and rather than an apology, it was a factual description of how the circumstances unfolded, the need for local church unity in even a very diverse mega church, and a sound doctrinal defense of why we should always be praying for those in authority over us. Secondly, who would not welcome the opportunity to pray for a nation's leader who had the humility— something President Trump is not usually accused of—to show up at a large evangelical church and publicly ask for prayer? What would you have done? Platt is obviously a far kinder person and a much more spiritually mature Christian than I. I am afraid that if I was their pastor, I would have told those carping Pharisees in his congregation that if they really believed what they complained about, they were in the wrong church and had probably slept through most of the teachings in the past couple years. Platt handled it much more maturely than I, as a seasoned pastor should—just another reason, I suppose, why you and many others are glad that I am not in a pulpit.

This is the very "Christian" isolationism, elitism, and failure to engage the world with our world view that I am attempting to highlight. It is not just a secular world problem; it is a local church problem. **If we won't even live a practical apologetic in our local church, what chance do we have to do it in our professional lives?** The Christian church is not a place for perfect people who all think alike. As a reminder, if you find the perfect church full of perfect people every time they gather together, you are in the wrong building. Whatever you do don't dare join it, because your presence would immediately sully their perfection. The local church is intended to be a place for messy Christians to gather in an effort to grow together spiritually as a diverse body to reflect Christ. It should always be a place where those imperfect human beings, whom we all know—where is the mirror?— come to gather for prayer, growth, and celebration. As Geoffrey Chaucer reminds us in the *Canterbury Tales*, "**The church is a sort of hospital for men's souls and as full of charlatans as the one for their bodies.**"

Let's shift from Sunday and go back to work on Monday through Saturday—or as in California and most of Europe, just Monday through

Thursday. With whom should we be working? What assignments should we accept? What is the believer's role in the world today? What is sacred work? What is secular work? **We are called to go into all the world, not just wrap ourselves in our pious robes and talk and pray only with fellow Christians who think as we do.** What after all is the Great Commission? Go to everyone except the President? Shame on all those who could not put aside their racial, gender, political, moral, and perhaps ethical differences for fifteen minutes to welcome a fellow sinner into their midst for corporate prayer.

Back to Indiana. We had a great day of learnings with this Episcopal group looking at the natural personality preferences of the fifteen individuals on the Vestry and relating their Type preferences to their roles in the ministry, their understanding of scripture, and the reasons to value their typological giftedness (diversity) when making decisions for the parish. After the day-long meeting, the priest asked if I would be willing to continue to coach her personally on her leadership style and help her bring the Vestry together as a more high-performing group. I was more than pleased to be asked to help despite our obvious theological differences. I was most pleased to be asked to help as she was very clear that Episcopal liturgy and approach to worship and church leadership was quite different from my more literal evangelical approach to church leadership and teamwork.

During one of our breaks, she was curious to know where I worshipped and why I went there. Before I even started to explain, she asked further if it was because of the particular minister that was there—apparently more focused on a too often cult of personality that drives so much of church attendance than a biblical local church model. I allowed that I really did appreciate our main Bible teacher who led the pastoral team but was mostly there because of the church's stated Core Values, its Statement of Faith, the way in which the overall ministry of the church was biblically based and tried both to lead others to Christ and to enable those who attended to grow in their faith, and also to impact the local community and the unreached peoples in other countries around the world with the Gospel.

At our next meeting in a Starbucks near her church, I discussed with her the need for any group that wants to become a real vestry "team" to be able to articulate their **Purpose** for existence and to be able to define their future **Vision** of what success would look like, the **Core Values** that they needed to agree upon to be faithful to their **Mission**, and their individual **Roles and Responsibilities** as they worked together on the basis of Common **Operating Principles and Norms** to achieve their **Vision.** In short, I reviewed for her those principles of teaming found in my books *Hannibal, Hummers, and Hot Air Balloons: High Performance Strategies for Tough Times, Culture and High Performance*, and my 2018 book, *Inliers: The Curse of Polarity Thinking.* While the kind of organization we consult for may vary between a Fortune 100 Company, a professional sports team, a small entrepreneurial software firm, a federal government agency, a Marine platoon in Fallujah Iraq, or a small local church in your community, the principles remain the same. Truth is Truth wherever it is found. *Muchas gracias Miguel Cervantes.*

The part of our discussion that really engaged her attention was when I discussed the need to have a set of Core Values that the vestry members needed to agree upon to hold one another accountable and to which the congregation could hold them accountable. I stated that, of course, they should be scripturally based and fit within their particular ecclesiastical framework, but should be unique to the shared values of all Vestry members. Her working assumption had been that because they were all Episcopalians, they must have the same unstated values. The priest explained that in her previous church there had also been some serious divisions, and they had brought in a diocese consultant to help resolve them. Rather than working the vestry through an often time consuming process (normally about 2-3 days) of examining their individual values, formulating their Purpose, Values, Vision, Mission, Operating Principles and Norms, and establishing key metrics to know if they were on their path to success, the consultant took the easy way out and simply issued them a generic Episcopal Diocese-blessed value statement to "recite together" at the start of each meeting—a statement that alleged to speak to their common Mission and Values as Episcopalians. Baptists do not all think alike; Lutherans do not all think alike, and neither do Episcopalians. "Team Values" are different from denominational expectations.

I asked her how successful that process had been, and the answer was... well, you guessed it. It failed, nothing changed, and the priest left that church and was hired by her current one. Such a cookie-cutter approach fails in the business world and it fails in church circles just as dramatically. I explained to the priest that the reason it had failed was that the statement was just something else imposed on the vestry from the "outside," and that none of the members were at all invested in its success. They were not able to tell their individual stories in the process of deciding on their guiding values. Values are personal and must be developed and affirmed by each group independently. They cannot be legitimately dictated by a group exterior to the organization.

When I suggested to the Rector that her Vestry Committee already had a set of well-thought-out Core Values to which they claimed agreement, one that had stood the test of time, she seemed rather perplexed by my statement. I reminded her that on the day I had met with them, they had started the meeting by corporately reciting the "Lord's Prayer" (the Our Father for Roman Catholics) and then also concluded the meeting with the same prayer at the end of the day. That approach pleasantly surprised me at the time and really opened the door for a serious biblical conversation as part of our work. That prayer could not only provide the routine bookends for the day but also form the scaffolding of all their work together. I challenged her by asking if they were just words on paper and a mantra they numbly recited or if they were a genuine statement of belief for the members. After all, we are not directed by scripture merely to repeat the same words each time, but to use the "Lord's Prayer" as a model for our prayers: "When you pray...." (Matthew 6:9-13). Getting her expected agreement to the latter, I asked her to consider the values implicit in that model for prayer.

Our Father—(not Mother, not parent) the value of family and hierarchy in God's kingdom.

> We are all children of God in his family and owe him the respect and honor that his role demands. Furthermore, with that title and role, come authority and leadership to which we need to assent.

Hallowed be thy name—the value of reverence for that which is holy, that we should be standing in awe of, with fear and trembling.

Thy kingdom come—a recognition of the temporal nature of our being and yet the eternal purpose of what we do, that this world is just a temporary stopping off place. The Vision for believers is that our future is with God. We should be preparing ourselves to be worthy of such a communion. What scripture calls ongoing sanctification.

Thy will be done—Obedience. We are to have the mind of Christ, so for believers, this should be a no brainer, so to speak.

On earth as it is in Heaven—the Christian community in this world—the local church—should be a microcosm of what Heaven will be like, hence the need for continuous sanctification. That means gender, racial, ethnic, and sociological reconciliation not only in our society but in our fellowships.

Give us this day our daily bread—our dependence on God for life itself. A recognition that all that we have comes from God the Father.

And forgive us our trespasses—The recognition of our need for God's forgiveness.

As we forgive—the need for a forgiving spirit in each of us to be somewhat worthy of God's forgiving others, *those who trespass against us.*

And lead us not into temptation and deliver us from evil—our need for God's Protection—deliverance.

For thine is the kingdom, etc. etc.—the all-powerful nature of God and our implicit humility. We are in his control now and for all eternity.

"Wow; listen to you," she exclaimed, shocked, I suppose that a business consultant knew her business well enough to highlight biblical truths for it. The values expressed in that prayer are hard to beat. I suggested to her that if they ask God for those things in a meaningful way, they should be willing to grant the same things to one another in their meetings and be held accountable for them as they serve in the vestry as administrative leaders of their church. Furthermore, vestry members should be ready to announce those shared values to the congregation so that the congregants could hold them accountable as well.

While not officially a "board of elders," a vestry committee serves essentially the same purpose for an Episcopal congregation, and could do far worse than be selected on the same criteria and values: all those virtues and values found in 1 Timothy 3:2-7, Titus 1:6-8, and Acts 20: 34-35. In any organization in which we work, we could call the following a good start to establishing a team's Core Values and Operating Principles and Norms.

> Be of good reputation
> Be above reproach
> Be respectable
> Be well thought of by outsiders
> Be hospitable
> If married, be above reproach in marital life
> Be mentors
> Manage their families well
> Be self-controlled
> Be sober minded
> Not be Quick tempered
> No greedy
> Not Quarrelsome
> Not a Drunkard
> Well-disciplined

CHAPTER XXV

Christian Apologetics: The Black Hole for the Local Church

So far, I have been dancing around this topic, poking at it from various angles. It's time to get more specific. Far too many pastors and teachers leading evangelical fellowships are scared off by any thought of engaging the mind instead of just the heart. They would much rather have the congregation sing the 15th verse of "Just as I Am" or repeat the last line of some contemporary Mercy Me or Hillsong tune over and over to stir up the emotions of the congregation, than express a clear argument for the faith. The more verses they sing, the louder and more emotional the congregation becomes, and the more hands get raised into the air and the more "a-men" and "praise Jesus" gets shouted from the congregation. Many charismatic and Holiness ministries rely on such emotions to buttress their faith. Last week alone in the church I was attending, the worship leader had the congregation repeat the same verse of a hymn 29 times. Yes, I counted; that's how bored I got after the 5th time through and being chastised by the worship leader for not raising my hands in praise when she told us to.

Those who do lift their hands in praise or adoration, often help to create a warm atmosphere of worship that I really appreciate. That openness and diversity of worship styles in large non-denominational fellowships is invigorating. Raising hands in praise, making the sign of the cross, spontaneously kneeling, emoting a-men's, or shouting "Yes, thank-you Jesus," or even dancing in the aisles are all great individual expressions of worship and born out of diverse Christian backgrounds and reactions to the leading of the Spirit. They are part of the diversity in the body of Christ that I value. Thank God for those individual expressions of worship. It's just not my style. I love glancing around the congregation and observing the different ways we have of worshipping the one true God. I can be just as worshipful and engaged, however, bowing my head from time to time and quietly thanking Christ for his mercy or celebrating the truth that He is worthy. Respect me for my worship style as well and don't assume that I have to mimic you to be a sincere believer. Too often the easy approach to coaxing superficial commitments out of a congregation is to work them up emotionally, steering them away from the challenges of rational thought that might get in the way. It is far easier to involve the emotions than make a logical case for conversion, which requires a change of mind as well as heart (Romans 12: 2b).

The "heart" (*kardia* in Greek; *leb* or *lebab* in Hebrew) is spoken of over 750 times in scripture; in most cases the word refers to the seat of emotions and involves a combination of the mind, the emotions, and the will. It is essentially synonymous with our word for "character." While the translation cannot denote intellect alone, that connotation is implied far more often than any other meaning. **Scripture emphasizes over and over the primacy of the intellect and the sovereignty of the claims of truth when making decisions.** Of the 750 times the "heart" is spoken of in scripture, it connotes "understanding" 278 times, implies the "mind" 135 times, and means the word "think" over 200 times. (Check out your *Strongs* or other favorite commentaries). Fewer than 150 times does the word "heart" actually convey primarily "emotions" and a related emotional approach to understanding.

The act of conversion itself involves a conscious act of the will and a movement of the mind in a new direction enabling one to "think" anew. The two bring about repentance and effects conversion. Think of it as a military "about face." He or she who once walked in one direction pivots and then, at the "command" of the Holy Spirit, goes in the other.

For some that pivot is immediate and undeniable; for others it is a slow motion turn that occurs over time.

Far from being an "also ran" in the Christian walk, an apologetics approach to understanding and conveying our faith is quintessential to a well-founded belief.

How does one do this? By standing on God's word. An apologetics approach starts with a solid understanding of scripture as well as an understanding of philosophy, science, and related disciplines.

> Study to show thyself approved unto God, a workman that needeth not to be ashamed, rightly dividing the word of truth. But shun profane and vain babblings, for they will increase unto more ungodliness (KJV, 2 Timothy 2:15).

Had the Apostle Paul been as afraid of engaging the mind as many Christians are today, the Gospel would have died a lonely death in Philippi, Thessalonica, Corinth, Colossae, and their environs. Let's be clear, no one has ever been argued into salvation. That is not what the Apostle Peter meant in 1 Peter 3:15:

> But sanctify the Lord God in your hearts and be ready always to give an answer to every man that asketh you a reason of the hope that is in you with meekness and fear (KJV, 1 Peter 3:15).

What a transformation for a simple, unlettered Galilean fisherman with far more experience mending a net and gutting fish than challenging the Jewish intellectual and religious hierarchy and, indeed, the whole world, with a pen! Under the guidance of the Holy Spirit, this unschooled fisherman had learned the power of reason, language, and rhetoric to further the kingdom. What began as a fledgling attempt to tell stories— what later 19th century theologians might call a narrative approach to apologetics—became under the guidance of the Holy Spirit, an ability to present reasoned arguments to Jewish leaders, scholars, and emperors. Only then could he become the founder of the Church whom Jesus told,

> I tell you, you are Peter, and on this rock I will build my church, and the gates of hell shall not prevail against it (NIV, Matthew 16:18).

If logic and arguments are not going to win the day, what place does an apologetics approach serve? Why bother? The word apologetics comes from the Greek word, *apologia*, meaning a defense in a legal sense. As our son, Paul, recently described it in a presentation he made on Christian Apologetics to a group in Washington, D.C., it "comes down to providing answers to life's most important questions—namely, those about truth and God. It means being able to articulate a compelling logical argument, tell personal stories that flesh out those principles, and making sound biblical applications to our lives. Deciding whether or not to pursue these answers is not something to be taken lightly; it is a biblical commandment." As those who have served in any military conflict know, before an attack on the enemy, there is often an artillery barrage to soften up the target and make the enemy more vulnerable. For some folks, so entrenched and fortified by years of Naturalistic propaganda and educational philosophy premised on secular Humanism, an apologetics approach can help to soften up their natural defenses to make a presentation of the gospel much easier. Think of it as biblical shock and awe.

I relate the following story with some hesitancy, recognizing as I do that the local church has many obligations and scriptural mandates and that as a member of any fellowship, I may not always be privy to the Holy Spirit's leading of the pastors or board of elders. It is certainly not my role to try to tell individual Christians, let alone church boards or evangelical fellowships, what aspects of ministry are the most important; that is up to them to decide based on how they perceive their Purpose for existing in the communities they serve and their perceived individual Roles. Every local church needs to be open to the leading of the Holy Spirit to know how and where to focus its ministry. Having a strong Spirit-led board of elders (you can fill in your model of church leadership) to decide the correct approach is critical. What is my purpose, however, is to call out an aspect of ministry I see missing in far too many fellowships—even the best—in this country and beyond; churches that as a result fail to prepare its membership, particularly its younger members to engage the world and leaves them vulnerable to attacks.

I could pick on any number of churches of several denominations that could improve their focus of ministry, but having said that, let me relate a short story of one particular church that does many things right—far more than most of the churches I have been involved with over the years: emphasizing sound doctrine, providing excellent teaching, providing loving support for families, growing youth work, acting on a biblical approach to church discipline, engaging the local community, attempting to reach unreached groups around the world, and celebrating our faith with excellent music. It is one whose ministry I actively support. God has truly blessed this fellowship and changed lives because of its ministry. What is lacking, however, is a well-thought-out approach to Christian apologetics. **If such an outstanding fellowship can miss out on this key aspect of ministry, it can happen anywhere,** and sadly does more often or not.

Every year this very fine Christ honoring church hosts a weekend conference that brings in outside speakers to engage the Christian community on some deeper theological topic. The idea, from my point of view, is to encourage Christians to delve deeper into the theological underpinnings of their faith and to understand that one need not give up her or his brain to be a Christian. Because Christ came to save the whole person, we are called not only to believe but to "think." Each year a two or three-day conference focuses on some important aspect of the faith. On the average, 100-150 churches from the local area are represented. In 2018 the church brought in Ravi Zacharias and Abdu Murray from Ravi Zacharias Ministries (RZIM), an evangelical ministry based in the Atlanta Georgia area, focusing on giving honest biblical answers to difficult questions. This is essentially the approach I learned from Francis Schaeffer and his staff in Huemoz, Switzerland and later working with bright young questioning minds from around the world in some of our consulting work, so our family was excited to attend and encouraged many others to attend as well, flying some in from out of state.

The sanctuary was packed for two days with thousands of attendees, some coming from as far away as California and the East coast and received great reviews from nearly everyone in attendance. Conversations over coffee during breaks were exhilarating! When the conference ended, I approached an elder who sponsors the conferences and asked what the follow-on plans were for ensuring that the many fires lit by the speakers did not get snuffed out by sheer neglect. The answer I received was that there was no plan to follow-up with classes on developing an apologetics approach to sharing our faith. During our brief conversation, he said he thought the church's basic "witnessing classes" that were already in place and ongoing would touch on the subject. I have not attended those classes, so he may be right, but when it comes to 1 Peter 3:15, "touching on the subject" doesn't hack it. Yes, we should honor the leadership of church elders, but when we believe they are wrong, out of brotherly love we should approach them and tell them. That is our Christian obligation. In this case, I believe he was naïve and wrong.

To be fair, even though we had been in the congregation for several years, he didn't know me (too often the case in larger mega-churches), so I briefly shared some of my background with him and offered to help him plan follow-on sessions to build on the RZIM work and got a very polite but perfunctory, "Okay, let me think about it as we go forward. I'll be in touch," response. It's been almost two years and . . . nothing. About ten months later, after church services, I approached another gentleman who is a member of the ministerial team, who had just made a brief presentation during the service regarding the church's youth ministries. After mentioning the RZIM presenters in the conference a year earlier, I asked him about his interest in perhaps developing an apologetics training ministry for the church's college age students and young professionals or even trying to take it to some of the many college campuses in the area. I expressed an interest in being part of that ministry should it fit within his role as youth minister or any other ministry of the church. He was polite but clearly distracted or disinterested and said, when you get a chance why don't you email me your thoughts.

We are already well past the subsequent 2019 conference, which focused on race and reconciliation and just concluded the 2020 conference. Not surprisingly, in an age when race, diversity, and inclusion are all the rage in the public arena and blaming anyone white and male for being a racist, or at best reacting to others on the basis of "unconscious bias," a topic we have already had one sermon on, is more or less the norm, several follow-on meetings regarding the topics of race and diversity, to include the whole gamut of unacknowledged bias—the topic seemingly required by every Fortune 500 company and public school district today—have already been scheduled. There is also a diversity working group that is well advertised for its weekly meetings, and two diversity trips to racial hotspots from previous generations. How *au currant*! We all have different gifts, talents, and interests as part of our Christian walk—that one is pretty far down my personal list of priorities.

I am sure that group is doing good work, and I am aware that the church has been and continues to be heavily involved in a center-city ministry—something I applaud and support but not one that engages my personal interest or gifts. I get enough of that topic rammed down my throat by the private sector during the week. Indeed, under my leadership, my company has worked in the area of diversity education for years with numerous schools and Fortune 500 Companies. I do not need to hear about racial ignorance and unacknowledged white bias—a vastly overhyped topic in our race obsessed "woke" culture—from the pulpit, even when it is approached biblically. I always want to trust church leadership to know the leading of the spirit when it comes to emphasis in ministries and can only assume that such is the case here, but local leadership should also expect its membership to push back when they see a problem. With this issue, I see a problem, a misplaced emphasis, and a really missed opportunity.

I reemphasize, I do not raise this issue just to be critical, particularly of what one excellent Bible believing church is neglecting in my opinion, because it does such very fine work in many areas of Christian development, particularly in the area of race relations. Indeed, one of the ministries recently spun off as a start-up church is in a severely racially impacted center city area. We even have an elder whose primary focus is race and diversity. The ministry team's involvement with persons of all races and cultures as well as those from differing theological backgrounds is exceptional and commendable. I raise the issue because of what I believe to be the tremendous loss of opportunities in regard to engaging the minds and hearts of a younger generation—a generation that the Christian church in general is losing because we are neglecting them and ignoring their serious questions.

We are in a war of world views, and at present, in North America alone, the church is losing. We dare not be found warming the bench on the sidelines and unprepared to enter the game. Our next generation is particularly at risk, because they are untrained. There have been several studies of the current high school generation and why they leave the church, but one recent troublesome survey by Lifeway Research indicates that of high school students who routinely attended protestant Sunday services while in high school, often times at the insistence of parents and guardians, once they graduate, 2/3rds between the ages of 18 and 22 stopped regularly attending. Even the Roman Catholic church that theoretically "requires" attendance at Sunday mass to be in fellowship, those attending most of the Sunday morning services are very long in the tooth and young people are hard to find among the gray hairs in the pews in most parishes.

Clearly this is my priority and not that of far too many church leaders caught up with other pastoral concerns that I do not pretend to know about. Once fires have been lit, however, we dare not let them die out due to inattention or neglect. Those of you who camp out from time to time know that when you do not tend a small fire in your campsite, it simply burns itself out and dies. What about your local church? Have the fires even been lit? If so, great! Who is tending the fire? What a shame to have stoked so many coals and encouraged so many—particularly college students at local universities and other schools in the area—members and non-members alike with ways to engage questioning friends and to be able to give a defense for the hope that is within them—in short ways to live a practical apologetic—and then simply drop the topic and move on.

In our current church, as in many of yours, we often have so many activities underway that I can barely stay up with them. I thank God for the many teachers, elders, and pastors we have to lead such ministries, but those of us in the pews have to choose our involvement carefully. I readily admit that where emphases are placed is probably mostly a matter of priorities and the interests as well as the capabilities of the elders. **Frenetic "activity,"** however, **in the local church—particularly in contemporary mega churches—too often masquerades as depth of theology.**

In our executive coaching work, we are very clear about our approach. We recommend a "Two-Push Approach" to helping leaders grow. When we are asked in and hired as executive coaches, we attempt two primary interventions. We will make recommendations for behavior changes and offer good reasons for making those changes and ways we can support them. If we see no changes take place over time, we try to encourage the leadership again, a second time. If we do not get any expected change the second time, we do not waste further time. Nobody likes a nag; we move on.

While admittedly, not the intention of the Apostle, we probably got this approach from Matthew 10:14: "And if anyone will not receive you or listen to your words, shake off the dust from your feet when you leave that house or town."

CHAPTER XXVI

Incompetence or Fear?

Let me speak more generally. Why the fear? Why the reluctance to tackle the hard questions head on? Part of the answer resides not just in a different ministerial emphasis but in a lack of preparation by those in local church ministries, and part of the answer arises from fear. What if I get a question, I can't answer? Consider the criteria for being a good pastor that the Apostle Paul lays out in First Thessalonians. The Apostle Paul's narrative in chapters one through three implies at least seven elements of an exemplary pastor's heart: compassion, protectiveness, gratitude, intercession, sacrifice, affection, and delight in seeing them. None of these directly relate to the apologists' concern for spreading the truth. The pastor's role, in short, is very different from the apologist's concern, which is why those concerned with such an approach are usually outside most local ministry teams and are found, if at all, at the level of elders, diversely educated lay people, outside speakers, professionals in the congregation, or others volunteering to assist with the parish ministries.

Furthermore, while **being a pastor, and by extension, an elder demands a healthy combination of "being"** (by this I mean good character and spiritual development—in short ongoing personal study and sanctification) **as well as "doing"** (performing specific tasks and fulfilling the duties required of a minister, lead pastor, or elder), there are many other stated and unstated expectations of the senior pastor. When we survey the major divinity schools to see what they say are a pastor's or minister's typical responsibilities, we find the more respected schools listing most of the following:

Parish or congregational leadership,
Preparing and delivering sermons,
Teaching children and adults,
Visiting and consoling the ill and grieving,
Responding to outside speaking engagements,
Administering the church office,
Resolving conflicts,
Building parish harmony,
Recruiting new members,
Leading a youth ministry,
Personal professional development,
Maintaining church discipline,
Maintaining a personal spiritual life,
Fund raising,
Baptizing and marrying,
Holding funerals,
Fostering fellowship,
Building a ministry team,
Planning unique holiday celebrations,
Recruiting and training parish leaders,
Supporting a Sunday School ministry,

Busy, busy, busy, and...the beat goes on. I am sure I have left out several specific responsibilities that you might add, depending on your denominational bent, but these are the usually advertised job requirements at most of the prominent pastor mills and often the requirements spoken of when advertising for a new staff member. Even with the support of elders, as the book of Ephesians and other Pauline epistles lay out as the normative pattern for the *New Testament* church, with all these responsibilities levied upon pastors and newly minted ministers, it is amazing that the burnout rate is not even higher than it is.

Several years ago, when guest lecturing for a few days on the Morality of Shakespeare's *Julius Caesar* at Vassar College, I attended a small Bible Church on a Sunday morning near Newburg, New York. I sat in the service, shocked and saddened, watching as the minister—someone whom I would guess was in his mid-forties or fifties—in the middle of his sermon, suddenly burst into tears and sobbed, "Oh, my God, I have never even been able to teach my son how to throw a baseball." He walked off the platform shaking his head and resigned. No wonder tackling a subject as heady as Christian apologetics seems too daunting a task for most ministers to add to their repertoire. It is tough to do. That is why it must be a legitimate calling not an add on career choice or an elective course or two in divinity school.

The aspect of ministry that can and should include an apologetics approach is "teaching," one of the principle duties of an elder, not just a pastor. We should be schooling our youth, young parents, and others in our assemblies to be able to answer specific questions that will be lobbed against them by teachers and peers alike from high school on, in not too veiled attempts to undermine their beliefs or simply embarrass them. Such a training program should be intellectually and spiritually rigorous—maybe call it an Apologetics Ranger School, that not everyone is prepared to undergo—but **preparing our brothers and sisters in Christ to give good answers to serious questions will go a long way to preparing the church to stand against the enemy** for another day or another century, until Christ returns. In the process, if you get a question or two that you can't answer, great. You have probably just found a serious seeker; go do your homework, so you can get off the bench and enter the fray when the coach calls.

If nothing else, in larger churches, where there is often thankfully a multitude of gifts and a desire to serve, and there are often numerous pastors or elders with specific responsibilities for being in charge of youth ministry, evangelism, hospital visitation, international missions, membership, small group development, elder care, finances, and a host of other ministries, there could just as easily be a Deacon of Apologetics or an elder specifically charged with growing a team of people schooled in practical apologetics, with a particular focus on preparing young people to be ready to provide a defense of the faith. **We face nothing less than a war for the souls and minds of this millennium.**

More often than not, the questions that are raised by skeptics to the faith fall under the framework of what we generally call apologetics ministries. Providing honest answers to such questions not only demands an in-depth understanding of scripture (2 Timothy 2:15) but also far more than a cursory knowledge of culture, philosophy, and science. How would you do in responding to some of the following questions from honest inquisitors? Has your local church helped to prepare you to give honest answers to these critical questions if they arise?

Have the *New Testament* documents been corrupted over time?
What was God doing in all the time before he created the earth?
Why did God create us if he is really all sufficient?
Is there any extra-biblical record of millions of Jews roaming the desert?
If God has always been, why did he wait so long to create people?
Why are a Christian's beliefs in divinity more correct than any other
    religion?
What is the difference between absolute and relative truth?
Where did dinosaurs come from? Where did they go?
Were the pyramids built before or after your worldwide flood?
Were there dinosaurs on the ark?
Do you actually believe that at one time giants roamed the earth?
What are the main traditional philosophical arguments for God's existence?
Where was the Garden of Eden? Must have been hot; they wore no clothes.
Why did Jesus have to endure such a gruesome death as that on the cross?
Why would God create so many planets and solar systems and put life
    on just 1?
Couldn't God have just pardoned Jesus and conveyed that pardon to us?
Why does an all-loving God need others to worship him?
Did dinosaurs roam the earth before or after Adam and Eve?
Were all animals vegetarians before death entered the world at the Fall?
Is there a non-biblical record of a day of darkness at the crucifixion?
Are all homosexuals headed to your hell?
How can you believe that angels and demons are real? Ever see one?

Did the earth actually slow in its spinning to create Joshua's "long day?

Should we obey governments that are evil?

Did people really live for hundreds of years during *Old Testament* times?

Is cremation at death allowed in scripture?

Did God ordain the leadership of Hitler, Kim Jon Il, Xi Jinping, and Idi Amin?

Are we really supposed to pray for such leaders?

Isn't capital punishment immoral?

Why did God pick the Jews as his "chosen people" and not some other group?

Why does God seem to have favorites like Jews and the Elect?

Is there any evidence that the resurrection of Jesus actually occurred?

Isn't Hell an unreasonable punishment for not believing a set of truth claims?

Hasn't science disproved God?

What happens to all those in other lands and times who never heard the Gospel?

Don't all religions point to the same God?

Why did God give black skin to some and white, brown, or yellow to others?

Why is Christianity right and Islam wrong?

Why don't Christian churches send more missionaries to Israel?

Why did Jesus pick the illiterate and unschooled to spread his gospel?

Do you believe that a flood once covered the whole earth, including Mt. Everest?

Why are Christians so upset by the science of evolution?

Does the *Bible* approve of or undermine the theory of evolution?

What is Young Earth Creationism (YEC)?

What is OEC (Old Earth Creationism), including the Gap Theory?

What Old Testament prophecies did Jesus fulfill?

Were the days (*Yom*) in Genesis 1-3 actually 24 hours in length?

What does the *Bible* say about Jesus' exclusivity as a savior?

Why would a good God allow evil to exist? Why not just kill Satan?

How can a loving Creator send his own creation to hell?

Do you really believe in an incarnate figure of Satan?

Why does God remain so obscure?

Does God predestine people to hell?

Doesn't the *Bible* condone slavery?

If Jesus is actually returning one day, come on man, why is he waiting?

Is there any evidence outside the *Bible* that Jesus ever existed?

Who selected which books were included and excluded from the modern *Bible*?

Why do Roman Catholic and Orthodox religions include different *Bible* books?

Are near death experiences real?

Why does your *Bible* contain so many passages that can be misinterpreted?

Are the Ten Commandments still applicable to modern society?

How can we know that the *Bible* we have today is a reliable record?

What does it mean that the whole earth appears to be "finely tuned?

Why doesn't the *Bible* set forth clearly the whole of creation and subsequent races?

Why are there so many denominations? Which one is right?

If everyone came from just Adam and Eve, and later from just Noah and his wife, where did the different races come from?

Why were Adam's and Eve's children and those of Noah allowed to intermarry with relatives? Isn't incest as crime if not a sin?

Can homosexuals become Christians?

What happens to primitive peoples living on islands in the Pacific and other remote jungle areas for centuries who never heard the good news? Are they all bound for hell? That sure doesn't sound like a fair loving God.

What happens to humans who existed before God began to appear to the Israelites?

Why don't miracles happen today if they happened in the past?

Do you actually believe that a real fish swallowed Jonah and later spit him out?

Why are women forbidden to preach in many protestant churches or serve as priests in the Roman Catholic Church?

How do you account for the existence of cavemen?

If Jesus picked all 12 of his disciples, why did he pick one he said was a devil?

Were there "real" giants at one time walking the earth? Who created them?

Did male demons once come to earth and have sex with female humans?

Will Judas Iscariot be in Heaven? After all he was just doing God's bidding.

Why would an all-powerful God create a person with the wrong sexual organs?

Are all transgendered human beings going to hell?

What happens to the millions of babies who have been aborted around the world?

Is work a result of Adam and Eve sinning or the natural response to God?

Is global warming upsetting God's plans? Didn't he foresee this problem?

Where did angels come from? Were they created or were they always with God?

If God is all good, doesn't that imply some absolute standard external to him?

If God has already chosen who will come to him (the elect), indeed has chosen them himself, why does your church waste so much money on missions, since these people are going to be saved, anyway, regardless of human effort?

What does God look like? How would you describe him to a child?

Will the Pope be in heaven? How about Mormons?

Some of these questions no doubt fall more under the category of theological issues than purely apologetic ones, but the two arenas often overlap. These are just a few that come to mind and that I have had lobbed at me over the years. I am sure you could add a few more, but the ability to provide honest answers to just these few legitimate questions posed by unbelievers sometimes even by questioning Christians, would form a good start. I know they will keep me busy. Just shouting "Jesus saves," won't hack it. This is most likely the table of contents for my next book. Feel free to send me more to consider (Esipres6@earthlink.net).

As you wrestle with these and other perplexing questions, you yourself will grow. You cannot start too early with children. Questions such as those few above were often the grist of question and answer games that we would play with our children, as they drifted off to sleep. In our family, in lieu of more formal nightly *Bible* reading, we would often play "Twenty Questions," or other more contemporaneous TV quiz games, always using some of the above questions to teach biblical principles related to the above questions, and answering them with scriptural references. Most of the kids seemed to love it and remember those games today. Unwittingly they were growing in their knowledge of scripture along the way. That way, the last thoughts they would have each night before saying their prayers and drifting off to sleep were biblical truths that we hoped would one day sustain them in life. At least that casual approach began to lay the groundwork for belief. Baby steps to chewing the wafer. The choice is theirs. **Apologetics starts in the home. Afterall, God created the family before Jesus established the local church.**

Fortunately there are some pastors, priests, and elders who take this responsibility seriously, but too often it is at best farmed out to others and at worst simply ignored. Today, there are groups like the CS Lewis Institute, RZIM, Answers in Genesis, Cross-Examined, and others, and several ministries founded by Ravi Zacharias, Josh McDowell, Norm Geisler, Tim Keller, Ken Ham, Tim McGrew, John Lennox, Os Guinness, Hugh Ross and other sound theologians that specialize in apologetics and in training lay people to provide this thoughtful approach to faith. The best graduate work in apologetics is at OCCA, Oxford Centre for Christian Apologetics, in England. Their faculty is nonpareil.

I would encourage you to seek out elders, teachers, and lay leaders in your fellowships schooled in dealing with such apologetic concerns and blessed with a passion to teach and serve and put them to work. Because this is a war of world views, you need some trained warriors to help out. Novices often throw in the towel and lose the battle. When they offer to help, don't turn them down out of fear or ignorance. As our son Paul reminded his class on apologetics held in the shadow of the Washington Monument, **"Pursuing these answers is not something to be taken lightly; it is a biblical commandment."**

CHAPTER XXVII

Truth and Team Building

As I have argued earlier, it is my clear professional bias that whether in your day job or in your church responsibilities, the most successful leaders, those whom we want to emulate, lead on the foundation of Vision and Values. Any other approach to crafting a philosophy of leadership is doomed to inefficacy and mediocrity. Many of the better reads, of the 192,345 books listed on Amazon in 2019 that deal with leadership principles, discuss the topic in one way or another. Two of my books, *Hannibal, Hummers, and Hot Air Balloons: High Performance Strategies for Tough Times*, and *Culture and High Performance: Creating a World Class Business and Organizational Culture* (www.execustrat.com, the Bookstore), make the business case for doing so with practical clarity. What this approach has to do with living a Christian world view, however, I trust is beginning to come into focus. That leaders need a trusted reference point—one not subject to the vagaries of experience—upon which to premise their decisions is fundamental to holding a non-Naturalistic philosophy of life, and I would argue it also has a keen Christian genesis. Without such an external reference point for our lives anything goes.

> In those days there was no king in Israel; everyone did what was right in their own eyes (ESV, Judges 17:6).

What was true then from the 13th to 15th century BC for the wandering tribes of Israel, is equally true in our more modern Humanistic culture— what for some, such as Richard Dawkins, is called the New Atheism and what philosophers will call a Naturalistic approach to values. **Without such an external absolute standard, we are too easily coerced to believe in anything, and our lives can crash and burn; our practical apologetic is reduced to ashes.**

My wife, Cheryl, is a private pilot. She decided to learn to fly while working as a chemical engineer at a plant in Corpus Christi, Texas and simultaneously attending graduate school to get her MBA in International Finance in Austin Texas, about 225 miles away. It was too far to drive twice a week after 12-hour shifts at her chemical plant and research center, so she took flying lessons and eventually bought her own Mooney—a single-engine private plane with a very distinctive backwards tail that you may have seen at local private airports—to make the trip. She had the privilege of learning to fly under the tutelage of a world war II fighter pilot. I'm not sure how much of a privilege she saw it as at the time, but clearly understands after the fact how powerful the various lessons were that he taught her to deal with on the fly with simulated, and sometimes authentic, emergencies that he would create—ones that few other pilots ever learned to handle during their training. As they would take off on a flight, for example, he would often lean back in his seat, open the *Wall Street Journal*, and seem to be unconcerned about her piloting until he would introduce some emergency for her to deal with such as engine failure, ice on the carburetor, or some other *faux* or authentic emergency. As Cheryl would scramble to identify the problem and then apply the correct remedy to restart their engine or simply keep their plane in the air, he would calmly ask, "Are you going through your checklist, Cheryl?"

One very clear and starry night he had her climb to increasing altitudes by spiraling in increasingly large turns as she gained altitude out over the Corpus Christi Bay. On such a night with the stars reflecting off the water below (or was it up?), the ground below looks very much like the sky above (or is it down?)—up cannot be distinguished from down or reality distinguished from reflection—and many a seasoned pilot without an external reference point has followed her or his deceived senses into the water or the ground. That was exactly what happened, for example, to John F. Kennedy, Jr who, temporarily lost in the fog, crashed his plane into the Atlantic Ocean, near Martha's Vineyard, in 1999, because he couldn't tell down from up, sky from water. While his instruments told him one thing, he trusted his senses and experiences that told him something else. Which do you trust at any point in time, your senses, or what your instruments tell you is the truth? The same is true of our theologies. Do you trust your emotions at any given moment or what scripture says? Are you using your checklist, or what you just feel is right? The person who "feels" redeemed on Sunday morning while singing the "Doxology" or "He is Worthy," can easily lose that feeling by Hump Day.

Not unusually, some of those who have been most prominent in such emotion-laden ministries for years, suddenly leave the faith saying they reject the authenticity of Christianity. They do not "feel" it is right for them anymore. It's not Christianity they are rejecting but the emotions that they were duped into thinking justified it. Recent apostates like Joshua Harris and Hillsong worship leader, Marty Simpson, are just the most recent public examples of previously confessed "Christians" relying on deceptive feelings and the crippling effects of not engaging the mind with a clear apologetic. Pray for them.

The teaching point is one that all pilots learn at some point in their training. Never trust the senses, always trust your instruments—your unchanging reference point based on magnetic north. This learning can be life or death when piloting a plane and, I would argue, determines success or failure in the Christian life as well. Our culture has been adrift in a post truth world ever since Hegel sent our heads spinning in moral and ethical relativism in the nineteenth century. No absolute truth can ever persist in Hegel's post-modern universe, when any truth—he called it a thesis—has an implicit implied (anti-truth) antithesis, which together then merge and lead inevitably to a synthesis (new truth). All truth then is temporary and relative until a new one emerges. The possibility of there being true truth then is demolished in Hegel's methodology and in most philosophies and their implicit Naturalistic Post Modern world views ever since. What is your checklist? Are you using it, particularly when things go badly, or just relying on how you feel?

Life is full of ups and downs, moral quandaries, temptations, and ethical dilemmas so complex it is often hard to know in which direction to head. Just tune into the evening news and you know it is hard to tell up from down and truth from falsity. Fake news now is the term we throw around, regardless of political affiliation, and few of us know what news sources to trust. Do you lean on FOX or MSNBC? Do you tune into CNN, Al Jazeera, or BBC? Which is most accurate, *The Huffington Post*, the *New York Times*, or the *Drudge Report*? When it comes to values or issues of faith, **Holy Scripture provides our only accurate instrumentation— our fixed reference point**—that does not fail as we experience life.

Those who trust their experiences are subject to the vagaries of emotions and spiritual temptations. Just because something feels good, does not make it right. **Satan specializes in helping us to feel good about our unbelief.** Nowhere will this deception become more lethal than in the last days when many *faux* messiahs and anti-Christs will arise. When the choice arises between what our emotions tell us and what the *Bible* says, the wise Christian piloting her or his life has but one rational choice: trust your instruments (Scripture), not your experiences. These are the Metrics we discuss as imperative in our model of exceptional team development. Let your story be that you choose wisely.

When one is lured into the faith by appealing solely to the emotions, one's confidence in that faith is easily shaken when the winds of life blow hard. They have no fixed reference point that they can trust. **The Word of God is our set of instruments that gives us a fixed reference point.** That, after all, is the thesis of the entire *Bible*, that the Apostle John expresses so well in his gospel:

> These things are written that ye might believe [that action verb we discussed earlier] that Jesus is the Messiah, the Son of God, and that by believing you may have life through his name (ESV, John 20:31).

It is one thing, however, to say that scripture is our fixed reference point but an altogether different thing to know what it actually says. That knowledge demands a daily immersion in scripture and the support of Christian brothers and sisters to encourage our ongoing study.

This is the basis for the model that we espouse when working with organizations. Our work is "secular," but the model is scriptural. Heads of businesses, NPOs, government agencies, and other exceptional leaders in every country all know that having a clear picture of what success will look like (five, seven, or ten years out)—we call that our **Vision** of success, and establishing a clear set of **Core Values** by which we should be known—is the starting point for creating a high performance culture. The **Vision** is what we expect the future to look like. That is why God gave us the Book of Revelation—our Vision of what our future will look like—and promises a special blessing to those who will actually *study* it.

> Blessed is he who reads and those who hear the words of
> this prophecy, and keep those things which are written in
> it; for the time is near. (KJV, Revelation 1:3).

Our **Core Values** provide the instruments to guide us there. Authentic leaders lead on the foundation of Vision and Values. **Effective pastors lead their flocks on the basis of scripture not emotions**. You can extrapolate that wisdom to your family.

CHAPTER XXVIII

Teams vs. Groups

Let me pursue this topic a bit more since it is one of the central foci of our business and a prime example of how one's Christian world view should inform the work one does. As I have insinuated, it excites me to know that the first time God addresses his creation, he does so as a team—the Trinity: Father, Son, and Holy Spirit. That team was present at the start of time and will be there at the end of time. **One of Satan's most potent tricks is to try to emulate and replicate the things of God and to counterfeit them for his purpose of undermining the Church.** You all know of churches in your city that Satan would be excited to have people attend faithfully, because the Gospel is never preached, and the congregations are being systematically coerced into believing in nothing. Once you believe in nothing, Satan's job is almost finished; you can be lured into believing anything. The minister, rector, pastor, or priest in such churches is just a modern embodiment of Nathaniel Hawthorne's "Preacher, Mr. Smooth-it-away," who replaces Bunyan's Evangelist, in his "Celestial Railroad," the nineteenth century allegorical parody of John Bunyan's *Pilgrim's Progress*.

We, therefore, should not be surprised at all that who should pop up in Daniel's seventieth week of prophecy and the Book of Revelation (what the majority of Evangelicals believe is a prophecy of the Tribulation period), but the unholy counterpart of the Trinity—the demonic team of Satan, the

False Prophet, and the Anti-Christ (Rev. 19: 19-20). Whereas the divine Trinity stands for Love, Truth, and Goodness, the unholy counterfeit stands for the diametrically opposed traits of hatred, deception, and unparalleled evil. What Satan knows well is that these unholy values will be much easier to insinuate once the Holy Spirit's restraining force has been removed for a period of time. After a brief but frightening seven years, during which this unholy team will terrorize the earth, it will ultimately fail abysmally and be cast into the Lake of Fire. Admittedly, then, there are good teams and bad teams.

I am more concerned with that good team—the Trinity—and how that triune nature of God is not only meant to inform humankind— our individual ontological, metaphysical, intellectual, and axiological natures—but is also intended to give us the framework for the local church (steep yourself in the Pauline epistles). Much of what we know about how a good team works and why others fail is by our experiences with poor ones. With that in mind, let's start with what believers do not mean by the Trinity.

1. **Christians do not believe in three Gods**. That is the premise of a medieval church heresy called Tritheism. Christianity is monotheistic like Judaism and Islam. **That similarity can often be a sound starting point for evangelism and practical apologetic arguments** particularly when witnessing to Jews and Muslims.

2. **We do not believe that the Father, Son, and the Holy Spirit are merely three different "forms" or manifestations of God— like, steam, water, and ice.** That understanding is the basis for the ancient Christian heresy called Modalism. And,

3. **Christians do not believe that the Father, Son, and Holy Spirit are each "parts" or "pieces" of God**. That would imply that Jesus is about 1/3rd God, the Father is about 1/3rd God, and the Holy Spirit is all the rest, about 1/3rd God. Jesus walked the earth as 100% man and 100% God. When the Holy Spirit speaks to us, He does so not as a vaporous spirit, winged messenger, or emanation of the Divinity, but as 100% God.

Granting the bias of any of the above hermeneutical errors as a legitimate premise in an argument attacking the Christian world view can undermine our practical apologetic. What we do mean is captured in Chapter X, titled "In the Beginning." The Trinity is *not three aspects of one God, but three beings: Father, Son, and Holy Spirit—three co-eternal, consubstantial persons, or hypostases—three parts of one divine nature.* As individual human beings, we are created in the image of God: body, mind, and spirit, which is why it follows that all human beings have a consciousness of God—someone far greater than ourselves. **Man alone, of all living creatures, has a such a God-consciousness.** Chinese pandas, Egyptian camels, Alaskan whales, Florida gators, ancient raptors, and amoebas in a university laboratory petri dish worship no one. If you accept that premise, it follows then that the local church is also probably meant to represent the triune nature of God in terms of how we work together to further the kingdom. While a team certainly has various parts, a real team—what in our secular business we call "Teams That Work"—prepares those various parts to function as one. The application is secular; the theoretical foundation is biblical.

I like to think of that as a holographic team model. Think of the holograph of Obi-wan Kenobi, played by Alec Guinness in the original *Star Wars* series. When that noble man skilled in the power of The Force comes to give advice to Anakin Skywalker, he appears as a complete form with every bit of the original Obi Wan—not a physical presence, but a virtual one—a holographic projection of Obi-wan. When my team of consultants represents me with a client, my name and reputation are at stake. They have to represent with clarity 100% of my Purpose, Core Values, Vision, and Mission. That requires we build our team first before trying to influence others. In like manner we as individual believers and, by extension, the local church should be representing 100% of the Triune God who relies on us to convey his message of salvation through Grace alone. We should build our church team first, as well.

The local church then is not just meant to be a group of people that gathers to worship, but a holographic team—the entire body of Christ—that collectively expresses the totality of God's goodness. Because man himself has been created in the image of God (Genesis 1: 26)—ie. as a human trinity (Body, Soul, and Spirit) or perhaps even a trinity of personality, rationality, and spirituality which allow us to relate to one another and also to the Creator—it stands to reason that the corporate Body of Christ ought to reflect that same trinitarian nature. Indeed, the very nature of the immortality of man cannot be understood apart from our trinitarian nature. For that reason among others the Catholic Church, as do a few higher church denominations, dedicate the first Sunday after Pentecost as Trinity Sunday to proclaim the Trinity to the world. The Apostle Paul affirms that doctrine in his benediction that closes his second epistle to the church in Corinth.

> The grace of the Lord Jesus *Christ* and the love of *God* and
> the fellowship of the Holy *Spirit* be with you all.
> (ESV, 2 Corinthians 13:14)

And again, at the end of his first letter to the Thessalonians, when Paul prays,

> Now may the God of Peace himself sanctify you
> completely, and may your whole spirit and soul and body
> be kept blameless at the coming of our Lord Jesus Christ
> (ESV, 1Thes. 5:23).

Again, in that curious inverted truth, the ultimate creation of man and woman is meant to reveal the triune nature of God. The Lord, himself, reaffirms this holy trinity with his Great Commission:

> Go ye therefore, and teach all nations, baptizing them in
> the name of the Father, and of the Son, and of the Holy
> Ghost (NKJ, Matthew 28:19).

Were we a physical body only, then our existence would end at death, stretched out on the slab in the morgue or drained of blood and pumped full of formaldehyde in some funeral parlor. By God's providence, we also have a spiritual nature that is separate and distinct from the body in which it dwells. Correspondingly, the church is meant to be a physical body—a team of individuals—who also have spiritual gifts differing according to the will of the Holy Spirit. Too often, in the local church, we make the same mistake that the business world does. We focus on the individual achiever—the believer—and that person's individual gifts, at the exclusion of the team. The Apostle Paul counsels otherwise; teams are important.

That our consulting and training work therefore continuously underscores the differences between a mere group of individual people who may be working together to do a job and a real team that has a whole different set of requirements—"Teams That Work"—has an unstated biblical principle undergirding it. We do not have to be methodically drawing subtle parallels to our world view to have our work stand as a model for it. In every case, one's world view must answer, either explicitly or implicitly, five fundamental questions:

Who are we?
Where did we come from?
Why are we here?
What has gone wrong with the world?
What solutions can we offer to fix it?

The team implications of the answers to these questions are set forth in my *Culture and High Performance* and *Inliers: The Curse of Polarity Thinking*.

To be clear, not every job needs a team approach. There are some jobs and assignments for which a qualified individual is just fine and others for which a well-functioning group is just what the doctor prescribed. But if you need a team, **if you really need a team**—I dare to allege that <u>the local church does</u>—**something dramatic has to happen to transform a group of people into a team. Such a transformation does not happen on its own.** It doesn't matter whether we are talking about the Indianapolis Colts, Qatar Gas in Doha Qatar, Bayer A.G. in Dusseldorf Germany, a Celanese textile manufacturing team in Queretaro Mexico, the New York Yankees in the Bronx, a PepsiCo sales team in Vietnam, a senior executive team leading Lockheed Martin in Bethesda Maryland, a Boeing diversity team in Seattle Washington, a Merck Pharmaceuticals manufacturing shift in Rahway New Jersey, an Episcopal church Vestry committee, or your board of elders. If a team effort is required, there are certain requirements to which one should attend to create a high performing team which will allow all the various gifts of its members to surface. The more you emphasize them and train towards them, the more of a Spirit-led team you will become. You have to work at it.

Using the biblical model, let's be clear what we are talking about. **A team is a small number of people with complimentary skills (or maybe gifts) who are committed to a common purpose, a set of performance goals, and an appropriate approach to accomplish their Purpose.** They may be centrally located at one geographical location or spread around the world as a virtual team. Teams must wrestle with the following questions. As you read through them, think about the team most important to you (at work, at home, or at church). More specifically, if you are a church leader, think about your current ministry team.

1. What is your sense of direction? What is the Purpose for your existence? What are you trying to accomplish? Have you clearly communicated that Purpose to all the appropriate members? Would they agree?
2. Does your team have the necessary talent and personal skills to accomplish its assigned tasks? If not, what is currently lacking? Who do you need to hire or ask to join your team to flesh it out?
3. Is each team member fulfilling her or his role and committed to the process? If not, what are you doing to coach them or replace them?
4. Does your team have the appropriate leadership and ongoing training?
5. What does success look like for this team? Have they taken the time to visualize success and articulate that Vision to the entire organization? Is everyone in agreement?
6. Who is the potential Judas on your team? You may have selected them for good reasons, but Jesus also selected his disciples, and one was "a devil."

7. Do individual team members respect one another and show appreciation to others on the team with different talents and or gifts?

8. Have they developed a set of Operating Principles and Norms by which they will operationalize these Values in meetings?

9. Has the team agreed on certain Core Values by which they want to be known and evaluated, and published them to the fellowship?

10. Are you training as a team or simply waiting for the Holy Spirit to stir the waters and get it done for you?

11. What is the heart of your team? How can you discover it?

12. Is your team holographic? In other words whether together or alone, does each member of your team at any one time project 100% of the team's declared Purpose, Vision, Values, Operating Principles, and Norms?

Then as this Team works together on a daily basis, you need to differentiate between key behavioral differences. We help organizations change behaviors below from Column A to Column B, because we believe such a transformation is not only effective but also based on biblical principles. Your homework is to figure out what they are. Column A is normal work force and traditional parish behavior. Exceptional performance requires our emphasizing the behaviors in Column B.

Column A	Column B
Groups hold discussions	Teams engage in respectful dialogues
Risk avoidance rules the day	Prudent risk taking is rewarded
The daily focus is on Not Failing	The persistent focus is on Succeeding
Meetings are characterized by hesitancy	Members are open and trustful
Information is filed away	Information is shared openly
Dysfunctional members are tolerated	Unsatisfactory behavior is addressed

Members feel directed	Members feel enabled
The members accept differences	The team cherishes diversity
Personal agendas are being worked	There is one team agenda

While these are the distinctives we teach regarding "secular" team behavioral differences, using the examples I discuss in several of my books, I would suggest they are all fundamentally biblical principles as well. As with all jobs, our approach to team building will reflect our world view. As a company, we are proud to base all our work on the fundamentals of faith and the elements of a Christian world view and would be pleased to join John Updike and Francis Schaeffer (probably the first time those two authors have ever been conjoined) in shouting the Creed at the top of our voices. As the "Apostle's Creed" begins,

> I believe in God, the Father almighty,
> maker of heaven and earth;

> And in Jesus Christ, his only Son, our Lord;
> who was conceived by the Holy Ghost,
> born of the Virgin Mary,
> suffered under Pontius Pilate,
> was crucified, dead, and buried.

It then continues with a few more absolute truths that need a little discussion from time to time, with,

> He descended into hell.
> The third day he rose again from the dead.
> He ascended into heaven,
> and sitteth on the right hand of God the Father almighty.
> From thence he shall come to judge the quick and the dead.

> I believe in the Holy Ghost,
> the holy catholic Church,
> the communion of saints,

the forgiveness of sins,
the resurrection of the body,
and the life everlasting. Amen.

It's hard to get a better start than this.

CHAPTER XXIX

An Emotionally Smart World View

The most recent technology impacting the development of exceptional leaders, high performing teams, organizational culture, innovation, and numerous other developmental issues impacting relationships, is the science of Emotional Intelligence (EI). Ever since Peter Salovey and John Mayer coined the term Emotional Intelligence in 1990, numerous self-appointed experts have tried to systematize our knowledge of the science and formulate ways to understand it in a more scientific way. Sadly there has been very little use of the technology in fostering the growth of the local church or training effective apologists for the faith, most likely because it is a "secular" tool based on a theory further developed by Daniel Goleman, someone raised as a Jew and who today also values the insights of the Dalai Lama. Cervantes where are you when we need you? "Where there is truth, there is God."

To date, there are a dozen or more different assessments that have been developed around the world to ascertain the extent to which individuals are capable of understanding the impact of emotions, theirs and others, on their communication style, problem solving, reasoning capability, stress management, and a plethora of other daily activities. Only three of these assessments have been scientifically validated and have psychometric credibility. Of those three, the one we believe does the best job at capturing this aspect of our being fearfully and wonderfully made, is the EQi 2.0, which is why we use it in all of our team building and executive coaching assignments. As with all of our professional developmental approaches, we ensure that it is first consistent with our Christian world view and helps us to reflect it in our daily work, before we adopt it.

I have previously called out what I believe to an improper use of and exploitive reliance on emotions in ministry, an approach that confuses, undermines, and lays fear at the feet of any attempt to be rational in our approach to faith. You know who you are. There is also an appropriate use of emotions, regardless of what gender you are or whether you are a T or F or E or an I in Myers-Briggs terms. Since God created us as emotional creatures, we have good reason to believe that such emotions can and should be used properly for our enjoyment and personal development as well as in the furtherance of his kingdom. **To be an effective practical apologist we have to be able to attract, understand, and engage others**. What is necessary is to assess what the proper uses of emotions may be. Not only is it critical to understand our own emotions and how they impact our decision making, communication style, worship styles, and interpersonal communications, but also to understand how emotions impact others when we interact with them to foster more effective relationships, to train and educate others, to present the Gospel, or to present clear arguments for the faith that is within us. Forget the numerical scores generated by any such an assessment. While they are extremely helpful in our managerial and executive coaching uses of the assessment, I want to focus here instead on the various categories of emotional functioning that have been identified, because they go to the heart of what it means to be made in the image of God.

The scientists who developed the questions used on the EQi2.0 for individuals' assessment of their use of emotions, took Goleman's five categories of emotional functioning, best described as, self-perception, self-expression, interpersonal reflections, decision making, and stress management, and broke them down into fifteen practical areas of concern in which our emotions play a critical role. We are convinced that understanding the appropriate use of these fifteen categories of emotional functioning is not only important in fostering our individual relationships, coaching, and organizational lives, but also critical in our desire to live out a Christian world view. **The improper use of any one of them can invalidate our practical apologetic and make us less effective telling our stories.**

In order to highlight the biblical background behind each of these various aspects of human emotionality, I'll start with a very basic definition of each category of emotional functioning and then point out a few of the scriptural implications (both good and bad) of each of the categories. To reiterate, the point is that **if we have chosen well, our story, our lives, the tools we use, and the work we do should reflect our Christian world view before we even speak a word.** Becoming more emotionally smart will help us in that endeavor. As I review them, **be thinking about how learning how to embrace each aspect of emotional functioning more appropriately can assist you in living a more effective practical apologetic and allow you to connect your Christian world view with someone who is a serious searcher.** If God created our emotions, it follows that he must want us to use them effectively. This leadership development tool has implicit biblical principles unwittingly embedded in every category of emotional functioning.

As you consider these aspects of EI, think about how each might be useful in improving conversations with others who may have sincere questions about your faith and confidence in Christ. Since we as Christians are called to understand our identity in Christ before we even explore our personality preferences, it is appropriate that an understanding of Emotional Intelligence (EI) should begin with an effort to understand what Goleman would call the whole composite category of our Self Perception. He begins with one's sense of personal Self Regard. Where does yours originate and how will I know it?

Self-Regard: <u>Respecting and having confidence in one's self</u>. This aspect of EI is associated with general feelings of confidence, security, inner strength, and self-adequacy. After all, we are told that God made us in his image and after his likeness . . . . "Male and female created he them"

(Genesis 1:26-27). Not a bad family tree. It doesn't get much better than that. Consider the applications in:

Genesis 1:27	Romans 12:3
Psalm 8:4	Romans 12:20
Psalm 144:3	1 Corinthians 25:10
Romans 5:8	1 Peter 2:9
James 4:6	Philippians 4:13
Jeremiah 17:7	Psalm 139: 13-14
Philippians 1:6	

Self-Actualization: <u>Pursuit of meaning and self-improvement</u>. Those who develop this trait have a finer awareness of the source of their impulses, desires, and opinions and the role the Holy Spirit plays in cultivating them. We dare not try to do this on our own. Humility trumps pride when we realize Christ's role in this appreciation of who we have become.

1 Corinthians 3:11	Matthew 6 (The entire Sermon on the Mount)
Isaiah 28:16	Philippians 4:19
Romans 14:12	Romans 8: 38-39
1 Corinthians 14:20	Philippians 1:21
Romans 12:3	2 Timothy 1:7
2 Corinthians 2:16-3:6	

Emotional Self-Awareness: <u>Understanding one's own emotions</u> is key to personal growth and success. Developing this trait is particularly valuable when trying to influence others or create meaningful change in organizations and other individuals' behavior. As we engage others with differing world views, it is critical that we not only understand when our emotions are under siege, but why. Several websites highlight passages of scripture that allow us to engage each emotion directly.

Proverbs 16:32	Romans 12:3
Ephesians 2:19-20	Ephesians 6:3
1 Timothy 4:16	Psalm 26:2

Proverbs 21:2   Galatians 6:3

Proverbs 20:5   Ephesians 4: 22-24

Emotional Expression: <u>This is the constructive expression of emotions</u> when working with others. The ability to do this well, helps to build trust between individuals and avoid misunderstandings and communication breakdowns, an aspect of emotional functioning particularly important when world views clash. Are your body language and expressions skeptical, welcoming, angry, dismissive, perplexed and so forth, and do they match the words coming out of your mouth? When you cite scripture to others, what does your body and face convey about the reasons why? Is your body language conveying excessive pride or compassion and understanding? Practice standing in front of a mirror speaking your favorite verses and even arguing key apologetic principles. What does your body communicate: compassion, skepticism, criticism, disgust, understanding, or hope? As I was coaching a well-known TV evangelist a few years ago, I pointed out to him that almost every time he quoted a *Bible* verse—something he was famous for being able to do better than almost any other well-known *Bible* scholar—he looked angry, I assume out of dire concern for his audience's souls and eternal destinies. Nobody is going to pay attention to a sourpuss. They change channels.

As we explain to interrogators in several law enforcement, political, and military venues, the mouth can often be misinterpreted and sometimes lies; the body never does. Check out any of the provocative books by renowned psychologist Paul Ekman, or take an afternoon to enjoy at a few Netflix episodes of *Lie to Me*, a TV crime series that ran for three seasons from 2009-2011. It will be time well spent. Time less well spent may be watching some TV evangelists who can't stop smiling like giddy teenagers their entire shows or others who come on late night TV who exude anger during the entire program. Neither is effective; neither should be trusted.

Ecclesiastes 3:4   Psalm 139:2

Romans 12:15   Daniel 5:6-9

Proverbs 10:18   2 Samuel 11:1-5

Proverbs 15:13   Jeremiah 7: 18-19
Psalm 2:5   John 11: 32-35
Matthew 27:46

Assertiveness: <u>Communicating feelings and beliefs in a non-offensive way</u>. Developing this skill helps prevent becoming a doormat in apologetic debates. Know what you believe and be willing to express it clearly. Be willing to challenge others' premises as well as their conclusions; Jesus certainly did. Just leave the scourges at home.

Proverbs 24:11   James 1:19-20
Ephesians 6:20   Philippians 2:5-8
Peter 5:16   2 Corinthians 3:12-13
James 5:20   Matthew 5:5
Philippians 4:13   Acts 4:29

Independence: <u>Being self-directed and free from emotional dependency</u>. It is the mark of an intelligent apologist to be able to entertain another's idea without necessarily accepting it. We must be able to understand others' stories before we can address them from the standpoint of our own. Sometimes our emotional attachments create uncertainty and limit our effectiveness as skillful practical apologists

2 Corinthians 5:7   Galatians 5:1
Galatians 5: 1-26   1 Corinthians 3:17
1 Peter 2:16   John 8:32
2 Corinthians 3:17   Romans 3:28
Romans 12:1-2

Interpersonal Relationships: <u>Fostering mutually satisfying ones</u>. Developing this aspect of EI helps us to understand others' stories and communicate our story to them more effectively. People rarely listen to others with whom they cannot relate. Is there someone in your life with whom you can discuss the most vital of issues? If not, you need to find one.

Luke 6:31	Galatians 6:2
1 Peter 4:10	1 Corinthians 10:33
John 13:34	Ephesians 4: 26-27
Galatians 5:14	Colossians 3:13
Matthew 7:12	Mark 12:26-31

Empathy: <u>Understanding and appreciating how others feel</u>. The ability to "walk a mile in another's sandals," without necessarily agreeing with them, is critical to success in both witnessing to the gospel message and living a Christian world view. Too many people erroneously equate empathy with sympathy. The two are vastly different. Even more important than simply understanding another's point of view is the ability to communicate to that person that you do. That approach can build bridges of grace that sustain the weight of truth into their world views.

Matthew 5:41	Thessalonians 5:11
Hebrews 4:15	1 Peter 4:
Hebrews 10:24-25	Romans 15:1
Romans 12:15	John 11:35
Galatians 6:2-3	1 Peter 3:8

Social Responsibility: <u>Having a healthy social consciousness</u>. This trait encompasses far more than the degree to which we worry about recycling or protecting the environment or even whether or not one helps to build homes for disabled veterans. These are certainly worthy aspects of such responsible social behavior, but the category captured by the EQi2.0 here pertains in larger terms to how willingly one contributes to the well-being of any group to which she or he belongs, regardless of whether or not one personally benefits from such efforts. In a business this may be the management team, the project team, or the shift you are on. In your church this may be the board of elders, your *Bible* study group, your Sunday School class, or your small group. When serving as a deacon or elder, besides performing your duties, how much do you assist others on the same committee to perform theirs? Are you a bunch of well-meaning, Bible-believing, capable loners or part of a team?

Ephesians 5:15	1 Corinthians 10:24
Romans 12:5	Romans 12:16
1 Peter 3:8	1 Corinthians 12:25-26
Galatians 6:2	Matthew 23:11-12
Proverbs 27:17	Ecclesiastes 4:9-12

Problem Solving: <u>Finding solutions when emotions become involved</u>. Developing this skill, helps us handle relationships more effectively, have more empathy with others' stories and their world views, and be able to collaborate on a team with greater effectiveness.

Proverbs 18:13	2 Corinthians 10:5
James 1:5	Proverbs 18:15
Philippians 4:13	Proverbs 18:17

The entire Book of Nehemiah: As you follow the story in this rarely studied book, you will discover a problem-solving model very similar to the **Z Model** I discussed earlier. As emotions become involved, try to…

Identify the Problem (S/N)
Pray (T/F)
Identify the causes (S/N)
Identify possible solutions (S/N)
Pick the best solution (T/F)
Devise and implement a plan, and (S/N)
Evaluate (T)

Then consider a popular Business School model such as a Force Field Analysis that helps you consider those forces compelling you to act or say certain things to another and those forces that may act as restraining forces. On which side is the weight of truth? Should you respond immediately or take time to study the issue from various sides and then respond after the fact more deliberately?

Reality Testing: <u>Being objective and seeing things as they really are</u> helps us not to be sucked into the vortex of another's premise or conclusions. It is hard to overestimate how important this aspect of emotional functioning is when debating apologetic issues. Demand truth and data, not suppositions and speculation. If someone's premise does not fit with yours, find out why. As Dr. Deming reminded us, "In God we trust; all others bring data." Don't buy into others' suppositions without testing their validity. For a quick course in demolishing other's arguments, check out an article on the Memoria Press website entitled, "How to Get to the Real Issue in an Argument." Martin Cothran offers some sage tips that will assist in debating others on apologetic concerns:

Colossians 2:18	1 Corinthians 2:14
Philippians 4:8	Proverbs 12:15

Impulse Control: <u>The ability to resist or delay the impulse to act.</u> This ability helps prevent us from responding too quickly when hearing another's story or debating an issue. This is certainly a trait Jesus had to teach Peter. We dare not get sucked into someone else's logic. A healthy sense of skepticism when debating can be helpful. This is an aspect of Emotional Intelligence (EI) that is often misunderstood. It is not enough just to think, well, I'll act more deliberately in the future, because you probably already pride yourself on making very deliberate decisions. When not properly understood, however, it is one aspect of EI that can often get a person's casual remarks deemed insulting or bullying when that was never the intent, particularly if the same person scores high in Independence, Self-Actualization, and Assertiveness. No one is born with good Impulse Control; it is a learned skill, even after having been in leadership positions for many years. Learn to count to 3 before you respond; better yet, count to 31, the number of Proverbs King Solomon gave us to foster prudence, morality, and wisdom, then respond.

Romans 12:2	1 Corinthians 9:22
2 Timothy 1:7	Proverbs 18:21
Proverbs 25:28	Romans 7:15-20
1 Corinthians 7:5	Romans 8:9
Proverbs 1:3	

Flexibility: <u>The ability to adapt emotions, thoughts, and behaviors</u>. This is a powerful trait within the body of Christ as we learn to appreciate the gifts, talents, practices, and idiosyncrasies of others. Appreciating how others praise, pray, preach, celebrate, and learn honors the God who created all of us. This is a critical EI trait not only when working in other cultures but simply when working with others whose psychological Types and ways of viewing reality and problem solving differ from our own. Cultivating this trait allows one to develop the best aspects of valuing diversity in the Body of Christ.

Romans 8:28	Mark 1:16-18
Romans 12:2	Genesis 12:1
Ephesians 4:1-32	2 Corinthians 1:23-2:4

Stress Tolerance: <u>The ability to cope with stressful situations</u>. Expect opposition to your beliefs and attacks on your world view. If your world view is not under attack from time to time, perhaps you are not living it as overtly as you think. Maybe you personally handle stress very well, but your actions can sometimes become a stress breeder for others. Check out your Facebook and Twitter postings over just the last month or two. At least once a month, go back and delete comments and sometimes even "likes" that may have offended others. Maybe it is time to start deleting offensive posts. Yes, I am talking to myself as well. When you are under stress, it's great to know that the Christian never bears that burden alone.

Philippians 4:6-7	Ephesians 4:29
Proverbs 29:11	Philippians 4:12
Proverbs 15:18	Ephesians 6:11
Joshua 1:9	Hebrews 13:5
1 John 14:1	Proverbs 17:22
Nahum 1:7	John 14:27
Philippians 4:6	

Optimism: <u>Maintaining a positive attitude and outlook on life</u>. The Christian above all others should allow her or his imagination and optimism to fly beyond the stars. We have the book of Revelation, so we already know how the grand story ends. Live like you believe it and are on the winning side.

Ephesians 6:13	Jeremiah 29:11
Philippians 4:13	Revelation 21:1-27
Matthew 7:7	Psalm 118:24
Psalms 50:15	Romans 8:28
Joshua 1:9	Romans 15:13
Philippians 4:13	

The above are all possible human expressions of emotions, and most importantly possibilities that God has instilled within us. Many of us are very good about exercising and working out to bulk up for the beach or improve our physical well-being by beefing up our cardio-vascular systems, but too often neglect the emotional part of our humanness as well. **Christ came to redeem the whole person: body, mind, and spirit as well as rationality and emotionality.** What is required of a believer is that we use each as the Holy Spirit guides us. It is our conviction that the appropriate use of our emotions and the ability to understand and respond to the emotions of others make us a much more credible practical apologist as we seek to live out a Christian world view. Ironically, the better we are at understanding the proper use of our own emotions and being capable of interpreting and responding to those of others, the better we become at presenting rational arguments for the faith. **The mind and the heart always work best as a team.**

We do not necessarily discuss the various biblical understandings of these issues as we work with teams, individuals, and businesses, unless they happen to be faith based organizations, or the door is opened by the client during personal coaching sessions, but the point is that any such tool we choose to use in our business life must be founded on sound biblical principles. They are part of the practical apologetic that reflects our world view. Consciously working to develop your Emotional Intelligence will reap tremendous value for you as you seek to become a more effective practical apologist for the Christian world view. As we have already seen a couple times, **when someone believes that we are willing to listen to**

and understand their personal story, they are much more likely to listen to ours. Those of us who want to be effective practical apologists should always be seeking to improve on these aspects of our Emotional Intelligence. So, how do you plan to get started?

What is your personal action plan for improving one or two of the above?
Which specific trait or traits (pick no more than three) do you want to improve?
What are some practical steps you can take to achieve it?
What is your projected time frame?
What outside assistance might you need to be successful?
What would be the benefit to yourself, your family, your board of elders, or your team if you succeeded?
Who would you want to share your efforts with to request assistance?
Do you have a trusted brother or sister in Christ whom you trust to give you honest feedback along the way? If not, find one.

Consider establishing SMART goals for your spiritual growth:
    Specific
    Measurable
    Actionable
    Realistic / **R**elevant and
    Timely

At least, **think about it**; after all, it is often more polite to chew the wafer with your mouth closed than with it open. Yes, I am a proud Introvert.

> Whoever guards his mouth preserves his life; he who opens wide his lips comes to ruin (ESV, Proverbs 13:3).

> Even a fool who keeps silent is considered wise; when he closes his lips, he is deemed intelligent (ESV, Proverbs 17:28).

Actions speak far more eloquently than do words.

CHAPTER XXX

Hiding Your Passport

If you buy my arguments so far that understanding one's world view is critical to your story and that simply by doing our jobs we can reflect that world view adequately enough to attract the attention of nonbelievers—what I have called **living a practical apologetic**—consider the challenge embedded in the somewhat depressing data below. As a reminder, our world view should reflect clear consequences of the following premises—all of which are implicit in God's story of mankind—the metanarrative of His created universe.

1. We are God's creation, designed to have fellowship with him and to govern the created world with his principles (Genesis 1:27-28; 2:15).
2. Because we disobeyed God at creation (violated his only commandment), we subjected the entire world to a perpetual curse (Genesis chapter 3).
3. God himself chose to redeem the world through the sacrifice of his son, Jesus Christ (Genesis, 3:15; Luke 19:10).
4. Because we sinned against a perfect God, the world needed a perfect sacrifice to be redeemed: "As in Adam all die, so in Christ will all be made alive" (1 Corinthians 15:22).

5. Because mankind is fallen and incapable of satisfying a perfect God, one day God himself will have to restore creation to its perfect state (Isaiah 65:17-25).
6. The Christian God, unlike the absentee landlord that the Deist worships, chooses to intervene directly in mankind's affairs.

As we nurture our Christian world view, therefore, it should necessarily lead us to believe in miracles (the intervention of *kairos* time into our mundane *chronos* existences), human dignity, absolute truth, and the possibility of personal and corporate redemption. Hence, a Christian world view is not only a driving force for existence, a Vision of our potential future, and a clear picture of God's Purpose and Core Values, but also as I have argued, it provides the only coherent framework for exceptional leadership. By now you should recognize these as key factors in our business's approach to fostering team excellence (Purpose, Vision, Values, Operating Principles, Roles, and Metrics). We didn't invent them; they are key elements of a non-Naturalistic Christian world view, with its origin in Genesis. The question is, how prevalent do you suppose such a view is in our culture?

Despite any number of very vocal current day detractors who would argue the contrary, it is a commonplace to say that traditionally the USA has been known as a Christian country. At least in the minds of the majority of the Founding Fathers, who came primarily from a Deist world view, Christian principles anchored our founding documents. As all evangelicals recognize, however, there are "little 'c' christians," as in a christian nation—a description under continual assault by the media, Hollywood A-listers and products, pandering politicians, and the court system—and "big" 'C' Christians who actually believe in the truths outlined primarily in the *New Testament*, who commonly are called Bible-believing or born-again Christians. I'd be one of the first to admit that there is a qualitative difference, therefore, between a "c"hristian world view and a biblical world view, but thus far I have been using the terms interchangeably, not only because these are the terms primarily conflated in the literature, but because ideally they should be the same. Even in academic (or intellectual) circles that may ostracize any attempt to discuss a biblical world view, they will allow an academic discussion of what can be called a Christian world view. I'll continue to run with that.

Given that distinction, however, where do you fit in the puzzle? How prevalent do you believe such a Christian world view is in American society? This is your chance to participate vicariously in one of those "person" in the street interviews. To that point, how prevalent do you think such a world view is even within the evangelical church in the United States? Let's take just a small subset of the local church today, born again believers. According to a wide-ranging recent national survey, **only 9% of church going Americans claim to be born again believers** (Barna Research Group). Not much of a surprise there. I suppose. Even more shocking, perhaps—unless you actually listen to the evening news—is that among all Americans, not just born-again believers, **only 4% claim to have a Christian world view**; yes, that is 4 without a zero after it. If we act day by day at work, watching your favorite sitcom, chatting with neighbors over a barbecue, or sitting on a jury on the unspoken premise that others share our similar world view, we are sadly mistaken. We hold world views with vastly differing major premises, therefore our conclusions regarding reality are remarkably different. The same survey finds that even though 26% of the US population are NONES (having no religious affiliation at all), 95% of Americans still believe in the existence of God (no doubt variously defined). At the same time, however, 75% do not believe in absolute truths. In short, God may exist in their various world views, but is not worthy of worship, and what He stands for apparently does not matter to three out of four "believers." That is simply a violation of logic and rational thought at best and a crippling indictment of what the organized church fails to teach at worst. No wonder the world is in such a mess. When we roam outside North American borders among the 17,500 ethnic/linguistic groups on the planet, the numbers become even more depressing. We have some work to do.

The unspoken assumption that we all believe in the same basics, even in this "Christian" country, is one reason why believers are frequently at a loss in arguments and debates. They assume both parties are starting from the same premises. Such is not the case. We must always test those premises. An incorrect premise leads to an inevitable erroneous conclusion. It is a misstep that is a further reason reinforcing why it is imperative for individuals as well as organizations to articulate clearly what they believe (Core Values) in order to have meaningful dialogues at home and abroad. Naturalists and non-Naturalists, Christians and non-Christians, each begin from different starting lines with totally different premises and rules. That is why an understanding of logic must precede any discussion of philosophical differences which in turn must precede any rational analysis of moral and ethical behavior.

The questions the researchers asked to ascertain these pitiful numbers above regarding one's world view are fairly basic; there were just seven:

1. Do absolute moral truths exist?
2. Are absolute moral truths defined by the *Bible*?
3. Is God the all-powerful and all-knowing Creator of the universe?
4. Does God still rule today?
5. Is salvation a gift of God that can't be earned?
6. Is Satan real?
7. Is the *Bible* accurate in all its teachings?

How about you? Can you answer "yes" to all seven of the above questions? If so, you "probably" have a Christian world view. They are at least the necessary if not sufficient conditions for such a position. The question is… are you living it, and would others know it? Again, if you do, you share that world view with only about 4% of your fellow Americans. Is it any wonder therefore that you feel like a foreigner sometimes in your own land when you watch a sitcom, chat with neighbors, watch the morning news, enter the voting booth, tune into a Superbowl halftime performance, listen to a political debate, or sit in a jury box?

"For our citizenship is in heaven" (Philippians 3:20).

Even more importantly, **if you admit to having such a world view, does anyone know it, or do you cleverly hide your passport?**

CHAPTER XXXI

Just Call Him JT

Return with me to my teaching assignment at National Defense University (NDU). The intermediate staff college within NDU where I joined General Jolemore's leadership team was, AFSC, the military's intermediate Joint Staff College in Norfolk, Virginia. Because the ostensible purpose of this college is to teach members of the five military services, senior executives from all US federal agencies, and those from several allied countries, how best to work together and team up for successful operations, each small seminar in the college is led by two senior officers from different services (army, navy, air force, Marines, or coast guard) to provide different service perspectives on all the professional and service-related issues discussed during what was, while I was on the faculty, a nine-month program. The two senior officers in charge of each of the seminars are responsible for teaching almost all of the courses in Executive and Professional Development, DOD policies, the US weapons acquisition process, ethics, professional writing, briefing styles, consensus building, conflict management, and joint operations (those involving more than one military service) of every variety to a group of twenty to twenty-five officers, mostly majors and lieutenant colonels from all of the above organizations as well as from fifteen to twenty allied countries.

In one of these sessions, I was the senior officer, hence my title of Seminar Chairman. My assigned associate, an air force lieutenant colonel, was new to the school faculty, having just arrived from the State Department, where he had been responsible for negotiating nuclear throw weight with the Soviets and other world powers in the SALT (Strategic Arms Limitation) talks in Geneva, Switzerland and Vienna, Austria for several years. He was a skilled political scientist with degrees from the Air Force Academy, the Institute d'Etudes Polytechnique de Paris, and Harvard University. I'll call him JT; you may also see him show up as a trusted colleague in a couple of my adventure novels like *Spirit of the Oryx* or *Concord*.

Since we shared an office, our conversations from the day he arrived centered not only on who would teach which subjects and our differing styles of engaging our students, but also on the values we wanted to pass on to our charges. JT was a natural teacher and had a passion for higher education as did I. We spent untold hours learning about one another's background, arguing our idiosyncratic views of the military and political strategy, and discussing our views of life, relationships, outlook on politics, and our interest in theology. I was a West Point grad; JT was an Air Force Academy grad. I was a combat veteran, JT was not. JT was an Olmsted Scholar and a respected State Department veteran, I was not. I was a born again believer; JT was a smorgasbord Catholic. JT was particularly perplexed that despite my educational background and experiences working with cultures all over the world, I could actually believe that the *Bible* was true and a trusted guide for life. Over the six semesters we stayed together—a unique amount of time for the staff college to allow the same seminar leadership team to stay together—they usually rotated after every class—we became best of friends and somewhat infamous within the college. When other faculty members would learn that a student was assigned to our Seminar 8, they would just shake their heads and tell them to get ready for the toughest graduate education they'd ever had. We took our mission to prepare military professionals and government officials very seriously and used every chance we had in class, in evenings, and on weekends at one another's homes and student quarters, and in activities of all varieties in the Tidewater Virginia area from cricket to fishing trips to surfing competitions to submarine visits to acting in County Fairs to speech competitions to grow our charges.

JT had been raised a Roman Catholic by Puerto Rican parents and was steeped in that theology but over time had come to see many of their beliefs at best as anachronisms in the modern world and at worst as contrived mythologies meant to engender a perpetual sense of guilt to control them and lure them to weekly masses to generate contributions and increase control through guilt. Religion had become mostly a cultural issue for JT not a compelling belief system. He rarely attended religious services, but even when a bachelor when he first arrived on the faculty was an occasional holiday attendee at Catholic masses in the Virginia Beach area where he lived—later, when married and a father, doing that more for the model it set for his kids than for himself—but he was never very vocal about his faith or personal beliefs.

When JT arrived at the college, he was at best a philosophical Naturalist with a relativistic teleological bent. You might recall that I described myself as a non-Naturalistic deontological absolutist. Yes, we were philosophical opposites. Our fellow staff college faculty referred to us as Mutt and Jeff. Yep, I was the Mutt—not the worst thing I have ever been called. Not only did the two sides of our office look very different, as an INTJ, mine was orderly, professional, and spartan, and JT's ENFP office area just kinda collected stuff and spilled into my half and sometimes the hallway and beyond. Our passports also were from very different worlds. For the Christian, "our citizenship is in heaven," (NIV, Philippians 3:20). God does have a way of giving us a chance to tell our stories, if we are willing.

Since I was serving as the President of the local base Chapel Board and led a faculty and student *Bible* study every Monday morning before classes, I had frequent student visitors from other seminars, as well as the Commandant of the College who was, himself, an active member our weekly staff college *Bible* study, in our office. Some came to discuss our lessons from the previous week's study, and others dropped by to discuss the Christian implications of the military and political doctrine we were teaching. Occasionally other believing faculty members would get difficult questions posed to them by their students and their fallback position had become, "Go talk with our colleague, Colonel Jeffries." For that reason, students, including a rather famous Saudi Prince in one of the seminars—the license plate on his Maserati said it all, "Number 3"—just popped in from time to time between and after classes and auditorium lectures to ask questions and argue their respective philosophical and theological points of view. JT, who was infamous in the college for being on the tennis courts, far more often than being in the office to meet with students, would invariably linger for these discussions sitting quietly at a desk just about ten feet away as our conversations regarding faith took place. At first, he would just listen quietly, but over time began to ask questions, pose difficult conundrums, and jot down notes furiously as our conversations took place.

What particularly intrigued JT was that while he was the director of all courses in Political Policy and State Department relations, I had been selected to direct all the courses in Personal and Executive Development and Ethics for officers who, upon graduation, would be assigned duties anything from flying combat sorties in the Middle East or Southwest Asia, directing policies of military involvement for the Joint Chiefs of Staff, leading special operations teams in numerous unfriendly countries in Africa, Asia, the Middle East, and South America, or serving on senior officer staffs in the Pentagon. In our almost continuous conversations, he would always probe how my Christian world view would impact our discussions of ethics and the consequences of our military actions. He eventually bought a *New Jerusalem Bible* (at the time, the best of contemporary Roman Catholic study *Bibles*) to bring to the office in order to quiz me on facts he was convinced I was probably making up.

What particularly intrigued JT was my view of the end times, which at first he saw as a fairy tale but within time began to view as "a real possibility" because of how he saw world events unwinding, and my apparent ability to tie John's eschatology in the Book of Revelation—a book that before Vatican 2, the Catholic Church told him never to read—Daniel's prophecies in the *Old Testament*, and the Apostle Paul's discussions of the Day of the Lord and the Day of Christ in Thessalonians to world affairs. JT was skilled in philosophy and political science, so our conversations were far more apologetic in character than salvatory or meditative, and JT's faith began to thrive during my multi-year-long "artillery barrage" on the integrity of his world view. Our relationship is just one practical example of why I believe it crucial for Christians to know their *Bibles* and, to be conversant with eschatology and know what they believe regarding the end times. If you are living a clear Christian world view, you will be asked about it and challenged because of it. That, after all, is what a Christian's ultimate Vision of success looks like—receiving an invitation to attend the Marriage Supper of the Lamb and spending an eternity with God. "Without a Vision, the people...". I'm sure you know the consequence. To reiterate, if you are not being asked about your vision of the future, that could be a problem; check your passport, and make sure it is up to date.

In addition to our seminar teaching, students from all the seminars would meet collectively three or four times a week during the nine month course for auditorium presentations by senior Flag officers (generals and admirals) from all five services and heads of federal government agencies. They, and other senior military leaders and a host of other well-known public officials, would lecture on highly classified foreign affairs, current combat activities, and cyber technologies, so that when students graduated and got to their next units or government agencies, they could hit the ground running armed with current policy information. We got to hear on a weekly basis from all the movers and shakers in our federal government and the civilian and military chiefs of the five US military services.

During one of our follow-on seminar discussions regarding the ethical use of nuclear weapons, subsequent to an auditorium lecture by the Air Force Chief of Staff (a four star general) on the preparedness of our nuclear missile forces, JT was surprised to learn that I had been previously assigned for a few months to partner with Bishop John O'Connor (former Chief Catholic Vicar of the armed forces and later appointed by the Pope as Cardinal John O'Connor from New York) to travel to several Minuteman missile sites in this country to discuss with their silo crews the ethics of the potential employment of nuclear weapons. The Bishop had been named to this assignment because the Pontiff had only recently re-issued a Papal encyclical reaffirming the Vatican's antagonism to the use and even the possession of nuclear weapons by nation states. Some practicing Roman Catholics in the air force missile force as well as some navy officers on boomers, nuclear strategic missile submarines had apparently voiced misgivings about their assignments. Some had even intimated that because of the Pope's pronouncements, they might not be able to comply with an order to launch nuclear weapons against an enemy because of this spiritual guidance, even if directed to do so by the Commander-in-Chief (President). That was a potential ethical crisis of momentous import during the Cold War years. The two of us were dispatched to hold focus groups and individual counselling with these individuals to present rational theological and philosophical arguments to the contrary.

I was assigned as the Bishop's junior partner for this assignment no doubt because of my previous assignment teaching philosophy and ethics at the Academy, my then current role teaching ethics at AFSC, and my initial army branch choice of Air Defense Artillery, during which I had personally commanded two different nuclear capable missile batteries within NATO, but truth be known, also because a couple of the Joint Chiefs of Staff (four star generals) knew that I represented a "protestant" counterpoint to the Bishop's view from the Papacy. What really intrigued JT was that the Bishop and I had at least three months of close contact to share our particular theological beliefs with one another, learn from each other, and debate one another behind closed doors, and that despite our obvious theological differences—sometimes very large, particularly regarding salvation—we had been able to present a unified position in taking an apologetic and scriptural approach to the most dire forms of national defense and global conflict. That the Jesuit trained Roman Catholic Bishop was willing to listen to me and study scriptures with me in our off time and that I had apparently been willing to learn from his story as well, provided more legitimacy to JT for our on-going office conversations. Our two Christian world view narrative apologetics crisscrossed at key points.

Over the time we had together, JT's appreciation for a how a Christian world view can provide a firm foundation for one's life as well as one's personal faith began to grow, and his interest in seeking honest answers from scripture, not just journals of political science, began to take root.

I am not aware that he ever shared any of these changes with his family, perhaps embarrassed at having stressed his Catholicism and ritual over personal faith to them for years. These days, as I have had conversations his wife and children about the changes that I had seen taking place in their dad before he died unexpectedly at a very young age, they seem very surprised to learn that he had been developing a strong personal faith outside the hierarchy of his former more formal theological belief system.

As a student of political strategy schooled in a *realpolitik* mentality from Harvard and the University of Paris for years, JT had always unconsciously hung his hat on a Naturalistic world view. That mostly Existential and thoroughly Humanistic world view had slowly morphed into a Christian world view because he began to see that one could not live consistently within such a Naturalistic framework and that a Christian world view was capable of offering honest answers to his brilliant and always questioning mind. Living consistently and ethically within his world view, had been one of JT's claims to fame while a State Department negotiator. He began to see that only a Christian world view (and underlying holy scriptures) actually provided honest answers to the most important questions of existence, and he had begun a gradual "about face." **Truth tends to do that to people**. He became a different person and eventually stood up for me as the best man at my wedding at West Point.

Our job as Christians is often just to live the truth—a practical apologetic—and let God take it from there.

> "And ye shall know the truth, and the truth shall make you free"
> (KJV, John, 8:32).

CHAPTER XXXII

Fatherhood

When God gives you children, he spreads a potential future before you. Each gift from God is so full of potential as to stagger human imagination, if we as parents with God's help are clever enough to nudge them in the right direction. I have been blessed with some wonderful children, most of whom still talk to me from time to time. Each one is different and extraordinarily gifted and is involved in activities and careers I could not have predicted. Several of my books are dedicated to them and the wonderful cognitive, spiritual, and physical diversity they represent.

Since I earlier mentioned the fact that one of them speaks on apologetics from time to time, let me relate a couple stories about his youth because that inquisitive theologically questioning nature began early in his life. Once, while Paul was just two, we were attending church in Madison, New Jersey. During the hominy, the preacher reminded the congregation about God's being present in our midst. At one all too quiet interlude in the homily, Paul asked far too loudly, "Mom is that really true?" Dozens of eyes in the church turned our way as Cheryl quietly answered, "Yes he is. We are promised that He's always here in our midst when two or more Christians gather together" (Matthew 18:20). Paul looked around and once again in an "outside" voice very atypical of a two-year-old asked, "Then which one is he?" The stares turned to ripples of laughter rolling across the nave. Early on Paul began to ask the difficult questions that demanded a serious response. That was toddler apologetics in action—genuine baby steps. **We as parents better have good answers to such questions, or they stop being asked**.

If we are going to engage the world, we should probably start in our homes. At another service, during one of the hymns, Paul wandered out of our pew and, before we could stop him, walked up front and sat on the edge of the platform during the sermon. The speaker, who had come to know Paul very well since his infant dedication, was unfazed and continued without missing a beat. So did Paul, remaining there for the rest of the service, nodding his head affirmatively from time to time in apparent support of key theological points, very comfortable being in front of the large congregation—probably why he enjoys speaking to large groups today on biblical subjects.

My parents guided me rigorously into God's kingdom, and as I have admitted, I fought them every step of the way, as they dragged me to youth groups, potluck suppers, prayer meetings, and church services morning and evening every Sunday. They were laying the foundation for my eventual world view before I knew what one was. They deserved better from me. I saw their Christian doting as such an inconvenience, that I probably never thanked them enough. I just pray that today if they have the ability to look down from Paradise—no doubt very bad theology—they somehow know that they did all the right things. Someday, "when I finally make it home…."

My frequent prayer to God is to thank him for all of our children, those I have named herein and those I have not, those with whom I stay close and those who have taken very different paths, and to make me somehow worthy of their love and respect and never allow me to let them down.

> **Train up a child in the way he should go,**
> **And when he is old he will not depart from it**.
> (KJV, Proverbs 22:6)

CHAPTER XXXIII

Coda

If you ever have the chance to travel to Vatican City, be sure to include a visit to the Apostolic Palace, the official residence for the sitting Pope. The central focus of the art in the Palace is a marvelous collection of frescos created by the Renaissance painter, Raffaello Sanzio, who is better known simply as Raphael, in about AD 1510. The fresco best known of the four today as "The School of Athens," was commissioned by the aging Pope Julius II to decorate the Papal Apartments where he lived. Raphael apparently saw this as his chance to create a work of art that would form the synthesis of the **worldly** (represented by the rational Greek Naturalistic world view) and the **spiritual** (represented by the Christian world view). How well he accomplished that goal is for you to decide when you visit. I, for one, stand in awe of his art, not only for its beauty but because it stands as a clarion call to his world view.

What he clearly accomplished by this particular masterpiece was to sum up the history of philosophy in magnificent artistic terms. One might even conclude that in one fresco, he combined a narrative and traditional approach to apologetics. Sprawled on the stone steps inside an elegant cruciform temple constructed in the shape of a large Greek cross, much like the floor plan of the West Point Cadet Chapel and the Duke University chapel, are portraits of virtually all the philosophers and scientists known to date: Euclid, Archimedes, Socrates, Pythagoras, Alexander the Great, Heraclitus and a dozen others, including many of the lesser known Pre-Socratics who formed the philosophical underpinnings of the more familiar names.

In the center of the fresco (If you are familiar with the artistic compositional theory of the Rule of Thirds—the very center of the 9 sections), however, are the two great philosophers upon whom Raphael wanted us to focus because, with apologies to my more scholarly Humanist friends, these two philosophers sum up the history of faith and reason. Walking side by side are Plato and Aristotle. As one views the painting, Plato is on the left with his hand and index finger pointing upward towards the heavens, indicating that there are higher truths that are eternal and unchanging (a non-Naturalistic understanding of the world), and Aristotle is on the right, with his hand extended with fingers splayed and pointing towards the ground, suggesting in his philosophy that the only reality is what we can see and experience by sight and touch (a Naturalistic approach to knowledge). Both of their thought forms have been incorporated not only in western rational thought, and the theory of psychological type, but also into the various versions of historic Christianity, which is why they are placed in the center of the painting. They are not only central to the fresco's art and the foundations of western thought but also serve unfortunately as a potential distraction from a larger principle that I believe is at stake.

The choices these two figures portray are the fundamental choices everyone must make regarding what they believe is true. Is truth embodied in ideas and concepts, what Plato would call *Forms* or *Ideals* (and Jung referred to as Intuition), or does truth reside in all those specifics of life, what Aristotle would call *Particulars* (Sensing for Jung*).* As a very pedestrian example of this difference, consider the following. If you are sitting in a chair reading this chapter, how do you know that what you are sitting in is actually a chair? Do you have a general idea, a concept of chair-ness (the *Form*) so that when you see a straight back dining room chair, a recliner with a New York Yankees logos on the back, a metal chair at your breakfast bar, a folding chair at your next pot luck supper, an over-stuffed chair in need of reupholstering that your grandmother loves, or even a swivel chair at your chess table, you recognize them all as chairs? Or, on the other hand, over time, have you seen all those individual contraptions used to accommodate sitting as well as dozens of others (*Particulars*) and as a result of your observations of all this data, developed a concept of chair-ness? I know, these are the kind of weird questions you tried to avoid by dropping PH101 and opting for 18th Century Romance Poetry or Gender Studies in college. You may have been able to avoid such questions in a formal class, but in different ways you have to wrestle with them every day, particularly when you reflect on the reasons you have adopted a particular world view and how yours clashes with another's.

Return with me to the Palace and glance up at the fresco. In Aristotle's hand is one of his books—The *Nicomachean Ethics*. The subtle implication is that from Aristotle's perspective, what is ethical does not have some absolute standard but is derived on the fly and pieced together as we confront particular experiences in life. Each can be as important as the others, because according to Aristotle everything is relative based on our individual experiences and observations. That book reflects Aristotle's world view. By his side, fortunately for our sake, is Plato pointing up to the sky and holding in his other hand the *Timaeus,* his treatise on space, time, change, and existence, all of which he declares have an ideal *Form*— some absolute standard—outside of our existences (the supernatural). This fundamental distinction between the created and the creator, what is and what can be, what is relative and what is absolute, what is Naturalistic or non-Naturalistic, what is experiential and empirical or known *apriori,* is essential to affirming a particular world view.

The Christian world view demands that we affirm an absolute standard outside of our earthly existence. As you declare your world view, this is your pre-flight checklist and the instruments you are advised to follow when things go awry. The Creator is always separate from and external to his creation. This is the non-Naturalistic approach to truth. Like Plato, our lives should always be pointing up. Becoming a practical apologist requires that we act on this truth in everything we do, so we can always be ready to give an answer for the faith that is within us.

Unlike most universities, where academic freedom knows no bounds and too often runs amok, at West Point instructors, even tenured ones, are evaluated each semester and provided very specific feedback on their effectiveness, teaching style, and approach to the subject matter content. Since we had just launched the new courses in philosophy and ethics while I was a PAP, our early civilian mentors external to the Academy would drop into our classes from time to time to see how we were doing and to offer suggestions. During one such session, a cadet had just asked me about "The School of Athens," the painting that he had remembered writing an essay about in Plebe English the year before and was curious about the philosophical implications embedded in the painting and why it had been selected for analysis. During our discussion, Will Barrett, one of our faculty mentors and the author of *Irrational Man*, stopped in for an unannounced visit to observe my class and evaluate my teaching.

We had been discussing philosophical Naturalism and its historic antecedents. Barrett, as one himself, was instantly engaged in the discussion. As it turned out, he loved this painting and particularly loved the fact that at the height of the High Renaissance, Raphael had included all the great philosophers of the ages in an apparent effort (as Barrett began to explain to the class) to demonstrate that all thought forms were represented with no apparent effort to emphasize one over the other. They were, in Barrett's opinion, all part of the history of rational thought and hence of equal importance in the development of Western culture. Human knowledge was key, not its particular origin or implications.

By describing his understanding of the fresco in this way, Barrett was merely reflecting his Naturalistic Existential world view. The Renaissance was a rebirth of knowledge, and to Barrett's understanding this painting was the highpoint of Humanistic thought; all truth shown as equal and the product of diverse thinkers. Man was to be the measure of all things, not some theoretical force outside of this world. As Barrett phrased it, all rational thought forms and systems of philosophy were relative and equally important elements of existence. His viewpoint was certainly expected as he was, after all, the leading Existentialist philosopher of his age. Barrett was a very charismatic figure and a great teacher and in short order had most of the cadets present nodding in affirmation of his interpretation of the painting.

As he prepared to leave, as any good teacher would, he pressed the class to see if they had any questions. After a short give and take, he thanked the class for their active participation, affirmed the need to raise such issues for future military professionals, and told them that he applauded the Military Academy for offering such a course. Upon exiting the classroom, he graciously thanked me for allowing him to sit in for a brief time and kindly remarked that he could see that "the class was in good hands." Seeing the opportunity, I asked him if I might ask one more question. "Certainly," he graciously affirmed, saying he thrived on questions from his fellow faculty members.

I reminded him that, as he had phrased it, all the great rational thinkers in math, science, and philosophy through the ages were present in the painting. Then I asked him what he thought Raphael might be trying to express in his work of art—his graphic story—by the fact that all of these philosophers, scientists, and purveyors of rational thought forms through the ages were depicted with their feet planted firmly on the ground but located inside of a building that had been created in the shape of a cross. I might phrase it differently these days, but as I phrased it at the time. "Don't you think, Professor Barrett, that it might be significant that all rational thought forms, philosophies, and ethics of the ages could be found under and expressed within a Christian framework. **The cross after all,"** I added, **"to the Greek mind was the intersection of the horizontal and the vertical, *chronos* and the *kairos*, the moment when the supernatural connects directly with the mundane, when Forms interact with the Particulars, and all rational thought can be seen as contributing to the glory of God."** "That is an interesting observation, Colonel Jeffries. I believe that...I think it is interesting that...Let me, um, let me think this over and I'll get back to you. Thank-you again Colonel for letting me sit in today." And he left.

To my knowledge, that was one of his few visits to our department and was his only visit to my class. And, no, he did not get back to me. After he departed, one cadet asked me if I had purposely tried to embarrass the professor by putting him on the spot to defend his observations. I assured the student that such was not my desire, but I merely wanted to give Mr. Barrett an opportunity to defend his view of the possible philosophical implications of the fresco, as it was clearly impacted by his personal Naturalistic and Existential world view. Our world views impact everything we observe, believe, say, and do. **This is a war of world views, and as Christians we need to be clear on which side we serve**.

I further told the cadet that he should learn immediately, if he had not yet learned it over his first two years at the Academy, always to stand for what he believed was truth whenever it might seem to be sullied by someone's point of view and always to be willing to defend whatever world view he found to be authoritative. His soldiers would expect that kind of clarity. The classroom, I reminded him, particularly a philosophy classroom should be a place where competing ideas can be presented with intellectual honesty and rational minds can discern the truth. A person's particular world view does not make one necessarily correct, but he or she should be able to justify it. The same could be said of any conversation regarding Christian apologetics. We practical apologists must be capable of making a cogent argument, highlighting it with pertinent stories that reflect those truths, and be sure to make some practical application regarding it in our lives. What I didn't say, because it was the wrong venue, was that our lives as Christians should reflect the same authenticity. I suggested to the class that **what we say, how we live, and what we declare we believe always sprout from our respective world views**.

This is the reason why living a practical apologetic is so critical to our Christian walk. The Christian never needs to take a back seat to Humanistic or Naturalistic anti-Christian arguments, nor should we ever be afraid to engage the mind as well as the heart.

If our faith is not capable of explaining every aspect of life, we should be ashamed and consider a world view more consistent with reality. "Study to shew thyself approved unto God, a workman that needeth not to be ashamed, rightly dividing the word of truth" (KJV, II Timothy 2:15).

AFTERWORD

I hope you will forgive all the preceding personal stories and anecdotes. They are irrelevant in the grand scheme of things, except as jumping off points to argue that what may seem at the time to be the most insignificant events in anyone's life contribute to one's developing world view and are capable of being used by Christ for his purposes. Both C. S. Lewis and J. R. R. Tolkien believed that "God has shaped the human mind and imagination to be receptive of stories, and that these stories are echoes or fragments of the Christian 'grand story'" (*Narrative Apologetics*, p. 8). **That is why our work always begins by telling stories and tries implicitly to tie those stories into the greatest metanarrative ever written**.

If you expected a carefully formulated step-by-step process by which a world view is formed, you have probably been disappointed over the previous pages; that is not how it works. Our unique individual experiences have been crafted by the Lord to provide insights and learnings we are capable of using to compile our unique stories. They are just a few of the ones I have singled out here. Our Lord came to redeem all of us, not just carefully selected parts of our lives. The simple point I want to make is that **each of us, regardless of our individual occupations, careers, and lives, has a story to tell and wafers to chew. Those stories should announce our Christian world view every day, before we ever say a word.** Not only do we each have such unique stories, but God expects us to share them with others—not just with words but with our lives.

> In the same way, let your light shine before others, so
> that they may see your good works and give glory to your
> Father who is in heaven (ESV, Matthew 5:16).

Every story worth telling has a Beginning, Middle and End as well as a Plot, a Setting, Characters, and a discernible Tone. As Shakespeare often reminded his audiences those stories can be comedies (where there are happy endings), histories dependent mostly on bare facts, or tragedies (where there are always deaths and sad endings). Because of the Fall of Adam and Eve in the Garden of Eden, God's perfect creation was cast by man into the form of a potential tragedy; death entered the world, as did a different emphasis on the meaning of life and work. Because of the second Adam (1 Corinthians 15:45-49), our Redeemer, Christ, transformed each of our lives into the potential for comedy, if we will but trust in Him. Hence John Milton's description of the events in Genesis as the *felix culpa*—the fortunate fall. No fall—no salvation. In between are the plots of our individual histories.

Whatever the setting of your story, whoever the characters happen to be, and what ever the tone at various times in your life (sad or happy, maudlin or celebratory, moody or ebullient, greedy, or thankful), we have the knowledge that, as God wills, our individual plots (events in *chronos* time) will intertwine with his grand story (interventions in *kairos* time) throughout our lifetime.

Recall that in John 8:12, Jesus says, "**I am** the Light of the world." By some extraordinary miracle of grace, in NIV, Matthew 5:14, he tells us, "**You are** the light of the world." For the time being, He is gone; we are here. In order to be a practical apologist, every plotline in our stories should reflect our Christian world view and shout to the world that we are bought and paid for by his mercy.

> "So whether you eat or drink or whatever you do, do it all
> for the glory of God" (NIV, I Corinthians 10:31).

Go, and live your story, remembering that, just as Chaucer's pilgrims, at the end of our pilgrimages there will be rewards for those who have told the best stories. The best stories are those that reflect God's metanarrative.

I hope to see you there, at the Tabard Inn.

APPENDIX I

Philosophical Distinctions to understand.

Agnosticism, (from Greek *agnōstos*, "unknowable"), strictly speaking, the doctrine that humans cannot know of the existence of anything beyond the phenomena of their experience. The term has come to be equated in popular parlance with skepticism about religious questions in general and in particular with the rejection of traditional Christian beliefs under the impact of modern scientific thought. Literally, this word comes from A- (or not) Gnostic—the belief that one simply does not and probably cannot know.

The word was first publicly coined in 1869 at a meeting of the Metaphysical Society in London by T. H. Huxley, a British biologist and champion of the Darwinian theory of evolution. He coined it as a suitable label for his own position. "It came into my head as suggestively antithetical to the 'Gnostic' of Church history who professed to know so much about the very things of which I was ignorant."

Atheism is, in the broadest sense, the absence of belief in the existence of deities. Less broadly, atheism is the rejection of belief that any deities exist. In an even narrower sense, atheism is specifically the position that there are no deities. Atheism is contrasted with theism, which, in its most general form, is the belief that at least one deity exists, even though he may be disinterested in what we do on earth.

The etymological root for the word atheism originated before the 5th century BC from the ancient Greek ἄθεος (atheos), meaning "without god(s)". In antiquity. it had multiple uses as a pejorative term applied to those thought to reject the gods worshiped by the larger society, those who were forsaken by the gods, or those who had no commitment to belief in the gods (*Wikipedia*).

Axiology (from the Greek *axios*, "worthy"; logos, "science"), also called theory of value, the philosophical study of goodness, or value, in the widest sense of these terms. Its significance lies in the considerable expansion that it has given to the meaning of the term value and in the unification that it has provided for the study of a variety of questions—economic, moral, aesthetic, and even logical—that had often been considered in relative isolation.

Constructivism claims that the job of philosophers is to do some kind of idea construction. This is most often applied to ethics (moral philosophy) and social/political philosophy, where the idea is that philosophers should have the job of building new ideas rather than just observing and analyzing the ideas that already exist in society. (*Encyclopedia of Philosophy*)

Deontology. In moral philosophy, deontological ethics or deontology (from Greek δέον, *deon*, "obligation, duty" is the normative ethical theory that the morality of an action should be based on whether that action itself is right or wrong under a series of rules, rather than based on the consequences of the action. It is sometimes described as duty-, obligation- or rule-based ethics, because rules "bind one to one's duty". Deontological ethics is commonly contrasted to consequentialism, virtue ethics, and pragmatic ethics.

It is an ethical framework that depends on the predefined sets of rules and policies for the proper functioning of a system in the environment. The deontology is simply based on the checklist which includes certain rules to be followed while performing a particular task. According to this framework, the work is considered virtuous only if this checklist is completed. This procedure is very simple to implement and understand.

The term deontological was first used to describe the current, specialized definition by C. D. Broad in his 1930 book, *Five Types of Ethical Theory*. Older usage of the term goes back to Jeremy Bentham, who coined it before 1816 as a synonym of Dicastic or Censorial Ethics (i.e. ethics based on judgment). The more general sense of the word is retained in French, especially in the term code *de déontologie* (ethical code), in the context of professional ethics. (Wikipedia)

Epistemology, is the study of knowledge and justified belief. As the study of knowledge, epistemology is concerned with the following questions: What are the necessary and sufficient conditions of knowledge? What are its sources? What is its structure, and what are its limits? As the study of justified belief, epistemology aims to answer questions such as: How we are to understand the concept of justification? What makes justified beliefs justified? Is justification internal or external to one's own mind? Understood more broadly, epistemology is about issues having to do with the creation and dissemination of knowledge, in particular areas of inquiry (*Stanford Encyclopedia of Philosophy*).

Existentialism, Like "rationalism" and "empiricism," "Existentialism" is a term that belongs to intellectual history. Its definition is thus to some extent one of historical convenience. The term was explicitly adopted as a self-description by Jean-Paul Sartre, and through the wide dissemination of the postwar literary and philosophical output of Sartre and his associates—notably Simone de Beauvoir, Maurice Merleau-Ponty, and Albert Camus—Existentialism became identified with a cultural movement that flourished in Europe in the 1940s and 1950s, but it is far more than just that historic footnote. Among the major philosophers identified as Existentialists (many of whom—for instance Camus and Heidegger—repudiated the label) were Karl Jaspers, Martin Heidegger, and Martin Buber in Germany, Jean Wahl and Gabriel Marcel in France, the Spaniards José Ortega y Gasset and Miguel de Unamuno, and the Russians Nikolai Berdyaev and Lev Shestov. The nineteenth-century philosophers Søren Kierkegaard and Friedrich Nietzsche came to be seen as precursors of the movement.

Existentialism was as much a literary phenomenon as a philosophical one. Sartre's own ideas were and are better known through his fictional works (such as *Nausea* and *No Exit*) than through his more purely philosophical ones (such as *Being and Nothingness* and *Critique of Dialectical Reason*), and the postwar years found a very diverse coterie of writers and artists linked under the term: retrospectively, Dostoevsky, Ibsen, and Kafka were conscripted; in Paris there were Jean Genet, André Gide, André Malraux, and the expatriate Samuel Beckett; the Norwegian Knut Hamsun and the Romanian Eugene Ionesco belong to the club; artists such as Alberto Giacometti and even Abstract Expressionists such as Jackson Pollock, Arshile Gorky, and Willem de Kooning, and filmmakers such as Jean-Luc Godard and Ingmar Bergman were understood in existential terms. (*Stanford Encyclopedia of Philosophy*)

Jural, Of or relating to rights and obligations.

Metaphysics, is the study of what is—the philosophical study whose object is to determine the real nature of things—to determine the meaning, structure, and principles of whatever is insofar as it is. Although this study is popularly conceived as referring to anything excessively subtle and highly theoretical and although it has been subjected to many criticisms, it is presented by metaphysicians as the most fundamental and most comprehensive of inquiries, inasmuch as it is concerned with reality as a whole (Britannica.com).

Naturalism, in philosophy, a theory that relates a scientific method to philosophy by affirming that all beings and events in the universe (whatever their inherent character may be) are natural. Such an approach necessarily impugns any attempt to posit a supernatural influence outside of nature or science. Consequently, all authentic knowledge of the universe should fall within the pale of scientific investigation. (*Stanford Encyclopedia of Philosophy*)

Non-Naturalism in meta-ethics is the idea that moral philosophy is fundamentally autonomous from the natural sciences. In some contexts, 'non-naturalism' denotes the semantic thesis that moral predicates cannot be analyzed in non-normative terms. In other contexts, 'non-naturalism' denotes the epistemological thesis that knowledge of basic moral principles and value judgments are in some sense self-evident. However, this view (which some self-styled naturalists would actually accept) is more often and more usefully referred to as 'intuitionism' (not to be confused with Jung's idea of Intuition). Most often, 'non-naturalism' denotes the metaphysical thesis that moral properties exist and are not identical with or reducible to any natural property or properties in some interesting sense of 'natural'. Understood in this way, non-naturalism is a form of moral realism and is opposed to non-cognitivist positions according to which moral utterances serve to express non-cognitive attitudes rather than beliefs that provide their truth conditions and is also opposed to error-theoretical positions according to which there are no moral facts. Moreover, each of these different conceptions of non-naturalism bears interesting relations of support to the others (*Stanford Encyclopedia of Philosophy*).

Ontology, the philosophical study of "being" in general, or of what applies neutrally to everything that is real. It was called "first philosophy" by Aristotle in Book IV of his *Metaphysics*. The Latin term *ontologia* ("science of being") was felicitously invented by the German philosopher Jacob Lorhard (Lorhardus) and first appeared in his work *Ogdoas Scholastica* (1st ed.) in 1606. It entered general circulation after being popularized by the German rationalist philosopher Christian Wolff in his Latin writings, especially *Philosophia Prima sive Ontologia* (1730; "First Philosophy or Ontology").

Positivism is the philosophical theory that theology and metaphysics are earlier imperfect modes of knowledge and that positive knowledge is based on natural phenomena and their properties and relations as verified by the empirical sciences. (*Meriam Webster's Dictionary*).

Postmodernism, also spelled post-modernism, in Western philosophy, is a late 20th-century movement characterized by broad skepticism, subjectivism, or relativism; a general suspicion of reason; and an acute sensitivity to the role of ideology in asserting and maintaining political and economic power (*Encyclopedia Britannica*).

Post-positivism (also called post-empiricism) is a metatheoretical stance that critiques and amends positivism. While positivists emphasize independence between the researcher and the researched person (or object), post-positivists argue that theories, background, knowledge and values of the researcher can influence what is observed. Post-positivists pursue objectivity by recognizing the possible effects of biases. While positivists emphasize quantitative methods, post-positivists consider both quantitative and qualitative methods to be valid approaches.

Post-positivists, therefore, believe that human knowledge is based not on *a priori* assessments from an objective individual, but rather upon human conjectures. Neither bias not actuality is superior. As human knowledge is thus unavoidably conjectural, the assertions of these conjectures are warranted, or more specifically, justified by a set of warrants, which can be modified or withdrawn in the light of further investigation. However, post-positivism is not a form of relativism, and "generally" retains the idea of objective truth. In regard to Ontology, Post-positivists believe that a reality exists, but, unlike positivists, they believe reality can be known only imperfectly and probabilistically. In terms of Axiology, while positivists believe that research is or can be value-free or value-neutral, post-positivists take the position that bias is undesired but inevitable, and therefore the investigator must work to detect and try to correct it. Post-positivists work to understand how their axiology (i.e. values and beliefs) may have influenced their research, including through their choice of measures, populations, questions, and definitions, as well as through their interpretation and analysis of their work. (Wikipedia).

Pragmatism is a philosophical tradition that very broadly understands knowing the world as inseparable from agency within it. This general idea has attracted a remarkably rich and at times contrary range of interpretations, including: that all philosophical concepts should be tested via scientific experimentation, that a claim is true if and only if it is useful (relatedly: if a philosophical theory does not contribute directly to social progress then it is not worth much), that experience consists in transacting with rather than representing nature, that articulate language rests on a deep bed of shared human practices that can never be fully 'made explicit' (*Encyclopedia Britannica*).

Pragmatism originated in the United States around 1870...Its first generation was initiated by the so-called 'classical pragmatists' Charles Sanders Peirce (1839–1914), who first defined and defended the view, and his close friend and colleague William James (1842–1910), who further developed and ably popularized it. During this initial period, pragmatists focused significantly on theorizing inquiry, meaning and the nature of truth, although James put these themes to work exploring truth in religion (*Stanford Encyclopedia of Philosophy*).

Spiritualism is a religious movement based on the belief that the spirits of the dead exist and have both the ability and the inclination to communicate with the living. The afterlife, or the "spirit world", is seen by spiritualists, not as a static place, but as one in which spirits continue to evolve. These two beliefs—that contact with spirits is possible, and that spirits are more advanced than humans—lead spiritualists to a third belief: that spirits are capable of providing useful knowledge about moral and ethical issues, as well as about the nature of God. Some spiritualists will speak of a concept which they refer to as "spirit guides"—specific spirits, often contacted, who are relied upon for spiritual guidance. Spiritism, a branch of spiritualism developed by Allan Kardec and today practiced mostly in Continental Europe and Latin America, especially in Brazil, emphasizes reincarnation.

This "ism" developed and reached its peak growth in membership from the 1840s to the 1920s, primarily in English-speaking countries. By 1897, spiritualism was said to have more than eight million followers in the United States and Europe, mostly drawn from the middle and upper classes. Spiritualism flourished for a half century without canonical texts or formal organization, attaining cohesion through periodicals, tours by trance lecturers, camp meetings, and the missionary activities of accomplished mediums. Many prominent spiritualists were women, and like most spiritualists, supported causes such as the abolition of slavery and women's suffrage. By the late 1880s the credibility of the informal movement had weakened due to accusations of fraud perpetrated by mediums, and formal spiritualist organizations began to appear. Spiritualism is currently practiced primarily through various denominational spiritualist churches in the United States, Canada and the United Kingdom (*Encyclopedia Britannica*).

Stoicism, Stoicism is a philosophy of personal ethics informed by its system of logic and its views on the natural world. According to its teachings, as social beings, the path to eudaimonia (happiness) for humans is found in accepting the moment as it presents itself, by not allowing oneself to be controlled by the desire for pleasure or fear of pain, by using one's mind to understand the world and to do one's part in nature's plan, and by working together and treating others fairly and justly (*Encyclopedia of Philosophy*).

The Stoics are especially known for teaching that "virtue is the only good" for human beings, and that external things—such as health, wealth, and pleasure—are not good or bad in themselves (adiaphora), but have value as "material for virtue to act upon." Alongside Aristotelian ethics, the Stoic tradition forms one of the major founding approaches to Western virtue ethics. The Stoics also held that certain destructive emotions resulted from errors of judgment, and they believed people should aim to maintain a will (called *prohairesis*) that is "in accord with nature". Because of this, the Stoics thought the best indication of an individual's philosophy was not what a person said, but how a person behaved. To live a good life, one had to understand the rules of the natural order since they thought everything was rooted in nature (Wikipedia).

Teleology, (from Greek *telos*, "end," and logos, "reason"), is an explanation rooted in some reference to some purpose, end, goal, or function. Traditionally, it was also described as final causality, in contrast with explanation solely in terms of efficient causes (the origin of a change or a state of rest in something). Human conduct, insofar as it is rational, is generally explained with reference to ends or goals pursued or alleged to be pursued, and humans have often understood the behavior of other things in nature on the basis of that analogy, either as of themselves pursuing ends or goals or as designed to fulfill a purpose devised by a mind that transcends nature. The most-celebrated account of teleology was that given by Aristotle when he declared that a full explanation of anything must consider its final cause as well as its efficient, material, and formal causes (the latter two being the stuff out of which a thing is made and the form or pattern of a thing, respectively). (Britannica.com).

Telic: A central argument of Teleology says that the world has clearly been constructed in a purposeful telic rather than a chaotic manner and must therefore have been made by a rational being, i.e. God.

Theism: You can subdivide theism in many ways. For example, you can divide it into separate historical / cultural traditions, such as Judaism, Christianity, Hinduism, and Islam (and each of these could be subdivided still further).

You can also define types of theism by its number of Gods:

> Monotheism: one god
> Polytheism: many gods
> Ditheism: two gods, usually one good and one evil
> Henotheism: one main god with many minor gods

Alternatively, you can divide it in terms of different ideas about the nature of the god or gods:

> Pantheism: God = everything or the universe
> Deism: God created the whole universe but does not interfere in events
> Autotheism: God = the self or is within the self
> Eutheism: God is entirely merciful and just
> Misotheism / Dystheism: God is evil and many others

APPENDIX II: BIBLIOGRAPHY

Aquinas, Thomas. *Summa Theologica*. 1594.

Arment, Ainsley. *The Call of the Wild and Free: Reclaiming Wonder in Your Child's Education*, 2019.

Atkins, Daniel. *A Theology for the Church*, 2014.

Barrett, William. *Irrational Man: A Study in Existential Philosophy*, 1962.
_____. *Death of the Soul*, 1987.

Barth, Karl. *Church Dogmatics (14 volumes)*, 1994.
_____. *The Epistle to the Romans,* 1968.

Bevins, Winfred. *Ever Ancient, Ever New*, 2019.

Browning, Robert. *Men and Women*, 1855.

Brumbarger, Ron. *You're Always Being Interviewed*, 2016.

Bultmann, Rudolph. *Interpreting Faith for the Modern Era,* 1987.

Chesterton. G. K. "The Ethics of Elfland," Chapter 4, *Orthodoxy*, 1908.

Clark, Gordon. *A Christian View of Man and Things: An Introduction to Philosophy*, 1951, 1981.

Clark, Malcolm. *Islam for Dummies*, 2003.

Craig, William Lane and J. P. Moreland. *Philosophical Foundations for a Christian World View*, 2003.

De Bono, Edward. *Six Thinking Hats,* 1999.

Deming, W. Edwards. *Out of the Crisis,* 1982.

Ekman, Paul, *Emotions Revealed*, 2007.
_____. *Non-Verbal Messages*, 2016.
_____. *Unmasking the Face*, 2003.

Gladwell, Malcolm. *Outliers: The Story of Success*, 2011.

Goleman, Daniel. *Emotional Intelligence*, 1995.

Gordon, Wayne. *Systematic Theology: An Introduction to Biblical Doctrine*, 1995.

Henry, Carl. *God, Revelation and Authority, 1976*.

Hick, John, *Philosophy of Religion, 1973*.

Jeffries, William. *Culture and High Performance,* 2011.

_____. *Hannibal, Hummers and Hot Air Balloons*, 2001.

_____. *Inliers: The Curse of Polarity Thinking*, 2017.

_____. *Spirit of the Oryx,* 2009.

_____. *Still True to Type*, 2002, 2005.

_____. *Profiles of the 16 Personality Types, 2005, 2009, 2011, 2015.*

Jung, Carl Gustav. *Modern Man in Search of a Soul,* 2017.

Kierkegaard, Soren. *Either / Or,* 1971.

_____. *Fear and Trembling*, 1959.

Kroeger, Otto, Janet Thuesen. *Type Talk*, 1988.

Lewis, C. S. *Mere Christianity, 1952.*

_____. *The Abolition of Man*, 1943.

_____. *The Screwtape Letters, 1942.*

_____. *Surprised by Joy: The Story of My Early Life, 1955.*

Lindsay, Hal. *The Late Great Planet Earth,* 1970.

_____. *The Rapture: Truth or Consequences,* 1983.

_____. *There's a New World Coming,* 1984.

Lowen, Walter. *Dichotomies of the Mind: A Systems Science of the Mind and Personality*, 1982.

McGrath, Alister. *Narrative Apologetics*: *Sharing the Relevance, Joy, and Wonder of the Christian Faith.* 2019.

Morris, Tom. *Philosophy for Dummies*, 1995.

Munitz, Milton. *Theories of the Universe from Babylonian Myth to Modern Science,* 1965.

Murray, Abdu. *Grand Central Question*, 2014.

_____. *Saving Truth: Finding Meaning and Clarity in a Post Truth World,* 2018.

Niebuhr, Reinhold. *Moral Man and Immoral Society*, 2013.

Orr, James. *The Christian View of God and the World*, 1893.

Pinkhurst, Adam. *The Hengwrt Manuscript,* 15th century.

Qureshi, Nabeel. *Answering Jihad*, 2016.

_____. *Seeking Allah and Finding Jesus*, 2018.

Rudnick, Milton. *Christian Ethics for Today*, 1979.

Salovey, Peter and John Mayer. *Emotional Intelligence*, 1990.

Schaeffer, Francis. *Escape from Reason*, 2006.

_____. *He is There and He is Not Silent*, 1981.

_____. *How Should We Then Live?* 2005.

_____. *The God Who Is There, 1998.*

_____. *True Spirituality*, 2001.

Simmons, Annette. *Whoever Tells the Best Story Wins,* 2015.

Solomon, Robert. *Introducing Philosophy*, 2013.

Sproul, R. C. *Christian Ethics* Ligonier Podcasts).

Strobel, Lee. *The Case for Christ*, 2016.

Strong, James. *The New Strong's Exhaustive Concordance of the Bible,* 2003.

Traeger, Sebastian and Greg Gilbert. *The Gospel at Work*, 2018.

Trent, Tyler. *The Upset*, 2019.

Vroegop, Mark. *Dark Clouds, Deep Mercy*, 2019.

APPENDIX III: ABOUT THE AUTHOR

William (Bill) Jeffries is an International Consultant and Executive Coach who specializes in human and organizational behavior. He has been a soldier, scholar, university professor, editor, business leader, prolific author, keynote speaker, and trusted personal coach for business, military, and political leaders around the world. As the President and CEO of Executive Strategies International, he leads a diverse team of consultants that bring global perspectives to the workplace of the future. His undergraduate studies at West Point were in engineering and management and his graduate work at Duke University was in language, literature, and values. His post graduate work through the University of Heidelberg was focused on nuclear weapons technology.

Bill's clientele includes a Who's Who of Fortune 500 Companies, professional athletes, senior business leaders, military leaders, and political leaders in over 35 countries. His international consulting company, Executive Strategies International, Inc., coaches, and provides team building, diversity, negotiation skills, strategic planning, Emotional Intelligence, Psychological Type, sales mastery, leadership development, and innovation and creativity training around the world for over 90 of the Fortune 500 Companies and dozens of smaller entrepreneurial businesses.

Bill has written on subjects as diverse as New Business Development, Business High Performance, Organizational Change, War and Morality, Poetry, Professional Ethics, English composition, Psychological Type, Emotional Intelligence, Generational issues, Christian Apologetics, Political analysis, and the Development of High Performance Teams. His book, *Still True To Type* is widely used in several countries as a leader's guide to personality diversity, and his book, *Taming the Scorpion: Preparing Business for the Third Millennium*, (named by Drew University as one of the best business books of the year) is used by over thirty companies as a leader's guide for understanding diversity and developing High Performance Organizations. The detailed profiles of leadership styles available in his *Profiles of the Sixteen Personality Types* have been hailed as the most comprehensive portraits available on Jungian personality styles. His book, *Hannibal, Hummers, and Hot Air Balloons: High Performance Strategies for Tough Times*, lays out a strategy for creating team and organizational high performance during times of tremendous organizational change and transition. *Culture and High Performance*, presents the nexus between organizational and national culture and culture's impact on creating exceptional performance, and his most recent book, *Inliers: The Curse of Polarity Thinking*, is intended as a companion piece to Malcolm Gladwell's *Outliers*, that identifies the all too frequent impediments to personal and organizational performance.

Bill is also a fiction writer and has published four adventure novels. *Trap Door to the Dark Side*, is a fictional personal memoir, set in the secret war in Laos, Cambodia, and Vietnam in the 1960's. *Spirit of the Oryx*, is a high-tech spy novel set in Qatar and Virginia. *Concord*, is a tale of international terrorism and political intrigue, spanning Switzerland, Russia, Utah, France, and Washington, DC, during the Obama administration. The 4th adventure novel in the Christian Madison series, *Framing The Sacred: The Shadow of Death*, is based on an Iranian terrorist plot to destroy the US Energy Grid and the potential of remotely rewiring anyone's neural pathways through social media, with the result of turning that innocent person with no former political, religious, or national leanings into an unsuspecting domestic terrorist

For over 24 years Bill served in the U. S. army in several locations, including Southeast Asia, Germany (NATO), Greece, and the United States as a unit commander, military advisor, joint staff officer, and military scholar. For seven years, he was an instructor and later a Permanent Associate Professor at West Point teaching language, literature, philosophy, and ethics, and for seven years served as Professor of Ethics and Executive Development at the Armed Forces Staff College, part of this country's Joint War College System (National Defense University). There he taught Ethics, Joint and Combined Special Operations, and Executive Fitness, and coached senior managers from all federal government agencies and senior military and political leaders from 30 countries helping them to understand combined military operations, strategic planning, the DOD weapons acquisition process, the need for inter-service planning, political collaboration, personal mastery, and international team work.

In addition to his international consulting and executive coaching activities, Bill is a frequent guest speaker and/or adjunct professor in the graduate business schools and departments of Executive Education of several universities, including Carnegie Mellon, Georgia Tech, Ball State, and the University of California at San Diego. For 15 years he was the most acclaimed lecturer at The Naval War College in Newport, Rhode Island speaking on Executive Fitness and family relations. Bill also advises the NFL Players Association on career transition for players starting new careers, and is a sought-out keynote speaker on several topics including the Mental Game, preparing athletes at every level of performance from high school to college to MLB and the NFL teams on the mental side of sports. As a keynote speaker for several professional organizations and Fortune 500 Companies, Bill speaks around the world on High Performance, Sales Mastery, Culture Creation, Blocks to Personal Creativity, Business Innovation, and Team Excellence.

Bill is affiliated with several scholarly and professional organizations including, The Association of Psychological Type (APTi), where he serves as the Interest Area Consultant on Management and Organizational Development, The Association for the Management of Organizational Design, The scholastic Honor Society of Phi Kappa Phi, The West Point Association of Graduates, and The International Society for Military Ethics. In 2016, Bill established IC³, The International Center for Creative Change in the Arab Emirates, a private consortium of multinational companies dedicated to sharing insights and learnings regarding new business development, Innovation, and Creativity in the workplace.

In 2008-09, Bill and his company were awarded the prestigious Keeping America Strong Award by William Shatner and Admiral Kevin Delaney, on Shatner's *Heartbeat of America* TV Special, for their acclaimed success at helping American business recover from the effects of 9-11. As Shatner said on his show, "William Jeffries' influence on organizations of every variety and prominent leaders from every possible walk of life extends beyond the USA to countries and cultures around the world."

Most importantly, Bill is an evangelical Christian with a passion for communicating the claims of Christ in every aspect of his teaching, consulting, and parenting responsibilities. His particular interest is in the apologetic aspect of ministry and believes that Christians' lives should shout their Christian world view before they ever open their mouths. Bill and his wife, Cheryl, currently reside in Zionsville, Indiana, and attend College Park Church in Carmel. When not consulting or coaching, they can be found skiing wherever the powder is deepest but always think of their second home as the God-kissed Wasatch mountains of Deer Valley, Utah.

Should you wish to contact Bill, you may do so through his email at Esipres6@earthlink.net, his company's website at www.execustrat.com, or through his LinkedIn site.

CPSIA information can be obtained
at www.ICGtesting.com
Printed in the USA
LVHW111037210720
661194LV00008B/135/J

9 781728 356914